Pregna...
Literature and Film

Pregnancy in Literature and Film

PARLEY ANN BOSWELL

McFarland & Company, Inc., Publishers

Jefferson, North Carolina

Library of Congress Cataloguing-in-Publication Data

Boswell, Parley Ann.
    Pregnancy in literature and film / Parley Ann Boswell.
        p.   cm.
    Includes bibliographical references and index.

    ISBN 978-0-7864-7366-3 (softcover : acid free paper) ∞
    ISBN 978-0-4766-1468-7 (ebook)

    1. Pregnancy in literature.   2. American fiction—History
and criticism.   3. Pregnancy in motion pictures.   I. Title.
    PS374.P645B67 2014
    810.9'354—dc23   2014004485

British Library cataloguing data are available

Front cover: Demi Moore in *The Scarlet Letter*,
1995 (Buena Vista Pictures/Photofest)

Manufactured in the United States of America

McFarland & Company, Inc., Publishers
  Box 611, Jefferson, North Carolina 28640
  www.mcfarlandpub.com

To my mother
Parley Kathryn Dabney Boswell
1924–2012

Table of Contents

Preface

My interest in fictional pregnancy began several years ago when I was working on a project on Edith Wharton, who uses pregnancy in masterful ways in her fiction. But like most scholarly projects, this one really came into focus because of the happenstance of everyday life. One Saturday night, I turned on *Saturday Night Live* and watched a remarkable opening monologue. Host Tina Fey, six months pregnant, and Maya Rudolph, eight months pregnant, were performing a duet in which they were singing to their unborn children about how babies are made. I was immediately reminded of an earlier pregnancy skit when nine-months-pregnant Amy Poehler and host Josh Brolin danced to "I'm No Angel." The songs, the acts, and even the performers' costumes were provocative. And funny. And for me, timely.

The book I had been reading earlier in the day—which was sitting at my bedside while I watched Tina Fey and Maya Rudolph gyrating through their final trimester of pregnancy—was Ann Fessler's *The Girls Who Went Away: The Hidden History of Women Who Surrendered Children for Adoption in the Decades Before Roe v. Wade* (2006).[1] Part memoir (Fessler, an adoptee, bookends her study with her own story) and part historical narrative, the book's real power lies in the oral histories that Fessler provides. Her interviewees tell us how they felt and what their lives were like when they were young, pregnant and frightened. They describe what happened to them before and after pregnancy changed their young lives. They relive their fear, helplessness and anguish. For some of them, the interviews in this book represented the first time they had told their pregnancy stories.

My *SNL*–Fessler evening should have been little more than a coincidence, really. Serious, heart-wrenching personal narratives and a

1

raunchy TV skit? After all, pregnant or not, Tina Fey, Maya Rudolph, and Amy Poehler are all mature professional entertainers, light years removed from the teenage girls in Fessler's book. And whether we are in 1960s America or the 2010s, pregnancy is rarely funny. Yet the juxtaposition of *SNL* and the Fessler book stayed with me. The more I thought about the robust pregnancy performances on *SNL* and the stories of Fessler's women, the more I realized that their coming together one Saturday night in my mind was not a simple coincidence. As I continued to research, listen, and watch, I understood that the Fessler book and the *SNL* skits are both part of a rich legacy of pregnancy narratives in American literature and art, one with a complicated, often subtle, and always challenging history. As different as they are, a collection of real pregnancy stories and a song-and-dance by three pregnant celebrities both suggest the ways in which pregnancy narratives function.[2]

In *Pregnancy in Literature and Film*, I will explore the ways in which pregnancy behaves in canonical American literature and mainstream Hollywood films. I will consider how pregnancy has been used by writers and filmmakers, so that we can gauge the ways that fictional pregnancy has reflected, and has been reflected by, audiences throughout the 20th and 21st centuries. I have chosen canonical and mainstream works for two reasons. First, I wanted to discuss texts and films that we think we already understand. Evaluating them through a frame of pregnancy will change them for us, revealing aspects that we have either never thought about, or have never taken seriously.

Second: I have chosen mainstream, canonical works because traditional anthologies of literature and Hollywood studios are always the last to know anything. Both rarely set trends or take risks; in terms of cultural changes, they are almost always behind the curve. This has proven to be useful to me. Because Hollywood productions and multi-volume anthologies of American literature change very slowly, when they do embrace new ideas, then we know that the ideas have probably already arrived. They have both afforded me the chance to gauge the changes in how we express pregnancy. If Hollywood is doing it, then everybody else has already done it.

I have designed this study as a loosely chronological narrative—a story—that begins with a discussion of literature, beginning with *The Scarlet Letter* and *Incidents in the Life of a Slave Girl*. Because we find pregnancy in every genre and every decade of literature and film, I have organized subsequent chapters within a sketchy but sturdy historical framework into which I have woven discussions of genres and trends. We begin with the pregnancy melodramas of the earliest decades of Hollywood film, moving on through noir and teenpics, to horror films, and beyond to science fiction, and finally to independent film. We will explore how these genres are related and linked, and where fictional pregnancy belongs in a historical context. I conclude with a theoretical discussion of "the gaze": how we frame, perceive, and evaluate these artistic expressions of pregnancy, and a final summary of how narrative pregnancy behaves with the integrity of language.

And "*behaves*" is a seminal verb to describe pregnancy, real or fictional, because all pregnancies are organic and eventually follow their own rules and take on their own lives. As we will discover, the history of fictional pregnancy actually suggests a real pregnancy, one which begins subtly and often secretly in the 19th century, and grows throughout the 20th century to reveal new life by the 21st century. Also, like a real pregnancy, fictional pregnancy suggests the unknown and the unknowable to us. We may not always understand *why* a pregnancy behaves as it does, but we can certainly figure out *how* it behaves.

Fessler's *The Girls Who Went Away* has been especially helpful to this work, as have other recent scholarly studies on childbirth, mothering, and motherhood, all subjects that are related—but not identical— to pregnancy studies. Many of these works have supplemented and complemented my own work on fictional pregnancy. I have drawn my research from a variety of disciplines, including gender studies, film studies, and literary studies. This is primarily a historical narrative, but in order for it to make any sense, I have examined these texts and films through a variety of lenses, especially through a theoretical frame. There are some great works on feminist film theory, genre theory, and cultural theory, and they have informed all of my own readings. Although I have chosen to concentrate on popular or canonical American titles, I have also referenced other texts and films from around the world when appropriate. I have included references to poetry, drama, medical journals, websites, YouTube videos, photographs, paintings, advertisements, and television shows, all of which have enriched my understanding of fictional pregnancy.

Preface

For all of the titles and examples that I have included, I have never intended this work to represent a comprehensive listing of every text or film in which pregnancy is featured—there can be no such list. For those texts which have also been adapted to film, I have tried to acknowledge both. However, some film adaptations are better than others, and some do not lend themselves to a discussion of pregnancy as narrative. For example, Nabokov's *Lolita* has been adapted by Stanley Kubrick in a way that contributes to our understanding of how pregnancy works, but the film version of Atwood's *The Handmaid's Tale* does not tell us much that we cannot discover from that great dystopian novel. I have tried to provide a balanced and complete approach to work with so many examples, which has been challenging, because there is a large number from which to choose. For every title I mention, there are probably ten others that come to mind. The Internet Movie Database has been indispensible; through IMDb and other websites, I have found multiple lists of titles and other helpful information.

Writers often compare working on a big project to being pregnant and giving birth. Having experienced both, I understand the comparison: both a real pregnancy and a major scholarly undertaking require consistency and great labor, and both eventually take on their own lives, often in unexpected ways. This project certainly surprised and delighted me. As often happens with scholarly endeavors, at the beginning of the process I expected certain things to happen. Especially in terms of film, I assumed that I would be studying and writing about the high-profile pregnancy narratives produced by Hollywood: the seamless cautionary melodramas of the 1950s (*Written on the Wind*, 1956; *A Summer Place*, 1959), and perhaps the Doris Day romantic comedies of the late 1950s and early 1960s (*Pillow Talk*, 1959; *Lover, Come Back*, 1961; *The Thrill of It All*, 1963). I assumed I would study romantic epics—from *Doctor Zhivago* in 1965 to *Cold Mountain* in 2003—that include pregnancy narratives of star-crossed lovers.

I was wrong about much of what I expected. Those mainstream films certainly represent pregnancy narratives, and they are all films that I love. But they are not the films that distinguish themselves as significant pregnancy narratives; they do not tell us much about the ways in which pregnancy stories can enrich the narratives through which they move. These conventional movies instead represent set pieces, useful to me as a beautiful control group against which I have been able to examine some wonderful surprises: pregnancy narratives from women's noir, horror, low-budget B movies, and science fiction. In many of these films, pregnancy behaves like a Trojan horse, opening a narrative to reveal all sorts of human emotions and behaviors that have little to do with pregnancy itself.

Pregnancy in Literature and Film has been a major undertaking for me, one that I would never have been able to realize by myself. I thank my family, who are champions: Kennedy Hutson for his patient loyalty, and Boswell Hutson for the honor of being his mother, but more importantly, for giving me his castoff laptop and the Netflix thing. I thank my teacher Robert Carringer for reading an early draft of part of this. I thank these friends who have allowed me to babble to them about *The Scarlet Letter*, *Leave Her to Heaven*, *Lolita*, and on and on. I am lucky to have them: Stephen Swords, Christopher Weedman, Marjorie Hanft, Randy Beebe, Dana Ringuette, Joe Mari, and Bill Searle. Thanks to Scott Hutson. I am grateful for a sabbatical leave from Eastern Illinois University, and to Jean Toothman and Sarah Miller for their help. Booth Library at EIU has done everything right, as usual. I am very grateful to Photofest, which is a national treasure. I thank my beloved students, who have helped me in multiple ways. I am grateful to Coral, Ruby, August, Robin, and Susanna, who all know how they have contributed.

Finally, I am especially indebted to Tina Fey, Maya Rudolph, and Amy Poehler, who all helped me realize, one fateful Saturday night, that when pregnancy dances, we should all celebrate.

Introduction
The Pregnancy Narrative

Kisses for My President

The Hollywood productions for 1964 include some impressive films: *Zorba the Greek, Becket, Mary Poppins* and *My Fair Lady* were all released that year.[1] The 1964 list also includes Hollywood's annual share of unremarkable movies and curiosities, including several horror and fantasy films such as *Santa Claus Conquers the Martians* and *The Creeping Terror*. Listed somewhere closer to the worst end of the 1964 list than to the best, is an almost forgettable movie called *Kisses for My President*, a Warner Bros. production starring Polly Bergen and Fred MacMurray, written for the screen by Claude Binyon and Robert G. Kane. The opening sequence concludes with Bergen, as Leslie Harrison McCloud, standing with one hand on the Bible while she is being sworn in as president of the United States.

There are really few characteristics of *Kisses for My President* that would have distinguished it from any other light Hollywood productions of the mid–twentieth century. The plot is a predictable single joke that centers on the new president's husband Thaddeus (MacMurray), who struggles to find a place for himself as first lady, and who spends a good deal of the film pining for his wife, who is always too busy running the free world to give him much attention. Near the end of the movie, after standing up to international bullies and staving off the attentions of a South American dictator (Eli Wallach), President McCloud holds a press conference in which she announces that she is resigning immediately. Why? Apparently, the little time the McClouds have had together has been fruitful: the president of the United States is resigning because she is pregnant.

Introduction

As *New York Times* reviewer Bosley Crowther wrote, the film is "heavy and unexciting, and all that one can say is that we hope the first woman to become president brings along a more amusing husband than Mr. MacMurray and a more imaginative team of writers than Mr. Binyon and Mr. Kane." To Crowther this film represents little more than frothy fantasy in which even the humor fails: "[T]he prospect of a woman as president [would] not be funny." A woman president would not have been the only unfunny thing, however. A *pregnant* woman president— one who did not decide to resign—would have defined *Kisses for My President* as a horror movie or science fiction instead of a light comedy in 1964 America.

A silly comedy from 1964 has become a marginally clever relic by the 21st century, and tells us more about what passed as mediocre in 1964 films than it tells us about pregnancy. But this film does suggest one of the ways that writers and filmmakers have used pregnancy to move their stories along (as the punchline of a joke). How we come to understand pregnancy in fiction and film depends on many variables, including when the fiction or film was generated, and how the writers and filmmakers frame and focus the pregnancies for us. The spectrum of pregnancy templates is vast. In American literature, there are unspoken pregnancies (*The Scarlet Letter*), unfortunate pregnancies (*The Grapes of Wrath*), poorly timed pregnancies (*An American Tragedy*), and tragic pregnancies (*The Bluest Eye*). In other fiction written in English through the centuries, there are punishing pregnancies (*Charlotte Temple*), deliberate pregnancies (*Incidents in the Life of a Slave Girl*), mysterious or creepy pregnancies (*Rosemary's Baby*, *The Handmaid's Tale*) and un-pregnancies (*Frankenstein*, *Never Let Me Go*). Perhaps the most common literary pregnancy is the unintended pregnancy—a category that would actually include many of the preceding titles. The unintended pregnancy has the most potential for dramatic effect, and represents most of all fictional pregnancies.[2]

In narrative film, pregnancies seem equally numerous and equally complicated, although for the first half of the 20th century, pregnancy was suggested but not depicted very often on film (there are exceptions, as we will see). In pre–Code Hollywood, audiences never heard the word "pregnant" come out of the mouth of any of the characters they saw onscreen, however ("I'm going to have a baby" or "I'm expecting" were the most delicate and popular ways to announce pregnancy).[3] However, many of the women's weepies from these years (1933's *Bed of Roses*, for example) focused on women whose unplanned pregnancies—and subsequent children—forced them into lives they might not otherwise have chosen. Several of the glossiest melodramas of the 1950s, adapted from popular fiction to conform to the rigorous rules of the Production Code, were able to include plot lines about unintended teenage pregnancy because they presented themselves as cautionary tales (*A Summer Place*; *Peyton Place*, 1957). In some of the other blockbuster adaptations of the 1950s, including *A Streetcar Named Desire* (1951), *A Place in the Sun* (1951) and *Cat on a Hot Tin Roof* (1958), pregnancy—or the suggestion of pregnancy—contributes significantly to the integrity of the film.

After the end of the Hays Code era in the 1960s, and for the rest of the 20th century, pregnancy blossomed in Hollywood movies, from staple plot device, to dénouement, to sight gag, and more. During the 1970s, pregnancy in all of its forms, including abortion, began to show up in all genres: musicals (*Cabaret*, 1972); westerns (*A Man Called Horse*, 1970); crime (*The Carey Treatment*, 1972); comedy (*Fast Times at Ridgemont High*, 1982); drama (*Rachel, Rachel*, 1968); horror (*Rosemary's Baby*, 1968). One pregnancy takes place on Mars (*Total Recall*, 1990), another in a film that defies category (*Fargo*, 1996). From the 1960s on, audiences heard the word "pregnant" and its many variations—the crude, the cute, and the curious—over and over. We also saw a variety of pregnancies on the large screen—so many, in fact, that by the turn of the 21st century, pregnancy has gestated and given birth to a new genre of American film: the pregnancy film.

In *Pregnancy in Literature and Film* we will explore the ways that pregnancy—from the silent or unintended, to the intergalactic, to the high-profile—behaves in a variety of American texts and on film. We will study pregnancy as narrative, surveying the ways in which fictional pregnancy moves and changes, investigating how pregnancy reveals and also obscures aspects of the human condition. We will ask questions as we explore. For example, although so often used as plot devices, tropes, and *deus ex machina*, why are the pregnancies in literature and film so rarely the focus of the narratives? In the same way that audiences dismiss the actual tiny babies that may or may not be born (President McCloud's unborn child, for example, will be born after the film concludes and is therefore not even important enough for screen time), the pregnancies themselves sometimes barely register.

Pregnancy may be the most used of all plot devices in narrative because no matter who we are, we all know something about pregnancy. Our recognition of pregnancy allows it, once introduced into a plot, to morph nimbly and become almost anything from a whispered word, to an abstract idea, to a visual image, to a consumable good. Although pregnancy has been used as comic relief in Hollywood film (*Kisses for My President* is a lame and dated example), most films, and the fiction and drama to which film narratives are related, do not elevate pregnancy beyond a stock plot device. Writers and filmmakers rely on pregnancy to emphasize moral complications, to reveal character flaws, or to twist plots in on themselves, much more often than they use pregnancy to telegraph promise or joy. Fictional pregnancy is almost never funny, and can suggest powerlessness and instability. Even poor Leslie McCloud has to make an unfunny, consequential decision because of her pregnancy in *Kisses for My President*.

Yet there are exceptional fictional pregnancies that engage us beyond predictability. We can recognize them because they always embody opposites: tiny and huge, growth and stasis, past and future, covert and overt, pain and joy, on and on. Some fictional pregnancy can reflect the many complications that define pregnancy in real life. For example, in our real world, only one group of people—females—can grow other human beings inside their bodies, a biological fact that seems simple enough. As simple as this seems, it belies the profoundly complex phenomenon that is pregnancy. That women can grow babies inside their bodies—and that men cannot— suggests one of the most fundamental (perhaps *the* most fundamental) power puzzles of our world, one that has influenced every aspect of the way we live and think, from how our institutions function, to our cultural stereotypes, to our values and taboos, to our language and communication, to our religious beliefs, to our art. Pregnancy represents a singular process with no parallel in the male experience, and exclusive female pregnancy permeates every aspect of our lives—including the ways we tell stories.[4]

Visually, all pregnancies develop subtly and slowly, gradually changing the way the pregnant female feels and looks during the forty-week process. However, depending on how the pregnant woman and the people around her behave toward her pregnancy, before her body begins to change, the pregnancy itself might seem real only to her. Depending on the circumstances of the pregnancy and the degree of secrecy involved, the early stages of pregnancy can engage an entire spectrum of behaviors and emotional responses: panic, shame, or horror, to surprise, delight, and celebration. In the real world, a woman's pregnancy can be secret for only so long, of course, which changes everything for the pregnant woman and for those around her. The physical evolution of a pregnancy can be remarkably daunting for everyone involved. The world of the pregnant woman changes daily as she shares her body with the unknown entity inside her. Those of us on the outside of her pregnancy can react to what we see in any number of ways, depending on who we think she is, and who we think we are.

However we react when we see a pregnant woman, we most likely assume one thing about her: we all think that we know how she became pregnant—at least technically. Because we think we know her story, we can leap to all kinds of assumptions and conclusions. This leap of logic actually suggests the most interesting complication of a real pregnancy: Pregnancy seems so predictable that we can project the pregnancy story every time. And it is a story. For those of us on the outside, a pregnant woman becomes a story that we think we already know, one that seems so familiar that we can appropriate it for ourselves, sometimes privately or individually (example: I give up a seat on the subway to a heavily pregnant woman), and sometimes as groups (example: a group of state legislators decides how all pregnancies in its state cannot end). We appropriate other people's pregnancies to our own needs because we think we understand how the story goes. We make any pregnancy part of our own stories. In many ways, we read—we consume—pregnancy. A growing female body gives us a screen wide enough to imagine and project our own stories onto hers.

Pregnancy as Narrative

If real pregnancy represents a muddle of complex ideas, images, feelings and assumptions, then fictional pregnancy reflects an even bigger mess. Fictional pregnancy operates almost in opposition to real pregnancy: if a real pregnancy stays hidden and mysterious until it reveals itself to be a predictable narrative, then a fictional pregnancy begins as a predictable narrative that becomes increasingly complex and inexplicable. Real and fictional pregnancies also become oppositional in terms of who can be pregnant: biology defines pregnancy as exclusive to the female human in the real world, but science fiction suggests that the boundaries of fictional pregnancy are limitless—women and men can both be pregnant in fiction and film, and what pregnant characters deliver may not necessarily be human babies. As we will discover, fictional pregnancy—either in text or onscreen—can behave in ways that both confirm and contradict everything we think we know about pregnancy, and in doing so, can both defy and reveal something about the real world to us, often simultaneously.

When writers and filmmakers ascribe their stories to the bodies of fictional pregnant characters, they are rarely telling us stories about mothers having babies. They are engaging a *pregnancy narrative*: a narrative that inscribes any suggestion of the wide spectrum of women's physical, emotional, and sexual relationships to pregnancy—from menstruation, to sex, to birth control, to conception, to pregnancy, to hysterectomy, to menopause. A pregnancy narrative may tell us something through a missed period, or a miscarriage, or a kick to the mother's belly by an unborn baby. We may suffer through cramps, labor pains, or hemorrhages. And we may be presented with the male counterparts, whose own physical, sexual, and emotional selves are often mirrored and projected to us. Sometimes in pregnancy narratives, men suffer along with their suffering women; sometimes they are nowhere to be found; sometimes they are the pregnant ones. A pregnancy narrative can take us almost anywhere and force us to move ourselves out of our own orbits. How? By telling us a story we already think we know.

Fictional pregnancy filters ideas to us through a system of signs that we already recognize, beginning with either explicit or implicit acknowledgment of how babies are made. Assuming our understanding of how women can grow other human beings inside their bodies, a narrative moves us from a familiar pregnancy tale, to ideas, conflicts, and problems that the narrative may or may not resolve for us. Associating pregnancy with all that we do *not* understand about pregnancy allows narrative pregnancy to function as metaphor, often displacing the aspects of pregnancy that we think we know (how a pregnant body looks, for example) with aspects of pregnancy that we may not really understand (how it feels to be pregnant, for example).

Pregnancy as Metaphor

No one understood the relationship between pregnancy and metaphor better than 27-year-old American poet Sylvia Plath, eight months pregnant with her first child, who puzzled through the language of pregnancy in her 1959 poem "Metaphors" (116).[5] The nine-syllable riddle that Plath presents in her first line has been explored by literary scholars who often discuss alternative solutions to the enigmatic riddle ("I am going to have a baby" might be one obvious answer).[6] Yet Plath's playfulness belies her more serious reflections on the phenomenon of pregnancy. Perhaps more self-aware than many pregnant women—or at least more articulate about her changing self through the pregnancy process—Plath seems to understand that her pregnancy might begin as her riddle, but will certainly reveal itself, after which time she will lose control over how she and her pregnancy will be defined. She describes for us how her pregnancy grows from something inside of her into something outside of her control. To others, her pregnant body becomes one cliché after another, each one increasingly heavy and inevitable, and each one diminishing her power to define herself. Her body becomes a series of words, all language that dismisses and trivializes her. She is reduced to a series of disparate metaphors, none of which can describe how she feels. She becomes instead a thing, a place, a farm animal.

In "Metaphors," Plath understands that pregnancy may begin as a clever riddle whose answer is known only to the pregnant person, but that eventually, a pregnancy will eclipse everything, including the riddle and the person who is pregnant. As a pregnant woman's body changes to accommodate a growing fetus—when she begins to show—then her riddle becomes moot and she becomes a public, visual fetish. As soon as a pregnancy shows, Plath tells us, the pregnant woman becomes just another tale in the public discourse, just another predictable, sometimes laughable caricature. Just as she is helpless to control how her own body behaves and looks during pregnancy, she is also helpless to control how her image is projected and defined by others. A pregnant woman, Plath suggests, becomes a game, a picture, and a joke that someone else is telling.

Other poets before and after Plath have written about both the perils of pregnancy and the valor of pregnancy.[7] Puritan poet Anne Bradstreet, in "Before the Birth of One of Her Children," cautions her husband not to remarry if she dies in childbirth. "And if thou love thyself, or loved'st me,/These O protect from stepdame's injury," she writes (Ferguson 464). Bradstreet, who endured pregnancy and childbirth eight times, knew that dying in childbirth was a real possibility in 17th-century New England. Her many domestic poems and elegies to lost grandchildren attest to her understanding of the dangers of pregnancy.[8] In *The Wasteland*, T.S. Eliot allows us to hear a conversation between two women in a pub. The speaker wants her friend Lil to do something about how bad she looks. "You ought to be ashamed, I said, to look so antique." Lil reminds the speaker that she looks bad because of a self-induced abortion: "I can't help it, she said, pulling a long face,/It's them pills I took, to bring it off, she said" (1348). Anthony Hecht describes his wife's miscarriage in the first line of "The Vow" as a sudden, shocking spot of blood that transforms his early joy into grief and helplessness by the end of the poem (42).

In "the mother," Gwendolyn Brooks's speaker delivers a eulogy in which she explains to us that terminating her pregnancies did not terminate her love for her never-born babies. Brooks concludes by assuring her unborn children that she will always love them (Lauter 2147). Lucille Clifton also expresses her grief in "the lost baby poem," in which she describes how her love for her aborted child transcends the memory of her abortion. Like Hecht in "The Vow," Clifton promises her never born child that her own life, and the lives of her living children, will testify to her love for the one not born (Baym 2801). In "The Language of the Brag," Sharon Olds's speaker boasts directly to two other American poets, both male, who also write about pregnancy and childbirth in their works. Olds's speaker reminds Walt Whitman and Allen Ginsberg that she has accomplished something that neither male poet could ever have done. The thing she has done and brags about? She has endured pregnancy and childbirth. Like a swaggering braggadocio, she boasts that giving birth rivals any manly heroics on any epic scale (57).[9]

Olds, together with Brooks, Hecht, Clifton and other contemporary poets, represent a significant cluster of 20th-century writers whose pregnancy poems "challenge us to examine our criteria regarding what constitutes a heroic act" (Argyros 141).

Pregnancy poetry (of which these few represent only a fraction) reveals another way in which the pregnancy story works: as if we are seeing a reflection in a mirror, a real pregnancy suggests increasing powerlessness for a pregnant woman as her pregnancy shows and increased power for those who see her. When a real pregnancy shows, the story is all but over for those of us on the outside. A woman is pregnant, and somehow that story will resolve itself one way or another. But fictional pregnancy suggests the opposite dynamic: the more we understand about a fictional pregnancy, the more powerful and complicated the pregnancy becomes. As a character begins to understand her own pregnancy narrative, the less control we have over her story. Pregnancy narratives are not as predictable as a bad Hollywood movie might suggest; they are living organisms that move and grow in ways that we cannot predict or control. The more we think we understand about how pregnancy works in storytelling, the less we probably really know.

Chapter Preview

"Film," writes Don DeLillo in his 2003 essay "That Day in Rome," "allows us to examine ourselves in ways earlier societies could not— examine ourselves, imitate ourselves, extend ourselves, reshape our reality. It permeates our lives, this double vision, and also detaches us, turns some of us into actors doing walk-throughs" (76). Although he is referring specifically to the power of cinema, we might argue that DeLillo's argument applies equally to textual storytelling as well, because any story that we see, hear, or read provides us with a "double vision" that engages us and changes the way we see the world. Our exploration of pregnancy narratives in *Pregnancy in Literature and Film* will provide us with ample confirmation of this power of the double vision of narrative. From American literature of the 19th century through narrative films of the 21st century, fictional pregnancy behaves in ways that both mirror and challenge our real world—sometimes serving as

Introduction

a moral compass, sometimes reflecting a dream world, sometimes portending a dystopian nightmare. By the 21st century, how we express and project pregnancy—especially on a screen—reflects and challenges some of our most profound cultural values. The pregnancy narrative has the power to change how we focus and how we frame anything we might experience, including pregnancy.

We begin *Pregnancy in Literature and Film* with a study of fiction in Chapter 1, "'A' Is for Pregnant: The Birth of American Pregnancy Literature." Hester Prynne's pregnancy (which takes place before the action begins) and Linda Brent's two pregnancies in Harriet Jacobs's *Incidents in the Life of a Slave Girl* will become our touchstones as we move from mid–19th century to consider the 20th-century pregnancy literature written by a variety of authors, including canonical authors Kate Chopin and Edith Wharton, both of whom privilege stories about pregnancy in their works. We will consider popular fiction of the mid–20th-century, and also review some of the pregnancy narratives by male authors, including Theodore Dreiser, Ernest Hemingway, and William Faulkner; we will note the pregnancy themes in several playwrights, including Tennessee Williams, Edward Albee, and August Wilson. We will conclude our discussion of pregnancy fiction by examining the pregnancy works of Toni Morrison, Alice Walker, and Sapphire.

In Chapter 2, "The Weepies: Pregnancy, Melodrama and Noir," we will study the relationship between pregnancy and melodrama in fiction and film. Beginning with Harriet Beecher Stowe's *Uncle Tom's Cabin*, we will consider a range of pregnancy narratives which might be classified as weepies in popular American fiction and film in order to understand how pregnancy narratives function in the formulaic melodramas of the 1930s, 1940s, and 1950s. Focusing on D.W. Griffith's epic *Way Down East* in 1920 as one of the first pregnancy narratives in motion picture form, we will trace how melodrama has been the genre in which pregnancy—especially the unintended kind—has always been a most effective part of the Hollywood melodrama formula. We will also consider the ways in which American filmmakers learned to negotiate the strict Production Code during these years through adaptation strategies, so that their audiences could also learn to see beyond the censorship into stories about pregnancy. During and after World War II, pregnancy shows up in a variety of ways in American film, perhaps most pointedly in film noir. By the 1950s, pregnancy became part of a nightmare vision—especially for men—unless we are watching television.

In Chapter 3, "Pregnant Teenagers and Other Monsters," we will consider two of the most distinctive pregnancy narratives, both of which included pregnancy narratives involving teenagers: *Peyton Place* and *Lolita*. We will explore the genre of "teenpics," a group of B-movies marketed specifically to American teenagers in the post–World War II era. Among the most popular of these were low-budget horror films. We will consider ways in which pregnancy haunts the horror genre, beginning with Mary Shelley's *Frankenstein,* moving on through James Whale's 1931 adaptation of the same, and beyond. By the 1960s, horror was a well-established and especially expressive American genre, often focusing the horror in suburban homes or upscale urban townhouses. We will conclude this chapter with a discussion of the creepiest American pregnancy story ever: *Rosemary's Baby*.

In Chapter 4, "The Mothership Arrives: Pregnancy in Science Fiction" we will explore how pregnancy moves around the science fiction genre. We will focus on several significant films, including the *Alien* trilogy. We will explore other kinds of motherless reproduction on film including cloning, and Margaret Atwood's nightmare vision of forced pregnancy in *The Handmaid's Tale*. We will consider what happens when men become pregnant on film, and how pregnancy technologies have encouraged cinematic adventures into the womb in *Look Who's Talking*. We will consider the ways in which space travel movies use the pregnancy narrative to help us understand the possibilities of rebirth. Finally, we will return to Earth, to where we began: *The Scarlet Letter*.

In Chapter 5, "Ways of Seeing Pregnancy," we will consider theoretical questions about how we evaluate artistic expressions of pregnancy. With the help of John Berger's *Ways of Seeing* and Laura Mulvey's study of the male gaze, we will consider how film frames pregnancy, and how we receive pregnancy. Our best guide will be artist Frida Kahlo, whose pregnancy self-portraits remain some of the most important pregnancy art to date. We will then review some of the most innovative pregnancy films of the 20th century. Beginning with *Breathless* in 1960, a diverse group of filmmakers—including women—began showing us pregnancy tales in ways that seemed especially original, including movies that feature abortion. We will study some of the most recent pregnancy narratives, including *Fargo* and *Juno,* and we will consider the ways in which film, as a collaborative art, reflects pregnancy, also a collaborative endeavor. We will conclude our study with a discussion of the linguistic characteristics of narrative pregnancy, as we consider the final lyrical sequence of *Daughters of the Dust.* Before we begin our narrative pregnancy journey, however, we need to return once more to 1964.

The Pumpkin Eater

Kisses for My President was not the only film to open in the fall of 1964 in which pregnancy showed. Jacques Demy's *The Umbrellas of Cherbourg* sang us the story of Genviève (Catherine Deneuve), a beautiful young Frenchwoman, desolate and pregnant, whose lover has left for the Army. Another 1964 film, *The Pumpkin Eater,* adapted by Harold Pinter from Penelope Mortimer's 1962 novel and directed by Jack Clayton, might have seemed shocking to some American audiences, because Pinter had faithfully adapted the entire novel, including scenes in which characters discuss pregnancy, abortion, and hysterectomies. Unless they were reading lurid dime novels or watching low-budget B movies, American audiences were not hearing these discussions in mainstream Hollywood fare at the time, and would only experience if they were buying tickets for theaters in urban areas that showed art films and foreign movies.[10]

The American audiences who saw the movie liked it, and so did American critics. *Time* described the film as a "slow, strong, incisive film version of the book, the ironing out of a well-kept wife's unkempt psyche" (125). Because it was produced in the UK, *The Pumpkin Eater* did not suffer the censorship that likely would have mutilated an American adaptation. The film is now considered an example of "the celebrated heyday of English social-realist cinema, influenced by Italian Neorealism and the French New Wave. Among such exceptional films as *Saturday Night and Sunday Morning* (1960), *A Taste of Honey* (1961), *The Loneliness of the Long Distance Runner* (1962), and *This Sporting Life* (1963)," *The Pumpkin Eater* remains a well-crafted and powerful film (Sterritt).[11] Anne Bancroft won a Golden Globe, a BAFTA, and a Best Actress Award from the Cannes Film Festival for her work in *The*

Pumpkin Eater, in which she played Jo Armitage, fragile wife to a philandering husband, mother of seven children, and pregnant off and on
throughout the film.

If *Kisses for My President* represents the most stereotypical way that
Hollywood used pregnancy until the 1960s—as a heavily censored plot
device—then *The Pumpkin Eater* anticipates how pregnancy will begin
to behave in American film after 1966. We watch Jo Armitage in various
stages of pregnancy. We hear her reveal her secret pregnancy to her
mother; we watch her struggling to do housework and care for children
while she is seven or eight months pregnant; we endure a close-up of her
anguished face while she is recovering from an abortion and hysterectomy; we gauge her reaction when she is told that her husband has impregnated a young actress. *The Pumpkin Eater* exemplifies the ways in which
pregnancy on film can be so compelling that it eventually overshadows
everything as it moves the narrative. Sylvia Plath, writing about how it
felt to be diminished by pregnancy at about the same time that Mortimer
was writing *The Pumpkin Eater*, certainly would have understood.

In fact, Penelope Mortimer and Sylvia Plath both published novels
in 1962 about women who have nervous breakdowns (*The Pumpkin
Eater* and *The Bell Jar*). Both authors represent two in a significant cluster
of 20th century women writers who came of age during and after World
War II, and whose fiction most often expressed something about the
female condition. Unlike earlier generations of women writers who
sometimes masked their gender through narrative techniques, these
writers identified themselves and their central women characters as
females. The group, all Mortimer's contemporaries, includes Iris Mur-
doch, Nadine Gordimer, Muriel Spark, Denise Levertov, and especially
Doris Lessing, in whose novels *The Golden Notebook* and *A Proper Marriage* (and later, in *The Fifth Child*) we experience the female perspective.
In all of these writers' works we read about how female characters think
and talk about everything from politics to their monthly cramps, from
world events to how they are supposed to navigate their own lives. In
The Golden Notebook, Ella, herself a fictional character created by Lessing's character Anna Wulf, explains the dilemma of these modern
women:

> My deep emotions, my real ones, are to do with my relationship with a
> man. One man. But I don't live that kind of life, and I know few women

who do. So what I feel is irrelevant and silly ... I am always coming to the conclusion that my real emotions are foolish; I am always having, as it were, to cancel myself out. I ought to be like a man, caring more for my work than for people; I ought to put my work first, and take men as they come, or find an ordinary comfortable man for bread and butter reasons— but I won't do it, I can't be like that ... [300].

Plath's generation of women writers followed. Many, like Plath herself, were college graduates with careers as scholars, journalists, editors, and teachers. They were almost all mothers as well: Adrienne Rich, Audre Lorde, Anne Sexton, Toni Morrison, Margaret Drabble, Joan Didion, Alice Munro, Maya Angelou, Margaret Atwood, and many other women all began exploring the female experience through poetry, essays and fiction during the middle decades of the 20th century.[12] Whether they were writing in Canada, the United States, the UK, or South Africa, all of these writers were "centering on women's consciousness and concerns" in their "exploration of female interiority" (Greene, 17). They explored differently and with various degrees of success, and their works, often difficult to categorize but generally considered postmodern, share at least one characteristic: at some point, they all explore pregnancy.

In her 1970 novel *Play It as It Lays*, Joan Didion's heroine Maria Wyeth, a divorced sometimes-actress, is recovering from a nervous breakdown. She has isolated herself from almost everyone she loves, including her four-year-old daughter Kate, and in short, terse snapshots, the narrator tells us the story of Maria's meltdown. Among the events that haunts her is an abortion, which she remembers in spite of trying not to think about it. She has trouble sleeping. When she wakes up, she remembers: "But by dawn she was always back in the house in Beverly Hills.... Instead of calling Les Goodwin she bought a silver vinyl dress, and tried to stop thinking about *what had he done with the baby. The tissue. The living dead thing, whatever you called it*" (115). In the same year, Toni Morrison published *The Bluest Eye*, in which we learn from our adult narrator Claudia in the second sentence that adolescent Pecola Breedlove "was having her father's baby" (9). In the second paragraph Claudia tells us how Pecola's pregnancy story ends: Pecola's father is now dead, "our innocence too. The seeds shriveled and died; her baby too" (9).

The Pregnancy Narrative

It is no coincidence that at the same time that these fiction writers were beginning to explore and experiment with new narrative perspectives that included pregnancy, a parallel dynamic was happening among screenwriters and filmmakers. *The Pumpkin Eater* represents only one of many postmodern works—by both women and men—that would be adapted to the screen in the 1960s and beyond, and not just among filmmakers outside the U.S. The heavily coded, stock plot device of Hollywood movies for decades, pregnancy would begin to show in all genres of American film as well. Some of the first American films to suggest the power of a pregnancy narrative were adaptations of stage plays or novels written by men. Tennessee Williams, especially, provided dramas in which pregnancy shows: *A Streetcar Named Desire*, first staged in 1947 and filmed in 1951, included a very pregnant Stella in almost every scene; in *Cat on a Hot Tin Roof* (staged in 1955 and filmed in 1958), Goober's wife Mae is pregnant throughout the action, and Maggie feigns pregnancy at the end of the play.

The same year that Penelope Mortimer published *The Pumpkin Eater*, Edward Albee's *Who's Afraid of Virginia Woolf?* opened on Broadway, a terse tragicomedy in which both married couples, George and Martha, and Nick and Honey, reveal their experiences with pregnancy, false pregnancy, and imaginary pregnancy—all pregnancy narratives that the characters use to hurt each other throughout their drunken howling night together. When Mike Nichols directed the film version of *Who's Afraid of Virginia Woolf?* in 1966, he kept the pregnancy narratives intact. The scenes in which we learn about the two couples' pregnancy issues remain some of the most electric—and disturbing—scenes in the film. Also electrifying is the pregnancy narrative in *Fences*, August Wilson's Pulitzer Prize–winning play, first produced on Broadway in 1987, in which we come to understand most clearly the characters of the difficult main character Troy and his long-suffering wife Rose through a pregnancy narrative. Troy enters his yard carrying his newborn daughter—whose mother, Troy's lover, has died in childbirth. He explains to a stunned Rose, who listens, then takes the baby from him. "You can't visit the sins of the father on the child," Rose says. "From right now," she continues, "this child got a mother. But you a womanless man" (Miller, 1081).

By the turn of the 21st century, discovering a pregnancy narrative

Introduction

Fanny Brice (Barbra Streisand) plays a pregnant bride onstage at the *Ziegfeld Follies* in *Funny Girl* (1968). Earlier in the 1960s, Hollywood's Production Code began to lose its long-held power to restrict images of pregnancy on film, allowing for movies of all genres to include images of pregnant women, whether they were sight gags or not.

on stage or on film does not seem out of the ordinary. Even American musical theater, always considered a close relative of melodrama, has provided us with pregnancies: the plot of Rodgers and Hammerstein's *Carousel,* first staged in 1945 and filmed in 1956, revolves around a pregnancy. The 1963 stage and 1968 screen productions of *Funny Girl* use pregnancy as a sight gag with Fanny Brice (Barbra Streisand) in the *Ziegfeld Follies.* Dressed in an elaborate wedding gown and enormously pregnant, she sings suggestively about how her love's affection is reflected in her appearance. More recently, the 1995 novel and the 2003 musical production of *Wicked* include embedded pregnancy narratives, as do the award-winning *Spring Awakening* (2006) and *American Idiot* (2009). The lists of novels, stage plays, screenplays, and memoirs that include references to any aspect of pregnancy are very long, and attest to the remarkable talents of artists—men and women—who through the

22

decades have transformed the pregnancy narrative from a predictable series of sight gags into a fully developed language. The contrast between conventional pregnancy narratives in earlier Hollywood films, and those pregnancies which suggest complication and power—especially in Hollywood productions since 2000—suggests that pregnancy has become an impressive and complicated cipher in film art.

Among films produced by Hollywood, by independent companies, or international productions, we now have some especially beautiful and complex pregnancy narratives, some of which stand out as magnificent images of pregnancy. The 1992 adaptation of E.M. Forster's *Howards End* includes some beautifully dressed pregnant characters, including Helen Schlegel (Helena Bonham Carter), whose pregnancy near the end of the film covers the entire screen; Pedro Almodóvar's *All About My Mother* (*Todo Sobre mi Madre*, 1999) allows us to watch the pregnancy of Rosa (Penelope Cruz) as she struggles with a series of complications; in Dai Sijie's *Balzac and the Little Chinese Seamstress* (*Balzac et la Petite Tailleuse Chinoise*, 2002), we see Luo (Chen Kun) and the Little Seamstress (Zhou Xun) try to arrange for an abortion in the midst of the Chinese Cultural Revolution. In *Junebug*, Ashley Johnson (Amy Adams) is a clear-eyed, smiling North Carolina girl, almost due when we meet her. Convinced that the baby she is carrying will solidify her rocky marriage, Ashley represents the deep heart of the film. Guillermo del Toro's *Pan's Labyrinth* (2006) includes the tragic pregnancy of beautiful Carmen (Adriana Gil), mother of Ofelia, a girl sustained by her own imagination during the Spanish Civil War.

Besides these recent independent and international pregnancy narratives, Hollywood films have also provided some compelling pregnancy narratives. High-profile examples include *Traffic* (2000), in which Helena Ayala (Catherine Zeta-Jones), the wife of drug kingpin Carlos Ayala, works the cocaine trade on her husband Carlos's behalf while he sits awaiting trial for drug trafficking in San Diego. Helena is visibly pregnant throughout the film; the only time we see any reference to her pregnancy is when she refuses to taste the cocaine she is selling to her Mexican associate. In the 2002 adaptation of Michael Cunningham's exquisite novel *The Hours*, we watch a very pregnant Laura Brown (Julianne Moore) try to negotiate her husband's birthday and her own deepening depression, all under the eye of her observant young son Richie (Jack

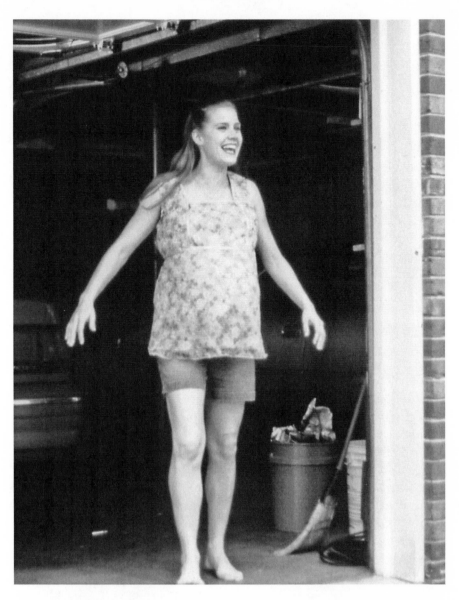

Ashley Johnson (Amy Adams) is only days away from having a baby when we meet her at the beginning of *Junebug* (2005). Although Ashley comes across as naïve, her pregnancy and complicated delivery near the conclusion of the film reveal remarkable facets of her character. *Junebug* exemplifies the power and sophistication of the pregnancy narrative in early twenty-first century films.

Rovello). And in *The Master* (2012), Peggy Dodd (Amy Adams), the young wife of charismatic leader of "The Cause," Lancaster Dodd (Philip Seymour Hoffman), appears to be pregnant throughout the film until the final scene, when she helps her husband expel Freddie Quell (Joaquin Phoenix) from the Cause. Like the pregnancies of Helena Ayala and Laura Brown, that of the steely-eyed, resolute Peggy suggests to us that she wields far deeper, more complex power than we know. Her pregnancy remains an unspoken but important story to which we are not privy. Her pregnancy is none of our business, and all of her own.

Eventually, all pregnancies become stories, whether publicly or privately, whether on a screen, in a text, or in our lives. Conversely, all stories suggest pregnancies as well. From the moment we conceive any idea, we are carrying within us a living organism, one that changes, grows, and eventually resolves into something else. This specter of pregnancy may have occurred to Nathaniel Hawthorne as he was conceiving perhaps the most famous fictional pregnancy ever, one shrouded in such silence that we might not recognize it. When Hawthorne secretly impregnated Hester Prynne, he made sure that she had conceived and delivered before his "tale of human frailty and sorrow" began. We have to assume and imagine Hester's unintended pregnancy. Hawthorne invites us to do so in many ways. However we imagine Hester's story, we can be sure of this: this pregnancy narrative will eventually transform our tale of human frailty and sorrow into something we cannot yet imagine.

1

"A" Is for Pregnant

The Birth of American Pregnancy Literature[1]

The Scarlet Letter

Nathaniel Hawthorne knew that the plot of *The Scarlet Letter* would likely be damned by some critics who, like the anonymous writer for *The Church Review and Ecclesiastical Register*, indeed found that Hawthorne's book encouraged "bad morals" (Wineapple, 217). Given the tastes and social mores of American readers in the 1840s, any depictions of secret passion in the forest, conception, labor pains, or childbirth would have relegated Hawthorne's tale to pulp or worse. Beyond any public distaste, several scholars have also suggested that Hawthorne had his own personal struggles with pregnancy and childbirth. "Although Hawthorne was confined by social values and rules, it is unlikely, given his temperament, fears, sexual guilt ... that he would have ... included the scene of the birth or the sex between Dimmesdale and Prynne that necessarily preceded the pregnancy" (Barlowe 108). For squeamish Hawthorne, pregnancy and childbirth were still the purview of women in the 1840s, which afforded his male narrator a convenient silence on both.[2]

For whatever reasons—practical and aesthetic, simple and complicated—Hawthorne left the details and circumstances of Hester's pregnancy to our imaginations, a narrative strategy of which he was a master.[3] Like all good storytellers, he understood that the less detail he provided, the more detail we would add ourselves. His silence on Hester's pregnancy allows us to imagine how Hester came to be pregnant in *The Scarlet Letter*. And his narrator, obsessed with Hester Prynne from the beginning, provides us with enough detail to encourage our projections of Hester as a pregnant woman, even as he is silent on her actual pregnancy. Hester may never be pregnant in the novel, but there would be no *The Scarlet Letter* without Hester Prynne's pregnancy. This great silent pregnancy represents the heart of the novel's power, that of "the absent presence of sex and childbirth, never mentioned, but always there shaping the narrative" (109). The silent yet always present pregnancy makes *The Scarlet Letter* one of the primary templates of American pregnancy literature.

When we meet Hester Prynne in the second chapter of the novel, she is a new mother with an infant daughter, both on display for all of Puritan Boston—and for us—to ogle. Hawthorne's narrator, the "gentlemanly moralist" who guides us with maddening deliberation through his "tale of human frailty and sorrow," makes us wait to see her until he has carefully introduced the scene: he describes the prison, the weeds beside the prison, the prison door, and the rose bush beside the prison door (Leverenz 264).[4] Before Hester comes through that very door, our narrator makes us wait further, while he describes some of the others who are also waiting to see Hester Prynne. Many of them are Puritan goodwives: sturdy, earthy Elizabethan women with "broad shoulders and well-developed busts" and a "boldness and rotundity of speech" (55). As we all wait for Hester to appear, our narrator allows us to listen to some of these goodwives, who speak plainly and ruthlessly about her, suggesting that she ought to be branded "with a hot iron" or should be executed (56).

Why are these women so savage toward Hester? Although she had lived among them for several years before her pregnancy, they talk about her as if they do not really know her well, calling her generic names ("hussy," "naughty baggage"). Like a slightly dim Greek chorus, these goodwives announce the entrance of someone whom they do not quite understand, but seem to fear. And they are jealous. They "envy [Hester's] beauty and resent her hauteur. They are fearful of her and suspicious of their own husbands, since the paternity of little Pearl is a mystery they surely do not want solved too close to their own homes" (Donohue 64).

Our narrator has used these hearty goodwives as his foil. He makes sure that when we see her, we will know that Hester Prynne is not just another of these stereotypical provincial women. Just before the prison door opens, he has prepared us for the remarkable "ritual set piece" that is this first pillory scene: "[A]ll mankind is present, but only Dimmesdale and Chillingworth know anything, the crowd below looks and sees not, hears and understands not" (51). What Dimmesdale and Chillingworth both know, and what the narrator wants us to understand through his protracted introduction of Hester is this: Hester is no goodwife. Hester is a knockout. Our narrator finds her ravishing, stunning, hot.

When Hester, with infant Pearl in her arms, steps into the fresh air and sunshine, our narrator describes her "burning blush," her "haughty smile," and finally, the scarlet A on her bosom, which is "so artistically done, and with so much fertility and gorgeous luxuriance of fancy," that the narrator questions whether or not this adornment challenges the limits of Puritan mores (57). But he only questions the A for a fleeting moment. Instead, he describes Hester for us in a way that mimics the embellished letter on her chest. He speaks in such rich and elaborate detail that we might begin to question the limits of *his* propriety:

> The young woman was tall, with a figure of perfect elegance, on a large scale. She had dark and abundant hair, so glossy that it threw off the sunshine with a gleam, and a face which, besides being beautiful from regularity of feature and richness of complexion, had the impressiveness belonging to a marked brow and deep black eyes [57].

He continues to describe Hester's outfit, which she had designed and assembled while she was in prison: "Her attire … seemed to express the attitude of her spirit, the desperate recklessness of her mood, by its wild and picturesque peculiarity" (57). The "point which drew all eyes," was "that SCARLET LETTER, so fantastically embroidered and illuminated upon her bosom. It had the effect of a spell" (57–58).

Hester's scarlet letter indeed casts a spell on us all throughout the novel. Perhaps the most spellbound is the storyteller himself. From the time he describes Hester on the scaffold until he describes her final resting place, this narrator cannot keep his mind or his eyes off Hester Prynne's bosom. He tells us everything about the letter: what it looks like, what other people think it means (Angel, Able, etc.), what popular legends have sprung up about it. In his calm ambiguous voice, he recounts one such fantastic legend in a chapter devoted almost exclusively to Hester's A, "Hester at Her Needle": "The vulgar … averred, that the symbol was not mere scarlet cloth, tinged in an earthly dye-pot, but was red-hot with infernal fire, and could be seen glowing all alight, whenever Hester Prynne walked abroad in the night-time" (81). Red-hot indeed.

His constant references to and descriptions of Hester's A reveal our narrator's own obsession with Hester, and his obsession with the scarlet A shapes the way he tells this story. This is an intelligent, careful voice, one who measures his words. He gives equal time to Dimmesdale, Chillingworth, and Pearl, letting all of them speak for themselves throughout the novel. He balances his descriptions of their clothing and appearances in ways that make them all complex, challenging characters. And yet although these characters have distinguishing features that the narrator describes (Chillingworth's dark brow, Dimmesdale's pale visage, Pearl's robust complexion, for example), not one of them commands his attention or requires his control with the same intensity as Hester does. Their posture is never so dignified as Hester's, nor do they have luxuriously dark hair that eludes him (the narrator wonders: Where is her hair? Did she cut it? Is it under her cap?). And none of them wears intricately embroidered scarlet letters on the ample bodices of their clothing.

Hester's A has a power over the narrator that no one and nothing else in the novel has. Even when he thinks he is telling us something else, he has Hester's bosom on his mind. For example, he thinks that he is describing Hester's nursing skills with this: "Hester's nature showed itself warm and rich; a well-spring of human tenderness, unfailing to every demand, and inexhaustible by the largest. Her breast, with its badge of shame, was but the softer pillow for the head that needed one" (131). Our narrator is preoccupied, obsessed, besotted with the elegant and silent Hester Prynne and her bosom.

"What are the sources of the A's residual power and why will it not fade with the story constructed to release its power?" asks Joanne Feit Diehl, in her essay on the Scarlet A as fetish (247). The "clue to its power," she continues, "is contact with the wearer and the ability of the A to draw all eyes toward it" (247). With his eyes drawn toward the A, the narrator indeed yearns for "contact with the wearer." The source of the letter's power is the one that the narrator does not tell us, but from which he cannot turn away: Hester as sexual, and then as lush pregnant woman. Sexually active Hester, the one whom our narrator projects when he describes her or the A, consumes him throughout the novel. And the more he tries to control Hester's story— by allowing her to speak fewer words than any other character—the less control he has over his fixation with sexual Hester. He cannot control his own distance from the story of Hester's A any more successfully than he can control Hester herself.

In the critical history of *The Scarlet Letter*, Hester's sexual history has been largely ignored or dismissed. For example, in "The Obliquity of Signs: *The Scarlet Letter*," Millicent Bell suggests that Hester's "sexual history is so private that it cannot be imagined when we gaze at her in the chaste aftermath" of the novel (Person, 461). Perhaps some readers cannot imagine Hester's sexual life, but Hawthorne's narrator suggests and projects it for us. In the most remarkable and revealing chapter of the novel, "Another View of Hester" (a chapter situated almost exactly in the middle—at the heart—of the book), our narrator projects us into Hester's most private place: her mind. In doing so, he also reveals something intimate about himself: the silent part of his story which he has never been able to tell or control—Hester's pregnancy—controls his entire narrative. The more he does not mention Hester as sexually active and pregnant woman, the more she stands before us as a radiant sexual woman in full bloom, one who is carrying a child.

The narrator tells us that seven years have passed since Pearl was born in "Another View of Hester," and now Hester supports herself and Pearl "by the faithful labor of her hands" as a seamstress (131). She has also become a nurse and confidant, "self-ordained" as a "Sister of Mercy" to the townspeople (131). "Hester's nature showed itself warm and rich," the narrator tells us with his usual reference to Hester's luxuriant visage, and of course, he describes her bosom. Hester has become a respected, if marginal member of her community and to the very men who had punished her with the Scarlet Letter seven years earlier, her badge of shame now "had the effect of the cross on a nun's bosom. It imparted to the wearer a kind of sacredness, which enabled her to walk securely amid all peril" (132).

The narrator devotes several paragraphs to a description of how her appearance has changed since the time we first met her (this chapter is, literally, a *view* of Hester). The "red-hot brand" has affected her in "powerful and peculiar" ways (132). She has replaced her artistically con-structed dress, which the narrator had described for us during the first pillory scene, with severely plain clothes. In an incredibly revealing passage, the narrator laments with sensuous longing that he cannot account for Hester's magnificent hair. Once "rich and luxuriant," her dark hair had "either been cut off, or was so completely hidden by a cap, that not a shining lock of it ever once gushed into the sunshine" (132). Hester is thin, plain, and she stands mute as a statue, yet this besotted narrator still conjures an image of the stunning new mother from seven years' earlier for us at this point. Another view of Hester, then, is not really another view at all, but a re-view of Hester in full bloom, as she appeared to us in the doorway of the prison.

"Another View of Hester" reveals a narrator who seems unwilling and unable to reconcile himself to Hester as a mature woman who is now raising a child. When he tries to describe her plain dress and vanished hair, he can only remember her as luxurious. When he tells us that Hester is now sexless, he instead reminds us of her as vibrant and sexual: "[T]here seemed to be no longer any thing in Hester's face for Love to dwell upon; nothing in Hester's form, though majestic and statue-like, that passion would ever dream of clasping in its embrace; nothing in Hester's bosom, to make it ever again the pillow of Affection" (133). Eventually, he stops his own elaborate narration—several times—and delivers to us instead single, simple declarations. He becomes a stern man of few words when he delivers these simple pronouncements in "Another View of Hester":

> "Hester Prynne imbibed this spirit" [133].
> "Everything was against her" [134].
> "The world was hostile" [134].

We can tell that our fluid narrator is himself changed by Hester's transformation by the way his narration of her story changes. He seems paralyzed to reconcile himself to this mature, self-reliant woman that Hester has made herself into without his attentions. His simple declarations represent "points in the text where [Hawthorne] abandons his technique of narrative and stylistic ambiguity" (Railton 496). Hawthorne's narrator, who has been playing with us in some ways until now, means business here: he realizes that he has lost control of Hester's story, even as he describes her thoughts and actions to us. In utter frustration at Hester's transformation from passive victim to determined head of her own household, and after babbling nonsense about the "ethereal essence" of woman, our narrator utters one last—and most baffling and brittle of all of his pronouncements: "The scarlet letter had not done its office" (134).[5] This confusing statement about Hester actually helps to reveal and explain Hester's particular power over him and over us in *The Scarlet Letter.*

If the scarlet letter did not do what it was supposed to do, what, exactly, was it supposed to do? How would any of us have known if the scarlet letter had done its office? Just before this odd pronouncement, our narrator has described how Hester, imagining a better world for herself and her child, realizes that "the whole system of society is to be torn down, and built up anew" (134). She understands that the "long hereditary habit" of men will never allow for such a revolution of institutions and ideas, and so she wanders "in the dark labyrinth" of her own mind, sometimes, at her most hopeless, trying to decide whether or not to kill Pearl and herself. And then: "The scarlet letter had not done its office." Would the scarlet letter have done its office if Hester had not thought about her and her child's place in the world in which they lived? Would the Scarlet A have accomplished something if Hester had killed Pearl and herself? There is nothing in Hawthorne's text to support the idea that Hester's projections of a different world, or her suicidal thoughts, would have validated her. But what she thinks about is important to understanding the change in the narrator here: whatever Hester thinks about or projects in this chapter, Pearl is *always* part of her equation. In the middle of his story, the narrator of *The Scarlet Letter* comes to realize that "Another View of Hester" is a view of Hester as mother, not as the narrator's fetish or pet.

The narrator recognizes that he cannot possibly understand Hester now—her distance from the story he thinks he is telling cannot be measured in years or in how her bosom has changed. The punishing scarlet letter that Hester has been forced to wear will never have chastened Hester in whatever ways the Puritan law might have imagined. After seven years' time, Hester answers only to her own living, breathing scarlet letter, Pearl. Pearl is Hester's punishment, but also her heart—our evidence lies in Hester's yearning for a new world for herself and Pearl; in her willingness to die with Pearl, and in the reaction of our narrator to this revelation. Pregnancy and childbirth, public and punishing for Hester, have transformed her from a lonely young widow into a mature, fearless woman who is no longer solitary, and who has learned to define herself as someone's mother. The narrator himself has described this transformed Hester, and has shown us why the scarlet letter did not do its office: because Hester does not regret her pregnancy.

Being pregnant, giving birth, and mothering Pearl have all empowered Hester and enriched her imagination. And our clueless narrator, obsessed with visions of Hester's bosom and luxurious hair, understands just enough here to know that the Hester he has described is merely his imaginary Hester. The real Hester, the one who will continue to move about in his story—on and off the pillory, in and out of the forest—will elude and defy him. After "Another View of Hester," he will not be able to explain or understand Hester as well as he does the other characters in the novel because he seems unable or unwilling to distinguish the profound difference between Hester's sin and those of the other players: her pregnancy. The scarlet A on Hester's bosom did not do its office because she doesn't regret being pregnant or having a baby.

As shamed, humbled and humiliated as Hester appears to have been, she harbors no regrets about giving birth to Pearl. Birthing and raising Pearl has delivered Hester from the life of an unhappy passive widow into an active thinker and participant in her own life. We learn this best from the narrator himself, who, in this same remarkable chapter, projects that without Pearl, Hester might have been an important revolutionary figure, "hand in hand with Ann Hutchinson," or perhaps a "prophetess" (134), only to remind us that Hester's pregnancy gave her a more compelling and challenging task: "Providence, in the person of this little girl, had assigned to Hester's charge the germ and blossom of womanhood, to be cherished and developed amid a host of difficulties" (134). With everything "against her," and confronting the "hostile" world of Puritan Boston, Hester has spent the first seven years of Pearl's life reflecting about whether she should "send Pearl at once to heaven, and go herself," and she has rejected this idea every time (134). Hester's pregnancy and her daughter are the best things she's ever done. They have provided her with real power. In "Another View of Hester," we discover that no matter how he tries, the narrator cannot make Hester wish that she hadn't gotten pregnant any more than the Puritan fathers can make her reveal her child's father.

1. "A" Is for Pregnant: The Birth of American Pregnancy Literature

In his excellent essay "The Address of *The Scarlet Letter*," Stephen Railton reminds us that Hawthorne's Victorian readers reacted differently to his novel than we do. For example, however a 19th-century reader might have anticipated the plot early on, "every modern reader already knows that Dimmesdale is Hester's lover" (496). Modern readers also evaluate Hester's stature and character differently as well when we first meet her on the scaffold. Where Hawthorne's 19th-century readers might "reject any identification with so dark a heroine," our modern sensibilities allow us to "prejudge Hester, so passionate a victim of a bad marriage and a repressive society" (496). Historical distance and cultural light years away from Hawthorne's 19th-century America, we can reassess more than Hester's bad marriage, however. Because of Hawthorne's careful storytelling, especially the authoritative yet ambiguous narrative voice that tells this dark tale through "euphemism" so as not to upset "his present day readers," Hawthorne was able to write "one of the nineteenth century's most mature explorations of adult sexuality" (497). As we plow through Hawthorne's ambiguous language and euphemistic devices in our 21st century readings, we can easily transcend his careful storyteller to project Hester as she might have looked just before the narrator appropriates her story: as a pregnant woman. Hawthorne's narrator himself admonishes us near the end of his tale to "be true," and undeterred by Victorian mores, we can read a different yet clear truth into Hawthorne's tale of sorrow: the only truth here is the power of Hester's pregnancy, without which this story would be nothing.

"Certainly for most readers, in Hawthorne's time and in ours," Railton writes, "the tragic waste of Hester's powers and passions is what resonates most deeply as we close the tale" (498). The tragic waste in *The Scarlet Letter* is that we are the only ones who can acknowledge Hester's powers and passions, which are manifest so clearly by the fruit of her womb and in the form of her daughter. For a modern reader, that which triumphs over our anguish is, finally, "the earthly fate of Pearl's self" (498). Indeed, Pearl also eludes Hawthorne's narrator throughout the novel—especially after he loses control of Hester in "Another View of Hester." Although he describes her throughout the novel as a wild, uncontrollable imp who bedevils everyone around her, including her own mother, the Pearl we come to see has characteristics consistent with many little girls: high-spirited, intelligent, and perceptive, a child who knows how to defend herself and how to manipulate her mother. The storyteller seems to sense that Pearl is out of his jurisdiction, that she is a creation beyond his power to control.[6] Our final image of Pearl in the final chapter is another ambiguous vision provided by the narrator who can no longer tell us much about the women in this tale. He describes Pearl as a grown woman, perhaps with a child of her own, who has thrived in Europe, far away from the grim Puritan community into which she was so un-ceremoniously born.

The great irony of Hawthorne's *The Scarlet Letter* is that the unspoken, uncontrollable pregnancy is the one absolute of the novel—the only unmovable element in the entire tale. Hester's power derives from her unspoken, offstage pregnancy, which grows from a secret shadow before the tale begins into the only fact—the only unmovable truth—of the novel. Throughout the novel, the narrator tries to keep Hester quiet, and he keeps quiet himself, on pregnancy and childbirth. For him, this silent pregnancy behaves as a wild card, allowing the shadow of pregnant Hester to become a moving target in *The Scarlet Letter*, both just out of his reach. But the power of the Scarlet A—the symbol of Hester's calling—is that she (and subsequently, her daughter) can bear children, and that she does not regret having borne one. While the other characters here—authoritarian narrator, wretched Reverend Dimmesdale and rotten Roger Chillingworth—all flounder, lose their grips, lose their moral compasses, and decay, Hester and Pearl escape and thrive. And although even as an old woman who has returned to New England voluntarily, Hester is not happy—she is lonely, isolated, chastened by how her life has destroyed the lives of others—she lives in a world that she created, one in which the fact of her pregnancy has defined all else. She may have endured her pregnancy in prison, but being pregnant is ultimately that which liberates her from the Puritan prison of her earthly life. Her pregnancy becomes her salvation.

"Although Hawthorne's characters in *The Scarlet Letter* are ritual figures," writes Agnes Donohue, "they nonetheless have a real life of their own. Hester is certainly Hawthorne's triumph" (52). He may not have intended Hester to be an unconventional feminist with subversive ideas about how the world should work, but Hawthorne had to have hoped that Hester would outlive the other Puritans in his tale, and his own age as well. Hawthorne enriched Hester Prynne with such complexity that her profile has survived many shifting signifiers through the centuries: she is a woman who can morph from humiliated sinner, chastened scarlet woman, and patient nurse in the 19th century to a woman who "brings up a child," "earns a living for two by needlework," and "suffers abuse in silence" in the 20th century (Baym 405). By the 21st century, she has survived the transmutation all the way from novel heroine to multiple turns as a larger-than-life heroine on a movie screen. In the age of film adaptation and revision, Hester Prynne will not only raise a child, but finally gets to conceive and bear her as well.

Incidents in the Life of a Slave Girl

Hester Prynne represents the most iconic of the 19th-century fictional pregnant characters in American literature, perhaps because the besotted and bewitched narrator leaves so much, including how she came to be pregnant with Pearl, to our imaginations. There had been pregnant American heroines before Hawthorne's Hester. In a popular sentimental novel with which Hawthorne was certainly familiar, Susanna Rowson's *Charlotte Temple* (1794), the title characters had also delivered an illegitimate daughter. Unlike Hester, whose story begins just after her daughter's birth, Charlotte's sad story concludes when she dies in childbirth.[7] Eleven years after Hawthorne published *The Scarlet Letter*, another American novel distinguished itself as a pregnancy narrative. But in Harriet Jacobs's *Incidents in the Life of a Slave Girl*, the pregnant narrator tells her own story, and she explains her pregnancies directly to her readers. When Linda Brent becomes pregnant, she wants us to know who fathered her child and why; she wants us to acknowledge that being pregnant represents much more than carrying and delivering a baby.

If *The Scarlet Letter* suggests the unintended pregnancy drama of 19th-century American literature, then *Incidents in the Life of a Slave Girl* represents the first clearly intentional pregnancy narrative in American literature. "The emergence of black women," writes Elaine Showalter in *A Jury of Her Peers*, "drew upon the conventions of the slave narrative, but also upon sentimental, domestic, feminist, and gothic fiction" (122). Jacobs was perhaps the most talented writer of a group of women who "began for the first time to speak in their own voices about slavery and race in a way that even a deeply sympathetic white writer like Stowe could not equal" (122). More importantly, Jacobs and other black writers "began to write about their lives as women and Americans" (122). Among the issues they dealt with was the rampant sexual abuse they endured as young slave women. None wrote more persuasively or more skillfully than Jacobs, who was able to negotiate the distance between the graphic details of her abuse and the sensibilities of a largely white female audience.[8]

By using metaphor and Biblical allusion, Jacobs's narrator, Linda, is able to relate to us that as a twelve-year-old orphaned slave, she began to endure—and also to resist—sexual abuse by her master, Dr. Flint. Early in the narrative she describes how her resistance began to take form:

> For my master, whose restless, craving, vicious nature roved about day and night, seeking whom to devour, had just left me, with stinging, scorching words that scathed ear and brain like fire.... When he told me that I was made for his use, made to obey his command in every thing; that I was nothing but a slave, whose will must and should surrender to his, never before had my puny arm felt half so strong [426].[9]

As Anne B. Dalton points out in "The Devil and the Virgin," Linda's description of Dr. Flint's whispering into her ear identifies his verbal abuse and "also suggests greater sexual abuse than the narrator literally reports" (42). As the years go by, Linda finds increasingly clever ways to stave off Dr. Flint. At fifteen, however, she knows she cannot remain where she is: "But I now entered on my fifteenth year—a sad epoch in the life of a slave girl. My master began to whisper foul words in my ear. Young as I was, I could not remain ignorant of their import" (437). Why was turning fifteen so sad for a slave girl? Why the sense of impending doom? Because, as Dalton points out, Linda is now able to become pregnant: although "during the nineteenth century, the age of menarche was considerably later than it is today—on the average fifteen ... this was the first year in which [Linda] was physically able to become pregnant" (52). Knowing that pregnancy is now a likely consequence of Dr. Flint's abuse—especially when he tells Linda that he is building a special cottage for her on his property—Linda decides to act. To avoid further abuse or becoming pregnant by Dr. Flint, she chooses to fight him with the most powerful weapon she has: pregnancy. She chooses to become pregnant by another man: "I knew what I did," she tells us, "and I did it with deliberate calculation" (464).

Brent's chapter on her first pregnancy, dramatically entitled "A Perilous Passage in the Slave Girl's Life," has become a standard excerpt of *Incidents* for anthologies of American literature, and has also garnered much attention from scholars who have studied the ways in which Jacobs is able to integrate "feminist abolitionist rhetoric" with the "plot of many a sentimental romance" (Ernest 188). She uses several rhetorical strategies in order to overcome the cultural problems she knew she would encounter among her Christian white women readers, who, ignorant of the realities of the lives of slave women, needed more than just narrative. Jacobs had to be able to teach her readers about something they did not understand by first showing them something that they did understand. Her audience needed to learn to see the monstrous "at home" in order to understand her situation (184). How best to bring white Christian women readers into Linda's story? Not by appealing to their religion, which, as Jacobs knew, could be "redirected back at the enslaved" by skilled proslavery forces (185). Appeals to justice would not be enough because she knew that "the justice of the heart can only echo, even at its best, the conceptions of justice defined by culture and habit" (185). How best to reach her readers? By "teaching them to see the invisible by giving voice to the unspeakable, forcing them beyond the gate of moral security and into a realm where all is uncertain, and where nothing can be addressed directly" (185). In other words, she reminds them of something they already understand: how being female means being vulnerable and silent, no matter who they are or where they live.

Linda stops her narrative at several points in this chapter to speak directly to her audience, or, as John Ernest so aptly describes, Linda "locks eyes, if only momentarily, in a quiet glance of mutual understanding" (187). In doing so, Linda disrupts her own narrative to suggest "unspeakable bonds," formed of common experiences between (black) narrator and (white) reader (187). What are these unspeakable bonds, these "gendered experiences for which women have no recognized public language?" (187). They are the physical characteristics and circumstances that define all women's lives: the menses, the cycles, the cramps, the missed periods, the pregnancies; and the unspoken realities of violence, rape, and abuse that many women readers would have recognized only too easily. Linda has proven that although she had been dehumanized by Dr. Flint, she "was still human and woman enough to be the object of [his] lust" (186). What she shares with her readers—who speak this unspeakable language—is a body that can be considered an object, one that can become pregnant. Her 19th-century women readers certainly understood what she meant, which made her story of willful pregnancy accessible—even silently reasonable—to them.

In what can only seem to be a remarkable act of self-determination to modern readers, Linda chooses to enter into a sexual relationship with an unmarried, respectable, professional white man, who eventually fathers both of her children. Becoming pregnant by Mr. Sands most likely saved her from further sexual molestation by Dr. Flint, and perhaps also saved her life. When Linda will not tell Dr. Flint who has fathered her child, he "sprang upon me like a wolf ... raised his hand to strike me; but it fell again," and Dr. Flint remarks that he doesn't "know what it is that keeps me from killing" Linda (470). What probably kept him from beating Linda was that she had just given birth to someone else's child, and he could not gauge the consequences of abusing Linda at this point because there was an unknown man in the equation. He backs off, and although he tells Linda that he will never sell her (Mr. Sands "was on the watch to buy" her), Linda's pregnancy has ensured that she will not be nearly as vulnerable as she was before conceiving.

Linda's two pregnancies will inform every aspect of the remainder of *Incidents*. Like Hester Prynne's secret admission that Pearl was worth the sacrifice in *The Scarlet Letter*, Linda's sin is that she never regrets that she has two children. Unlike Hester, whose story is told by a narrator always obsessed with Hester's secret sexual life, Linda has control of her own story.[10] By explaining to us how she became pregnant, she defuses the issue of her children's paternity. Because we know how Linda conceived, she frees us to consider how she continues to free herself during the rest of her narrative. Her pregnancies make Linda Brent powerful as a character and as a storyteller who continues to share with us not only her pregnancy story, but those of other pregnancies defined by the slave culture in which she lives.

Jacobs's strategy of making silent eye contact with her readers allows her to "speak through the stories she tells," allowing for those "untold and untellable stories" that she implicitly draws from her readers"

(Ernest 188). Every story she relates about pregnancy or childbirth has strategic placement and importance, including her own story of how Dr. Flint, the "venomous old reprobate," tries to shame her. In language that rivals Hawthorne's, Linda tells us that she "felt humiliated enough. My unconscious babe was the ever-present witness of my shame" (487). When Linda becomes pregnant a second time, she tells us how Dr. Flint cuts off all of her hair, but stops throwing her down staircases, and becomes verbally abusive instead. When her second child is a girl, Linda stops her narrative to remind us of the dangers of being a female slave: "Slavery is terrible for men; but it is far more terrible for women. Super-added to the burden common to all, *they* have wrongs, and sufferings, and mortifications peculiarly their own" (488). Female slaves, Linda says without saying, must endure the hazards that their own bodies represent in the slave culture.

Linda reinforces stories of her pregnancies with stories of other women, both slave and free, black and white. Indeed, pregnancy, child-birth, and babies are the most prevalent signifiers throughout the entire text of *Incidents in the Life of a Slave Girl*. Nestled in the chapter where Linda herself becomes pregnant for the first time is the story of a white woman slave owner whose new husband fathers a child by a young slave woman. When "the slaveholder's wife looked at the babe, she wept bit-terly. She knew that her own husband had violated the purity she had so carefully inculcated" (460). Linda also tells us about her mother's twin sister, Aunt Nancy, slave and wet nurse to Mrs. Flint, who gave "premature birth to a child" on a night when she was supposed to be attending her mistress, and was forced back to work within two weeks. After delivering six children prematurely, Aunt Nancy finally delivered two "feeble babes" who both died shortly after birth. "I well remember," Linda tells us, "[Aunt Nancy's] patient sorrow as she held the last dead baby in her arms" (556).

Two of the earliest and saddest stories that Linda imbeds into her own involve Dr. Flint, who beats a male slave for accusing Flint of impregnating the slave's wife. When Dr. Flint sells both slaves, he reminds the pregnant female slave that she is being sold away because she "let your tongue run too far." Linda explains to us that "it was a crime for a slave to tell who was the father of her child" (422). Imme-diately after that story, Linda relates perhaps the most wrenching and

41

dramatic of all of the pregnancy stories in *Incidents*: a young slave girl, dying in childbirth while her own mother and her mistress look on, cries out in agony, "O Lord, come and take me!" Her mistress, who assumes that the baby was fathered by her husband, replies, "You suffer, do you? ... I am glad of it. You deserve it all, and more too." The dying slave girl's mother adds, "The baby is dead, thank God; and I hope my poor child will soon be in heaven, too" (422).

Harriet Jacobs uses pregnancy as her most profound and effective trope in *Incidents in the Life of a Slave Girl*, a novel that demands that we consider not just the cruel realities of slave culture, but that we also confront the physical bodies of slave girls and women who become pregnant. She provides both her 19th-century audience and readers of our time with a remarkable insight when she suggests that she has become a girl who now has periods (especially considering that Jacobs's novel was published only eleven years after *The Scarlet Letter*, in which never could the narrator have even subtly implied anything about Hester's missed period). But Jacobs knew that this was fundamental information, and that women readers, white or black, North or South, married or unmarried, would be able to relate to this aspect of her story.

Jacobs's insistence that we accept the reality of how female bodies worked, and that we confront the significance of menstruation, suggests the first—and one of the most powerful—representations of American pregnancy literature written by women. *Incidents in the Life of a Slave Girl* anticipates and influences some of the most remarkable pregnancy fiction of the 20th century, fiction in which we must engage fully with how female bodies work in order to evaluate the narratives. From Harriet Jacobs to Toni Morrison and beyond, pregnancy fiction—fiction that privileges narratives of pregnancy and women's pregnant lives—began to flourish in the twentieth century. Some of these pregnancy narratives are reminiscent of Hawthorne's *The Scarlet Letter*: stories that are silent and vague, yet able to overshadow and haunt their entire text. Some of the 20th-century pregnancy narratives will testify to the graphic nature of the slave narrative of Harriet Jacobs. However we categorize them, pregnancy narratives in modern fiction transcend genre, gender and decade, and confront us everywhere in 20th century literature. By our own century, pregnancy fiction will be so vital that, as Adrienne Rich suggested in *Of Woman Born*, it will have given birth to itself.

The Awakening

With a few exceptions (most notably Harriet Jacobs), fiction writers of the 19th century did not mention pregnancy, and fiction readers did not read about pregnancy. The "domestic fiction" of the century (a genre mocked by Hawthorne in *The Scarlet Letter* and employed by Jacobs in *Incidents in the Life of a Slave Girl*) included only suggestions of pregnancy. Although "frequent pregnancies were the lot of most nineteenth-century married women, domestic fiction novels written by, for and about these women gloss over this incredibly central part of their lives" (Lippincott 56). In these novels, "new babies are revealed, blandly, in their mothers' beds without explanation as to how they got there" (Riley 77). Certainly a male publisher would never have published a graphic depiction of pregnancy or childbirth, and authors continued to be careful of the "bounds of good taste regarding the details of pregnancy and childbirth" into the early 20th century (Lippincott 56).

All of that began to change dramatically as the century turned, when women readers became a more powerful force in the public sphere and the marketplace. Women's "growing confidence in their own individualism as readers" afforded them the opportunity to "read what they wanted to read" instead of what they thought they were supposed to read (Jack 271–72). By the early 20th century, "90 percent of the populations of the UK, France, Germany and the U.S. were functionally literate," and of those, many were women (279). American women began writing and publishing fiction regularly. Although the publishing industry was decidedly powered by men, women were becoming vital consumers of books and magazines, often devoted to fiction by women, some of whom were beginning to mention pregnancy and childbirth in their works.[11] Kate Chopin, whose reputation as a canonical writer would not be established until much later in the 20th century, was one of the first fiction writers to "openly write about pregnancy" in her works (Lippincott 56).[12] With Chopin's novel *The Awakening*, which includes dialog about "the intimate details of pregnancy and childbirth," the gestation period of pregnancy fiction begins. Pregnancy narratives—written by women and men, in various genres and forms—will soon begin to show.

Chopin understood that being dismissed as a "local colorist" afforded her the freedom to write in ways that mainstream authors could not, and she integrated many "details of women's lives as she contrasts various experiences during pregnancy" (59). *The Awakening* includes two pregnancy stories, "the dominant discourse of Adele's pregnancy," and "through a muted, subversive voice," Edna's own awakening, which grows like a pregnancy as well throughout the text (57).[13] Edna experiences Adele Ratignolle's pregnancy as Adele's intimate friend, even (reluctantly) attending to Adele during the birth. Being in the birthing room reminds Edna of her own pregnancy and birth experiences: "She recalled faintly an ecstasy of pain, the heavy odor of chloroform, a stupor which had deadened sensation, and an awakening to find a little new life to which she had given being..." (Chopin 131).

Always careful not to "transgress the bounds of good taste regarding the details of pregnancy and childbirth," Chopin nevertheless included enough details that pregnancy becomes the "dominant discourse" of the text (Lippincott 55, 57). Adele's birthing scene, although vaguely described through Edna's memories of her own pregnancies, leaves Edna "stunned and speechless with emotion" (Chopin 132). Even after she tries to regain her composure by getting some fresh air, Edna still feels "dazed" and exhausted by what she has seen (132). Through Adele's real pregnancy and childbirth scenes, Edna's pregnancy of self progresses as well: both women endure fainting and nausea; both women experience "quickening, when a woman first feels the movements of the fetus"; both women experience labor (Lippencott 60–61). In the final chapter of the novel, after Adele has literally given birth, Edna also gives birth: she strips naked, "like a new-born creature," and delivers herself into the sea (Chopin 175–80).

Kate Chopin, who had delivered six children by the age of 28, understood only too well how pregnancy worked. Like Harriet Jacobs before her, she was able to integrate the details of women's sexuality and pregnancy into her novel in ways that women might recognize easily, and also in ways subtle enough that the male-dominated publishing industry did not object. Her narrative of female awakening relies on an especially specific discourse—that of gestation, pregnancy, and child-birth—that continued to grow during the 20th century. "Chopin's brilliant use of the language of pregnancy," Lippincott writes, "underscores the centrality of universality of this natural process for women" (65). *The Awakening* articulates the distinctive language of pregnancy in ways that begin to find a stronger and stronger voice in fiction throughout the 20th century. And although it "would be decades before another American woman novelist combined Kate Chopin's artistic maturity with her sophisticated outlook on sexuality," it would not take decades for other writers to privilege pregnancy in their works (Showalter, "Tradition," 187).

Edith Wharton

If Edith Wharton wrote fiction in which pregnancy became a central focus, then pregnancy fiction was finding its voice. Wharton, a childless American expatriate who felt more comfortable among men than women, wrote fiction that represented a sharp contrast to the sentimental fiction of the 19th century in which she had been born. She privileged pregnancy in some of her best works, and in ways that suggest both Hawthorne's silent pregnancy in *The Scarlet Letter* and Jacobs's deliberate pregnancy in *Incidents in the Life of a Slave Girl*. All of Wharton's fiction makes us confront systemic institutional hypocrisy and decay, especially for women characters, who often struggle to find a place for themselves in a man's world. When any of Wharton's characters becomes pregnant in this indifferent and unstable world, we can be assured that whatever we think we understand will be undermined. Especially in *Summer* (1917), *The Old Maid* (1924), and *The Age of Innocence* (1920), Wharton uses pregnancy as a way to explore the ironies suggested by pregnancy: that pregnancy can mean powerlessness and power simultaneously.

In *Summer*, Charity Royall, an impoverished, dreamy-eyed seventeen-year-old ward of Mr. Royall, spends a summer secretly meeting her lover, Lucius Harney, in a deserted mountain cabin in the Berkshire Mountains outside of their village of North Dormer, Massachusetts. When Charity discovers that she is pregnant, she knows that she has nothing but trouble ahead. She hears through the small-town gossip mill that Lucius is recently engaged to a young woman of his own social class (he is studying to be an architect). Charity realizes that she must deal with her pregnancy alone, so she keeps an appointment in a neighboring town where she knows of a doctor who not only confirms her pregnancy, but offers to perform an abortion for her.

We have actually heard about Dr. Merkle twice in *Summer* before

Charity actually goes to see him. Early in the novella, Charity's friend Ally reminded Charity of the time that Ally accompanied another friend, Julia, to see the doctor for an abortion. Ally had described the sign on the office: "Dr. Merkle; Private Consultations at all hours. Lady Attendants" (148).[14] Later, Charity recognized this office when she and Lucius walked by it on July 4, a hot evening when they were on their first (hot) date. When Charity realized that she and Lucius were standing in front of Dr. Merkle's office, she remembered Julia's sad story, and although she was overwhelmed by "the heat and the rapture, a shiver of cold ran over her" (148). By the time Charity herself goes to see Dr. Merkle, we understand Charity's early portentous fears.

Wharton allows us to go inside the doctor's office, where a "mulatto girl with a bushy head and a frilled apron" eventually takes her in to be examined by Dr. Merkle.[15] We do not experience the exam (Wharton lets her ellipses work on our imaginations here), but afterwards, we learn that Dr. Merkle's "hands were large and smooth, and quick in all their movements" (183).[16] Charity insists to herself that she had come to see the doctor only to make sure "that she was not mistaken about her state," and she leaves, but not before Dr. Merkle makes her pay for the visit with her brooch, Charity's only gift from Lucius (183). Instead of feeling distraught by all of this, Charity begins to feel "immense and unexpected quietude" (184). In language that suggests Hester Prynne's "Pearl of great price," Charity laments that although it "had been horrible to have to leave Harney's gift in the woman's hands," she feels vaguely delighted that she is pregnant: "even at that price the news she brought away had not been too dearly bought" (184).[17]

In her biography of Edith Wharton, Hermione Lee points out that *Summer* reveals Wharton's ability to focus on the cruelties of gender injustice for young women. The novella is "particularly bitter about female oppression. Charity is at the mercy of a male double standard" (512). We understand clearly that Charity's "choices are to return to the 'animal' life of her mother, or to have an abortion, or to become a prostitute. These options are very clearly spelt out, much more openly than in any previous novel of Wharton's" (512). Wharton's narrator allows us to understand gradually how Charity comes to weigh her options. The evening of her appointment confirming her pregnancy, Charity sits alone and, as if reviewing a film, "she began to relive, with a dreadful poignancy, each separate stage of her poor romance" with Lucius Harney (185). She decides that her memories of the romance are only part of her consolation: "These things were hers; they had passed into her blood, and become a part of her" (186). Her memories "were building the child in her womb; it was impossible to tear asunder strands of life so interwoven" (186).

After weighing other options, including becoming a prostitute ("She knew that girls of that kind sometimes made enough to have their children nicely cared for," she thinks to herself), Charity feels lost and tired (198). What keeps her from total collapse is "the weight of reality; it was the bodily burden of her child" (199). Although she still has no plan, Charity realizes that being pregnant can be both a burden and an impetus for action: The "child was like a load that held her down, and yet like a hand that pulled her to her feet" (200). At this point, Charity is no longer the romantic girl that she was before she met Lucius Harney. She has become pragmatic: the pregnancy will demand no less of her. Her decision to marry Mr. Royall attests to her grim realism. Her pregnancy, the only relic of her love affair with Lucius Harney, becomes the most important factor in her decision.

In the same way that Hester Prynne's pregnancy eventually affords her a private sense of accomplishment and dignity, Charity is energized and motivated at the conclusion of *Summer* by her pregnancy. Like Hester, Charity must do things she finds difficult or humiliating. When she marries Mr. Royall, she acts dazed, then repulsed, but finally reconciled to her fate. When he gives her money with which to buy clothes, she instead retrieves her brooch from Dr. Merkle, wanting this piece of jewelry for her baby, as "a link between Harney's child and its unknown father" (209). In retrieving her jewelry—like Hester retrieving her A— Charity "has preserved a space within herself that neither Lawyer Royall nor the Law of the Father can invade" (Skillern 134). Her pregnancy triumphs at the conclusion of *Summer*. In a life where she never had much power, her uncontrollable pregnancy has given her some control over how she sees herself, and defines how we see her at the conclusion of the novella, as a pregnant woman whose body first betrayed her, and then confirmed her.

Summer represents a stunning example of a pregnancy narrative but not the only one that Wharton contributed to the body of pregnancy works in the early 20th century. The plot of *The Old Maid*, one of the quartet of short stories collected as *Old New York*, revolves around Charlotte Lovell's secret pregnancy—one that we never see at all—and the old maid's life that she must lead in order to watch her illegitimate daughter Tina grow up in the household of Charlotte's cousin Delia. Like *The Scarlet Letter*, *The Old Maid* includes nothing about the actual pregnancy—which we learn about in vague hindsight—which allows Charlotte's pregnancy to haunt the text. The unintended pregnancy around which the plot of *The Old Maid* swirls was enough of a problem that Wharton had trouble selling the short story to women's magazines in 1924. She would have no trouble, however, selling the story to Hollywood. The successful film version of *The Old Maid*, produced two years after Wharton died in 1937, reveals dark aspects of the short story that help to bring Charlotte's silent pregnancy out of the shadows.[18]

Charlotte and Delia are not the only pair of cousins affected by pregnancy in Wharton's work. In *The Age of Innocence*, cousins May Welland Archer and Ellen Olenska have to deal with a pregnancy as well. In this, her most celebrated novel, Wharton uses pregnancy like a weapon, one that is so deliberately and skillfully managed that, like unsuspecting Newland Archer, we never see what has hit us. Near the end of the novel, Archer has determined to leave his wife May and run away to "another country" with May's cousin Ellen Olenska, when word reaches him that Madame Olenska has decided to return to her estranged husband in Paris. As if that news weren't stunning enough for Archer, his wife May announces that she and Archer are "giving a farewell dinner" for Madame Olenska. At the dinner, Archer is in shock, floating "somewhere between chandelier and ceiling," as he slowly realizes that his wife and her tribe of "dumb conspirators" have staged this entire dinner because they believe that Archer and Madame Olenska are lovers (200).[19]

Archer knows that he has been handled "like a prisoner in the center of an armed camp," but still plans to tell May that he wants to leave New York and travel to "India or Japan" (200, 205). When he attempts this conversation, May, "hovering over him," tells him directly that he cannot go without her, and then tells him that her doctors will never allow her to travel. Delicately, May continues: "For you, see, Newland, I've been sure since this morning of something I've been so longing and hoping for" (205). With a pounding headache and a "sick stare," Archer realizes that he is, indeed, a prisoner. His wife is pregnant. Having told Archer just enough that he now knows that May has probably engineered Madame Olenska's exit with premature news of her pregnancy, Archer questions his wife's timing: "I thought you said you weren't sure until today" (205). She replies, looking him straight in the eyes, "No; I wasn't sure [when I told Ellen]—but I told her I was. And you see I was right!" (206).[20] The final image we have in this scene is of May's "blue eyes wet with victory" (206).

Wharton's narrator never allows us to know anything more about Archer's reaction to news of his impending fatherhood. When the novel concludes in the next chapter, thirty years have passed; Archer is fifty-seven years old; and May is now dead. When Archer's son suggests that Archer meet Madame Olenska again in Paris—both of them are now single—Archer must "deal all at once with the packed regrets and stifled memories of an inarticulate lifetime" (214). He chooses not meet her again, but instead declines his son's offer to take him to her apartment. His son—the same son whose impending birth was so carefully calculated to bind Archer to his real life—walks toward Madame Olenska's. Archer walks "back alone to his hotel" and the novel closes (217).

Before he walks away from the story in the final chapter, Archer has had time to think, and he has thought not about Ellen Olenska, but about May, which seems fitting, considering the commanding role that May played in Archer's drama. Indeed, May Welland Archer will have been the victor among the three characters who make up Wharton's love triangle in The Age of Innocence. Archer always underestimated and trivialized her, for example, earlier in the novel dismissively likening her to the Greek goddess Diana for her adept archery. Yet, as Cynthia Griffin Wolff points out, Diana is not merely the goddess of the hunt, but "is the divinity of childbirth and fertility; she presides over the generation of life itself" (428). May's power derives from her legitimate claim to pregnancy, and from the timing of her pregnancy. However else May might seem simple or unsophisticated to Archer and to us, her pregnancy reveals that she understands that she has the most effective, calculated weapon in the arsenal that is Old New York: pregnancy. A master archer who hits the bull's eye, May is clear-eyed and completely unsentimental about her victory over

Archer and Madame Olenska. She "is committed to the most funda-mental human processes, and in this commitment she is as ruthless as nature itself" (428). In *The Age of Innocence*, May is a hustler, and not just any hustler. Her strategy is so sophisticated that she plays all of us.

May's pregnancy may conceal her calculations, but it also reveals how fictional pregnancy works. Wharton uses pregnancy as a tool and a weapon in her fiction, to both conceal and reveal reality to us. In doing so, she continues the legacy of pregnancy narrative from the 19th cen-tury. Like Hester Prynne, May becomes the character who survives and triumphs: Chillingworth and Dimmesdale are dead; Newland Archer and Ellen Olenska are separated forever. Like Linda Brent, May looks like she should have limited power, but uses pregnancy skillfully as a way to sustain herself and improve the quality of her life.

The dual nature of Wharton's characters reflects the dual nature of how Wharton saw herself as a 20th-century writer. Wharton "regarded herself as a man's woman," yet she also "realized that at best she com-bined a masculine and intellectual approach to fiction with a feminine attention to detail and feeling" (Showalter 271). If a man's woman was writing about morning sickness, pregnancy, and abortion, then those topics were now fair game for men writers as well. By the middle of the 20th century, pregnancy and its attendant issues would become increas-ingly common elements in fiction, poetry and drama, written by women and men. American pregnancy literature would begin to mature in a multitude of ways.

Popular Pregnancy Literature: Kitty Foyle

"The major experiences of women," writes Elaine Showalter, include "menstruation, loss of virginity, pregnancy, childbirth, and abortion. All of these subjects occurred in women's literature of the thirties" (Showal-ter, *Jury*, 335). Male authors had never shied away from writing about the experiences of women (Hawthorne, for example, whose male nar-rator in *The Scarlet Letter* lectures his audience more than once on the essence of woman). By the middle of the 20th century, reading audiences would have had trouble reading fiction written by either sex in which some character was not secretly pregnant, wanted to be pregnant, had to have an abortion, had had an abortion, used birth control, did not use birth control, etc. Pregnancy shows everywhere from the pages of women's magazines, to novels written by Nobel laureates, to dramas staged on Broadway, to poetry published in small art periodicals. In the 20th century, American pregnancy fiction becomes abundantly, and radiantly, pregnant with life.

Mary McCarthy's character Dorothy goes to be fitted for a pessary in *The Group* (1936), and learns how to "insert the pessary herself" from a female doctor who puts her at ease by not asking any questions but clinical ones. While Dorothy struggles with the diaphragm, the doctor gives her "a little lecture" about birth control: "how a medicated plug had been known to the ancient Greeks and Jews and Egyptians, how Margaret Sanger had found the present diaphragm in Holland, how the long fight had been waged through the courts here" (73). Later in the novel, another member of The Group, Priss, is treated as "a special pet because she had been in Obstetrics and Gynecology three times with miscarriages before she had made the grade" (238). For Priss, whose husband is an authoritarian taskmaster of an MD, pregnancy has been frought with struggle, heartache, and now physical terror: after being bedridden for the final five months of her pregnancy, "she had had a kidney complication … delivery had been normal, though labor had been protracted—twenty-two hours" (238).

Other lesser known (but widely read) writers included pregnancy as part of their work, including Meridel LeSueur, whose short fiction explores the lives of young working-class women as they struggle with unintended pregnancy, abortion, and dangerous childbirth.[21] Popular serialized stories and novels sometimes included characters who were pregnant and decided to have abortions, like Christopher Morley's best-seller from 1939, *Kitty Foyle*. Kitty, a wisecracking working girl who narrates her own story, tells us that a "girl can't kid herself very long if things go wrong. Female plumbing is just one big burglar alarm" (262). When she sees in a newspaper that the father of her baby is engaged to be married to someone of his own class (Charity Royall? Lucius Harney?), Kitty does not hesitate. She has the "operation," telling us that the doctor was "skillful and decent," and that afterwards, she "tried to think things over a bit. Maybe I just haven't any moral sense. I felt sorry, and selfish maybe, and like I'd lost something beautiful and real, but I couldn't feel any kind of wrongness. I did what I had to do" (270).

Men Writing Pregnancy

Men were writing fiction in which pregnancy played a role as early as 1911, when Theodore Dreiser's title character in *Jennie Gerhardt* (based loosely on the life of his sister) becomes pregnant by her lover, who does not want children. She decides to keep the baby anyway, and eventually her lover buys a house for Jennie and her daughter in Chicago.[22] In one of his most anthologized short stories, "Hills Like White Elephants," Ernest Hemingway includes a minimal and disturbing conversation between two characters about an abortion he hopes that she will have. "It's really an awfully simple operation, Jig," the man in the story says to the girl as they drink their beer. "It's not really an operation at all" (Lauter 1423). Eventually the girl says, "Then I'll do it. Because I don't care about me" (1424). After more talking around the abortion, the two finish their beers while they wait for a train. "I feel fine," the girl says in the last lines of the story. "There's nothing wrong with me. I feel fine" (1424).

One of the most poignant characters in John Steinbeck's novel *The Grapes of Wrath* is Rose of Sharon, whose pregnancy is so compromised by the hardships of the Joads' journey to California that her baby is still-born. In the stunning final scene in the novel, Rose of Sharon, having just delivered a dead baby, nurses a starving boy as she smiles "mysteriously" (581). In James M. Cain's *Mildred Pierce*, Mildred's calculating daughter Vida tells everyone that she is pregnant, so that she can extort money from her naïve lover's parents. And in almost all of his novels, William Faulkner represents pregnancy in one way or another, especially in *Absalom, Absalom!* and *Light in August*, a novel that takes its name from a colloquial Southern farm term that refers to pregnancy and birth among livestock. Faulkner left a legacy of pregnancy narratives that has inspired and engaged other writers, including one of his most successful literary heirs, Toni Morrison.

Toni Morrison

In 1970, when one of Toni Morrison's characters in *The Bluest Eye* describes her pregnancies to us, and then her childbirth experiences, we might recognize the legacy of pregnancy narratives from earlier decades. As Pauline Breedlove tells us about her babies, we should be reminded of Jacobs's Linda Brent, Faulkner's Lena Grove, and perhaps Chopin's Adele Ratignolle:

> I don't recollect trying to get pregnant that first time. But that second time, I actually tried to get pregnant. Maybe 'cause I'd had one already and wasn't scairt to do it. Anyway, I felt good, and wasn't thinking on the carrying, just the baby itself. I used to talk to it whilst it be still in the womb. Like good friends we was.... I went to the hospital when my time come. So I could be easeful.... The pains was coming, but not too bad ... some more doctors come. One old one and some young ones. The old one was learning the young ones about babies.... When he got to me he said now these here women you don't have any trouble with. They deliver right away and with no pain. Just like horses... Only one [doctor] looked at me.... He knowed, I reckon, that maybe I weren't no horse foaling [98–99].

Like Faulkner, Morrison often relies on the language of the natural world to tell us about circumstances and situations that are not natural. Pregnancy and women's sexuality are fundamentals in Morrison's storytelling, and characters in all of her novels, from Pecola in *The Bluest Eye* to Cee in *Home*, must struggle when their female bodies are abused unnaturally by others.[23] The two most powerful pregnancy narratives that Morrison provides are those in *The Bluest Eye*, where we not only hear Pauline Breedlove's pregnancy soliloquy, but we also experience her daughter Pecola Breedlove's first period, her rape by her father, and her final madness, and in *Beloved*, where we must confront, simultaneously, the cruelty and the majesty of pregnancy.

In her excellent essay "Maternal Narrative," Marianne Hirsch describes the value of mothering in Morrison's *Sula*, but her description could apply to *Beloved* as well: "The mother's discourse, when it can be voiced at all, is always repetitive, literal, hopelessly representational. It is rooted in the body which shivers, hurts, bleeds, suffers, burns, rather than in the eyes or in the voice which can utter its cries of pain" (269). Certainly the body of Sethe represents the matrix in *Beloved*, but there are multiple pregnancy stories in the novel, which not only suggest Harriet Jacobs's imbedded pregnancy tales in *Incidents in the Life of a Slave Girl*, but also remind us that, like *The Awakening*, *Beloved* transforms storytelling itself into a kind of pregnancy.

Among the pregnancy stories in *Beloved*, Denver's birth story is one of the most complicated, and one we hear more than once. In many ways, the birth scene represents a restructured telling of *Huckleberry Finn*, in which Morrison "alters the original story" into one where a poor white girl, Amy Denver, assists a runaway slave, Sethe, in delivering her baby. In this reconstructed *Huckleberry Finn*, Amy and Sethe are "two throw-away people" on a riverbank who together bring Denver into the world. Huck and Jim might be "afforded the luxury of escape," writes Ellen Argyros, but "there is no escape available for the hugely swollen Sethe: she is captive to her body and must give birth when and where that body goes into labor with the help of whomever strolls by" (153). The two women perform a miracle on the riverbank, whereby we are allowed to watch as Sethe and Amy do "something together appropriately and well" (84). Denver's birth suggests that "women like Sethe and Amy are the greater heroes ... for men can easily escape... but women ... are held captive [to their bodies] throughout the process of reproduction" (Argyros 154). This story of courage on the river will become one of Denver's most prized possessions as she grows up in the house where the spirit of the dead baby terrorizes everyone.

The story of Denver's birth becomes one of Beloved's favorite stories to listen to while she is living with Sethe and Denver. Denver relives her mother's pregnancy for Beloved over and over, describing how Sethe was "by herself and inside of her is another baby she has to think about too" (78). Denver provides enough detail and "fine points" that her story becomes "a duet" with Beloved (78). The more Beloved hears this story, the more she wants to integrate Sethe's pregnancy into herself, which she does. She craves the strength of pregnancy that she hears from Denver. However, as Trudier Harris points out, stories—especially birth stories—for Morrison are "not just effects; they are effects with consequences" (168). Denver's understanding of her birth story helps her "to form the basis upon which to grow into an adult human being." For Beloved, however, "learning about herself is much more destructive" (168). Sethe's history of courageous pregnancy and devastating infanticide are both stories that inform Beloved's profile: she becomes both a pregnant warrior and a potential killer.

Sethe tells Beloved and Denver the story of her own African mother who, according to Sethe's caregiver Nan, had been pregnant multiple times, but only kept "small girl Sethe." Sethe tells the girls what Nan had told her as a young girl:

She threw them all away but you. The one from the crew she threw away on the island. The others from more whites she also threw away. Without names, she threw them. You she gave the name of the black man. She put her arms around him. The others she did not put her arms around. Never. Never. Telling you. I am telling you, small girl Sethe [62].

Sethe's mother, who died by hanging, most likely for trying to cut, left Sethe a legacy of self-determination and subversive action, which Sethe cherishes in this story. We hear this same sense of determination and action when Sethe tries to explain to Paul D all that she has done. She sounds as decidedly determined as her own mother must have been:

I did it. I got us all out. Without Halle too. Up till then it was the only thing I ever did on my own. Decided. And it came off right, like it was supposed to. We was here. Each and every one of my babies and me too. I birthed them and I got em out and it wasn't no accident. I did that. I had help, of course, lots of that, but still it was me doing it; me saying, *Go on*, and *Now....* It felt good. Good and right. I was big, Paul D, and deep and wide and when I stretched out my arms all my children could get in between [162].

Like her mother before her, Sethe has defied the institutional structure of her life, and has determined who her family will be. We understand Sethe's resolve and determination not just through her stories, but through projections of her pregnant body as well.

Much of the terror, pain, and cruelty in *Beloved* are projected onto Sethe's body—the worst onto her *pregnant* body: she is held down while the two nephews of her mistress nurse from her breasts; she is beaten afterwards, for reporting the boys' crime, and bears the scars on her back. As Amy Denver tells her, "Your back got a whole tree on it. In bloom" (79). As horrible as those scars are, by the end of the novel, they will have become one of the symbols of Sethe's healing and reconciliation with the people who love her. Like Hester Prynne's A, Sethe's chokecherry scars represent the symbol of "a repressive law inscribed" on her body, one that, like Hester's, is "positively reinterpreted" by the end of the novel (Wolter 31).[24] In *Beloved*, Morrison, like Hawthorne before her, takes apart the "significations of power" and replaces them with "a semiotics of the woman marginalized" who triumphs (31).

As Paul D remembers, Sethe was pregnant "every year including the year she sat by the fire telling him she was going to run" (9). Sethe's pregnant body, used and abused by the slavers, becomes finally a clear projection to us of Sethe as matrix and locus in *Beloved*.[25] Through her pregnancies and her body, we understand her will and her heart. In *Beloved*, as in *Huckleberry Finn, The Scarlet Letter*, and many other novels, pregnancy allows us to understand that women not only "are more captive to their bodies than men are," but that women who are pregnant and bear children in literature can confirm "the importance of responsibility" to themselves and to their children (Argyros 151). Pregnancy, a phenomenon that happens where we cannot watch it, and with all of its invisible, mysterious workings that we cannot see, allows us to gauge values and see growth and rebirth in literature. *Beloved* represents the most powerful pregnancy narrative of the 20th century. We cannot understand the values of the novel unless we recognize the woman at the center of the tale as a *pregnant* woman, one whose body determines her actions. Because Sethe's pregnancies and pregnancy stories dominate the novel, we must consider the nature of pregnancy itself: organic, uncontrollable, powerful beyond our understanding.

Beloved, and all of Morrison's works, also represent a historical moment in American literary history: when pregnancy began not just to show, but to show off. By the end of the 20th century, many writers had relied on the pregnancies of their characters to help enlighten us. Gloria Naylor, Louise Erdrich, Joyce Carol Oates, Alice Munro, Jane Smiley, Margaret Atwood, and Margaret Drabble represent just a few names on a long list of contemporary women fiction writers for whom pregnancy has functioned as a lightning rod.[26] By the time Sapphire published her novel *Push* in 1997, savvy readers could have probably guessed that its title might refer to childbirth. The novel reveals that through another powerful narrative pregnancy, Precious Jones learns to read her own life.[27] One of Precious's favorite books is Alice Walker's *The Color Purple*, which Precious realizes tells a story not unlike hers. She recognizes that like Celie, she has had two babies by her father, and that learning to read has empowered her. "Things going good in my life," she tells us, "almost like *The Color Purple* ... I love *The Color Purple*, that book give me so much strength" (82–83).

From Hester to Sethe; from Charlotte Temple to Pauline and Pecola; from Linda to Precious; pregnancy behaves in American literature as a conduit, one that moves us from the punishing eyes of Puritans through the institution of American slavery, to 20th-century technology. As storytellers become more open about the details of pregnancy—as we learn, for instance, when Pecola gets her first period, or why Sethe must lie down in a riverbed with labor pains—they enrich their texts and our reading experiences. That writers can include every detail of a woman's pregnancy in any piece of fiction now has not diminished the power of the pregnancy in storytelling, but instead has allowed storytelling itself to grow in new ways.

Real pregnancy, which begins in microscopic movement, grows dramatically into a vital life force. In the parallel universe of fiction, narrative pregnancy begins with its roots in sentimental melodrama—a significant enough genre to be appropriated by Hawthorne and Jacobs in the 19th century—and has also grown into a vital body. But melodrama did not merely spawn what would become a genre of pregnancy fiction. It is no coincidence that while writers were beginning to mention pregnancy and childbirth in fiction in the early 20th century, filmmakers were also beginning to project pregnancy stories on film. In the same way that narrative pregnancy in text begins with a silent pregnancy that becomes a fully developed genre with a vitality of its own, pregnancy on film begins with a similar gestation period. We will first discover narrative pregnancy on film at its source, in melodrama. Pregnancy will attach itself to the weepies and never let go.

2

The Weepies
Pregnancy, Melodrama and Noir

Melodrama and Uncle Tom's Cabin

Both Nathaniel Hawthorne in *The Scarlet Letter,* and Harriet Jacobs in *Incidents in the Life of a Slave Girl,* appropriated elements of the melodrama in order to engage their audiences—Hawthorne for ironic purposes and Jacobs for propriety. Nothing about their use of melodrama would have seemed exceptional to readers in the middle of the 19th century. Melodrama was by that time a popular mode for both stage plays and fiction throughout Europe and the United States.[1] With its roots in post–Revolutionary France, melodrama flourished on stage and in novels in the 19th century, when institutional power structures were unstable and in crisis throughout Europe and the United States. Instead of relating stories of aristocrats and high priests, melodramatic stage plays and novels focused on the trials of the little people. By privileging the complex conflicts and challenges of the bourgeoisie, melodrama proved to be malleable, accessible, and vital.

Charles Dickens was the master of blending social critique with melodrama in his popular novels, and he inspired "hundreds of novels and plays in mid-nineteenth century England and America" (Cawelti 37). Among those hundreds of novels, one—published two years after *The Scarlet Letter* and a decade before *Incidents*—was destined to become the most popular American novel of the entire 19th century: *Uncle Tom's Cabin* by Harriet Beecher Stowe. Stowe's novel employed all of "the melodramatic conventions her readers were predisposed to respond to," but with a twist: she was able to adapt the conventions of melodrama, including her use of conventional characterizations, stereotypes and plot construction, in her portrayals of "black characters as well as white" (37). *Uncle Tom's Cabin* was unlike any other published American melodrama because her characters' stereotypes defied the expectations of her middle-class reading audience. The characters' skin colors did not prescribe their moral characters in stereotypical ways: George and Eliza Harris were noble; Little Eva was an angel; and Simon Legree was worse than a scoundrel.

As the most popular example of a domestic melodrama of the 19th century, one that emphasized "feminine purity and the ideal of motherhood" as "dominant symbols of virtue, the chief objects of the noble hero's protection and the villain's attack," *Uncle Tom's Cabin* best represents the suppleness of the melodramatic mode in American literature of the time. Stowe's bestseller used the slavery issue as part of the melodramatic scheme, and consequently many novels began to incorporate their plots into a larger social background, one in which that larger society was no longer "static," no longer a generic place where characters might come and go while "society went on in much the same way" (40). By the end of the 19th century, most melodramas, on stage or in print, were reacting successfully to the ongoing upheavals and changes in American culture. "Social melodramas" now presented protagonists "faced with a rapidly changing society" who struggled to adjust their values to the changing times (40). Part of the changing times included the advent of the moving picture, where melodrama could be duplicated and replicated to audiences, who themselves made an easy transition to film melodrama in the first few decades of the 20th century.

Melodrama has never been unpopular in print, on stage, or on screen because it always moves stories along by "drawing its material from the everyday" (Byars 11). Melodrama "expresses a reality experienced by most of the people most of the time. This means also that melodrama expresses the contradiction that most people live most of the time, as well as the negotiations over the conflicts they cause" (18). By referring to "shared, public symbols," drawn from the workaday world (among them religious, ritualistic, and economic symbols), melodrama focuses on "the problems of the individual within established social structures" (11). Whether we label it "social melodrama," "domestic melodrama," or "maternal melodrama," the melodramatic mode has been a standard feature of narrative for two centuries. Melodrama provides flexibility and variety; it reflects and projects the complexities of our private habits and ordinary lives. No matter who we are, melodrama allows us to recognize certain familiar inconsistencies and hypocrisies, especially those drawn from our most private and vulnerable moments. Among those most private and vulnerable of times, of course, are those times when we encounter pregnancy.

Way Down East

Pregnancy has always represented a fundamental building block, indeed one of the most profound defining elements, of the melodramatic schema. *Way Down East* (1920), D.W. Griffith's "simple story of plain people," was one of the first American feature films to include pregnancy as part of the melodramatic narrative. Adapted by Lottie Blair Parker from a very popular stage melodrama by William Brady, *Way Down East* presents the story of Anna Moore (Lillian Gish), a poor, beautiful, trusting young woman who is tricked into a fake marriage by lothario Lennox Sanderson (Lowell Sherman).[2] Anna, who does not understand as we do that she has been duped, sends Sanderson an "urgent letter" telling him that they need to make their marriage public. The camera shows us a close-up of her delicately worded letter: he needs to come to get her because of "the tender new reason why the secret cannot be kept any longer." Sanderson tells Anna that they are not married; that they can never be married because he would lose his inheritance; and that all he can offer her is some money (which she refuses). After a series of tortured, backlit close-ups, Anna faints, and the sequence ends when Anna's elderly mother finds her daughter prostrate on the floor.

We never see a visibly pregnant Anna, of course; even before Hollywood's years of censorship began in the late 1920s, cultural norms dictated that we would never see a shot of a visibly pregnant woman on a film screen for several more decades. We do see a sequence of Anna in bed, with a doctor and her landlady hovering, and we understand how things are going for her through the four captions that are edited into the sequence as we continue to see the hovering figures over Anna's bed:

"Anna hides away with her shame."
"Maternity—Woman's Gethsemane."
"Shadows Across the Time Dial."

And finally, we know that Anna has delivered when we see: "The baby without a name."

Anna baptizes her baby (naming him "Trust Lennox") by herself in her little dark rented room, and almost immediately we see a sequence where her baby sickens and dies. We watch her rocking her sick son, her birthing bed behind her; we see the doctor come to pronounce the baby dead, and then we see a stunning backlit close-up of Anna's howling face. Soon after, Anna's suspicious and menacing landlady shows her the door. The rest of the plot of *Way Down East* involves Anna's attempts to find work, her growing relationship with the family with whom she eventually finds employment, and her climactic betrayal by the family patriarch who, having learned about her illegitimate dead baby, ejects her from the house during a blinding snowstorm. After enduring the melting ice on the rushing river, Anna is plucked from a moving ice floe and saved by the patriarch's son David (Richard Barthelmess). In the final sequence of the film, Anna, dressed in a lavish white lace wedding gown and veil, marries David.

Way Down East was an immediate hit, but its popularity most likely had to do with Griffith's mastery of filmmaking, not with the plot of the adaptation. Since its initial release, its spectacular ice floe sequence has taken on a life of its own; viewers who know nothing else about the film might recognize this sequence. Yet *Way Down East* represents more than an example of the spectacular on film. In several ways, it serves as the clearest link between earlier textual pregnancy narratives and the melodramatic mode in film. *Way Down East* shares with *The Scarlet Letter*, *Incidents in the Life of a Slave Girl*, and other pregnancy narratives, a story in which the marginalized woman gives birth and then tries to survive in a small dark space (a 17th-century colonial prison, a small attic room, etc.), only to free herself eventually by moving outdoors. Like earlier pregnancy narratives, Anna's story includes "traditional elements such as the secret, the illegitimate child, the rejected woman," and also "the city/country dichotomy ... the permanence of the earth, the counterpoint of the elements of nature unleashed" (Viviani 174).

Yet for all *Way Down East* shares with earlier pregnancy narratives, it also suggests how vitally distinct a pregnancy story told on film can be. A motion picture camera and some careful editing allow Anna's story to move in powerful visual ways that are particular to film. Her journey not only moves from the dark shabbiness of her rented room to the open howling sky of a winter's storm, but we are allowed to attend her delivery, however subtly—we at least see her in her childbearing bed. The childbirth scene is cluttered, uneven, repeatedly interrupted with captions, all of which mimics the instability and dissonance of her childbirth experience. Throughout that scene and subsequent sequences, we watch a series of close-ups of faces, and we learn to recognize Anna's anguish and pain, her determination, and finally her reconciliation with the world around her.

In Anna's close-ups, in fact, we begin to perceive the beginnings of the pregnancy narrative on film, one that will distinguish itself from stage melodrama and fiction. As scholar Charles Affron has pointed out, *Way Down East* provides us with an example of how close-ups in particular work with melodrama by subverting it. "A victimized, unwed mother who baptizes her dying baby is a melodramatic configuration" but a close-up of Gish "subverts melodramatic moral typage" (110). A motion picture camera captures something beyond melodramatic excess and artifice. The photographic movement of a motion picture camera captures the real—in the case of *Way Down East*, it shows us the profound shock and grief of a human being, larger than life, in our faces. For a fleeting moment at least, Anna has no back story; in that moment, the audience does not see that she is an unwed mother. What we see is the reality provided by "the photographic naturalism of cinema" (110). Anna's pain is real, the melodramatic formula has transmuted into something else: reality. And no matter how we learn about it on film, nothing is more real than pregnancy.

The pregnancy and childbirth sequences in *Way Down East* that suggest a backwards look toward Hester Prynne also project the future: a long line of screen pregnancies that move in the dark and are barely perceptible in 1920. The enduring characteristics of melodrama—the emphasis on the personal, the vulnerable, the secret—provide pregnancy narratives with some of the sustenance they would need as they transitioned from silence to sound, and from an independent film company to a corporate studio system. Melodrama's contributions to pregnancy films from the 1920s forward are significant and lasting. By the time movies could talk, there was an entire genre of Hollywood films devoted to and marketed to women, and pregnancy played a role in many of these movies. In fact, "maternal melodramas," affectionately known as the "weepies," constituted a substantial subgenre of the "woman's film." And weepies they were. This is what everyone was weeping about: although an audience would have been able to hear a character say that she was pregnant in a talking picture in the 1930s, not one pregnant character ever uttered that word out loud.

From the late 1920s through the studio years in Hollywood, how pregnancy behaved on American movie screens was strictly regulated by an increasingly institutionalized and corporate Hollywood. Characters could be pregnant, and could talk about their pregnancies in euphemisms, but several years would pass before American audiences would see a character who looked pregnant or uttered the word. How screenwriters and filmmakers responded to these restrictions becomes part of our pregnancy story, because the repressed pregnancy narrative in American movies was defined by creativity, resourcefulness, and subversion. Whatever censors and arbiters of good taste thought they were doing, this is what they actually did: the more regulation they insisted on, the more inventive and complex the pregnancy narratives became. Whether or not audiences heard the words or saw an obviously pregnant profile, audiences already knew all about pregnancy, and they learned to read it clearly and fluently on a movie screen. Anna from *Way Down East* might have told the Hollywood studios that they had a tender new reason why they could not keep their secret any longer. They could try and repress it, but pregnancy in film from the melodramatic weepies and beyond, could not be concealed for much longer.

The Production Code and Pregnancy

In the 1934 Warner Brothers production *Mary Stevens, M.D.*, Kay Francis plays a physician who finds herself pregnant by her married lover. She feels elated, and immediately announces the happy news to her office assistant: "Take a good grip on that desk, plant your feet firmly and prepare for the shock of your life. I'm going to have a baby.... What's so funny about it? I didn't invent the idea. Women have been having babies for a long while" (LaSalle 182). When her assistant asks her if she is happy about being pregnant, Stevens replies, "Walking on air." Her assistant responds, "Well, then, darling, so am I" (183). About this exchange, Mick LaSalle points out in his lively study of pre–Code Hollywood that it "would be a long time before such a reasonable exchange between single ladies would again be possible in an American film" (183). By the end of the very year that *Mary Stevens, M.D.* was released, the Motion Picture Production Code was being implemented. For the next few decades, pregnancy in Hollywood films would be on lock-down.

A single professional woman, happy about being pregnant with her married lover's child, represents one of the cinematic scenarios that likely secured the power of the Production Code Association after 1934.[3] Since the early 1920s, religious groups, especially in the largest American cities, had been lobbying and boycotting Hollywood movies that they found lascivious, and the Hollywood moguls had appropriated an office, run by Will Hays and his assistant Joseph Breen, to encourage the studios to regulate themselves more carefully. Among those films famously boycotted was an early talkie, *The Trial of Mary Dugan* (1929), starring Norma Shearer as a woman accused of having murdered her married lover. At the end of the film, the jury finds Mary not guilty and she is released, never "made to atone or reform" for the immoral life she has lived; she is free to live as she pleases with her values and dignity intact (59). Shearer, and other young female actors, among them Joan Crawford, Greta Garbo, and Jean Harlow, were starring in pre–Code films in which they were portraying women whose roles were not prescribed. Movie audiences were surprised and delighted, and the film was very successful at the box office, or audiences were alarmed and offended by what they considered the immorality of the film.[4]

These actors played a spectrum of characters, some professionals like Mary in *Mary Stevens M.D.* and some working class, like Barbara Stanwyck in *Forbidden* (1932). Many of them become pregnant by men who cannot marry them for one reason or another, and they choose pregnancy and single parenthood. In her delightful review of women's movies in Hollywood, Jeanine Basinger describes the winning formula for studio movies about unwed mothers:

> These stories are about women who have no one to help them ... they either give their babies over to their married lovers' wives, or they have to marry wealthy Englishmen.... [M]ovies offered two polarized kinds of stories to women on this subject. One was cautionary (prostitution and loss of the child) and one was escapist (fame and the peerage) [394].

2. The Weepies: Pregnancy, Melodrama and Noir

Basinger points out that many of the pregnancy narratives of the early 1930s used World War I as their backstory, allowing for melodramatic affect. She gives the example of *Born to Love* (1931), where "Constance Bennett goes to a little French inn with Joel McCrea, and he is pronounced dead and she is pronounced pregnant only seconds later" (396).[5]

Bennett starred in several pregnancy films of the time, and enjoyed great critical and popular success. Like Barbara Stanwyck, Ann Harding, and others, she found roles where she could play the brave unwed mother to be challenging and complex. Whether they were rich or poor, married or unmarried, working girls or common criminals, characters like Bennett's in *Born to Love* were articulate and attractive, and had all sorts of appetites. Until they were reined in by the Production Code, women characters "were conceived of as having sexual desire without being freaks, villains.... [They] were entitled to initiate sexual encounters [and] to pursue men" (Haskell 93). When they became pregnant, the stories of their pregnancies developed into the impetus for their drive, courage, and resiliency. In that short span of years between the earliest talkies and the Production Code of 1934, pregnant characters in Hollywood were lionesses, and their (unseen, early) pregnancies revealed the most poignant and heartbreaking of the Great Depression tragedies, that of the family in peril of being separated.

The narratives of pre–Code Hollywood films had less to do with sex appeal than they did with money: "Pre-Code Hollywood was driven by economics, not erotics," writes Thomas Doherty. "Scarred by the beaten-down quality of the harshest years of the Great Depression, the [pre–Code] films careen through a universe cut loose from sure moorings and friendly ports, adrift and unanchored.... In its most radical guise, pre–Code Hollywood questioned the justice of American institutions and traditions" (53). When Depression-era audiences watched Mary Dugan walk free after her murder trial, or Dr. Stevens and her young son happy together, these audiences were experiencing a cinematic world that looked in many ways like the opposite of their real world, that "spun its own topsy-turvy tales" (53). Among the best examples of the mixed-up nature of this era are the pregnancy narratives, in which unmarried women are happy about being pregnant, unwed mothers work valiantly to keep their babies, and even women who terminate pregnancies (off-screen, of course) do not suffer only ill consequences.[6]

"To be alone and broke and pregnant under any circumstances was bad enough," explains LaSalle, "but to be in that condition during the Depression was that much worse" (179). Audiences were so sympathetic to pregnancy on film during the pre–Code years that we have countless examples of pregnancy narratives in which we sympathize and admire the pluck of these pregnant characters. Constance Bennett made a career of playing pregnant or unwed mothers, in *Common Clay* (1930), *The Easiest Way* (1931), and *Born to Love*. Irene Dunne endures two unintended pregnancies in *Ann Vickers* (1933); Claudette Colbert becomes pregnant and decides to give up her baby in *Torch Singer* (1933); and Loretta Young, living in a tent city with Spencer Tracy, becomes pregnant in *A Man's Castle* (1933). By late 1934 when the official Production Code went into effect, audiences had enjoyed a variety of pregnancies onscreen. All of that—and much more—would change, of course, after the Production Code took effect.[7]

Many of these pre–Code films provided audiences with portrayals of thoughtful, mature, complex women, portrayals that would become anomalies soon enough. Among the first changes that audiences would notice: "[E]very female character in movies got her virginity back" (LaSalle 191). There were pregnant characters during the Production Code years, but they would have more in common with Hawthorne's Hester Prynne than they would with any pregnant film characters who had preceded them. Pregnancy was not only silent and invisible in American film, but almost any suggestion of pregnancy as part of the narrative of a Hollywood film was suppressed. And if a film did include any hint of pregnancy, that pregnancy would have to suggest either a happy marriage storyline, or else a punishment for some female character who had done the wrong thing. For much of the 20th century, the Production Code ensured that pregnancy, especially the unintended kind, signified retribution, penalty, and comeuppance for women characters. Pregnancy implied something evil, dirty, or twisted. No more sympathy for unmarried pregnant women; no more understanding for single mothers; no more slack for poor women who find themselves in the family way.

As Kelly Oliver reminds us in *Knock Me Up, Knock Me Down*, until recently American popular culture has a long tradition of treating visible pregnancy, and the language we use to describe pregnancy, with careful modesty. During the Code years, Hollywood films reinforced this cultural norm; studios might as well have taken their cue from Nathaniel Hawthorne, when they "mostly avoided the issue of pregnancy, preferring to skip from romance and marriage to instant family. Women characters had children, but they were never seen giving birth to them" (Oliver 27). Hawthorne's narrator in *The Scarlet Letter* could never have explained why the silence on pregnancy, but Oliver reveals why the Hollywood censors snuffed out any suggestion: Pregnancy "was not only a private affair, but also somehow shameful. It signaled that a woman had sex and seemingly stimulated the public imagination in 'unwholesome' ways" (27).

Breen's office coordinated the Production Code from 1934 to 1954, setting the standards by which Hollywood films would be judged. One of the Code's most complex set of rules had to do with the sanctity of marriage. Adultery could show up in movies, because even Breen understood that adultery represented "the plot complication and narrative lynchpin of comedy, melodrama, and mystery" (Doherty, *Censor*, 92). However, adulterers were now always to be punished in films—no more gold-diggers who find happiness, like Barbara Stanwyck in *Baby Face* (1933); no more fulfilled unwed mothers like Constance Bennett in *Rockabye* (1932). After 1934, women most often paid for the transgressions of all of the characters. "Women," writes LaSalle, "got the worst of it. Under the Code, it wasn't only crime that didn't pay. Sex outside of marriage didn't pay. Adultery didn't pay. Divorce didn't pay. Leaving your husband didn't pay. Getting pregnant outside of wedlock didn't pay. Even having a job often didn't pay. Nothing paid" (190).

The Production Code ensured that women characters embody Breen's backward-looking Victorian stereotype. "To my way of thinking," Breen wrote in 1923, "our good women, our mothers, wives, and sweethearts, may be moved to come to the rescue of the nation and State" (Doherty, *Censor*, 95). By putting women back on a Victorian pedestal in their well-run homes, and simultaneously suggesting "Catholic veneration of the Blessed Virgin Mary," Hollywood began to project "backlit halos and divine close-ups of the female face" with a kind of "religious adoration" (95). Women characters who in earlier Hollywood films had afforded audiences the chance to question institutions and consider alternatives to the status quo, now deferred to the authority of those very institutions; they were, with a few major exceptions, safely ensconced within the traditional family structure. Pregnant women had to pay for their sins, and during the Code years, they became the "celestial chiaroscuro in a Renaissance painting" that was the Hollywood screen (95). Yet like the Virgin Mary on whom Breen had modeled the roles of these characters, these pregnant virgins had vitality and power beyond the imaginings of the authorities who controlled them.

Within five years of the official 1934 Production Code enforcement, Hollywood films were already deviating from Breen's tight grasp. As World War II began in Europe and threatened to engage the United States, the Code guidelines began to change, first slowly and subtly, but eventually in noticeable ways by the late 1940s. Audiences detected changes in how Hollywood portrayed ethnic groups (in particular, Jews were treated with more sensitivity onscreen), in the language allowed in films (GIs used the word "hell" and "damn" regularly in war movies), and in how women were featured in Hollywood fare. One of the most telling gauges to how censorship rules changed has to do with how pregnancy was presented during the wartime years. Beginning in 1939, American audiences began seeing women in films who were more than barely pregnant, and who talked about their pregnancies.

To film historians, the year 1939 represents one of Hollywood's "golden years," and even at the time, audiences knew that the movies they were going to see at the theaters were spectacular. *The Wizard of Oz, Dark Victory, Mr. Smith Goes to Washington, Wuthering Heights, Ninotchka, Stagecoach,* and *Goodbye, Mr. Chips* were some of the 1939 films that would endure beyond that year. Three other remarkable films from 1939, including *Gone with the Wind, The Old Maid* and *The Women*, all included pregnancy narratives. In *Gone with the Wind*, Scarlett (Vivien Leigh) and Prissy (Butterfly McQueen) deliver Melanie's baby in a dramatic birthing sequence unlike any other presented on American screens since Anna delivered her baby in *Way Down East*. Beyond that sequence, Scarlett's own second pregnancy, one she never wanted (and one that has been suggested to us is the result of marital rape by Rhett Butler), ends with her stunning fall down a flight of elegant red stairs in her opulent Atlanta home. Finally, near the end of the film, Melanie (Olivia de Havilland) dies of complications from her second pregnancy.

In *The Old Maid*, adapted from the stage play based on Edith Wharton's novella, we see Charlotte Lovell (Bette Davis) only in her earliest stages of pregnancy, but her off-screen pregnancy drives the plot of the entire film. Agreeing to allow her cousin Delia (Miriam Hopkins) to raise the daughter she bore out of wedlock, Charlotte endures a lifetime of defining herself as the old maid aunt to Tina, her biological daughter. In *The Women*, a clever and stylish adaptation of the popular play by Clare Boothe Luce and directed by George Cukor, we do not see childbirth or hear about a past pregnancy, but a perpetually pregnant character, Edith Potter (Phyllis Povah), provides comic relief. At one point we see her talking on the telephone about her upcoming doctor's appointment while her six young daughters run around causing a racket, and in a subsequent scene, we see her running toward the bathroom with morning sickness.

The Great Lie

In 1941, audiences of mainstream Hollywood fare watched a character's body change from the early stages of pregnancy until she was too big for her clothes. Sandra Kovak (Mary Astor, who won an Academy Award for her performance) in Warner Brothers's melodrama *The Great Lie*, is a professional concert pianist who had been married very briefly (and, because of "a technicality," not legally) to aviator Peter Van Allen (George Brent). After they go their separate ways, Van Allen marries heiress Maggie Patterson (Bette Davis). Just after Van Allen's plane goes missing in South America and he is presumed dead, Sandra reveals to Maggie that she is pregnant with Peter's child. Maggie talks Sandra into an arrangement whereby Maggie will raise the child as hers, and she will support Sandra financially. When Sandra agrees to this proposal, the two women leave New York and spend the rest of Sandra's pregnancy in a secluded cabin somewhere in Arizona.

Compared to the earlier sequences of the film in which Peter and Sandra are married and divorced; Peter and Maggie are married; and Peter leaves for South America, the Arizona sequences move slowly, which simulates how annoyed, bored, and bedraggled both women—

especially pregnant Sandra—are feeling by this point. Our best gauge to how time moves during this part of the film becomes the visual display of Sandra's pregnant body. She wears the same chenille bathrobe that we had seen her in during an earlier New York scene, but in Arizona the bathrobe becomes more and more ill-fitting, to the point that when Sandra stands, we can see the outline of her pregnant belly. We also see her pregnant body from a distance, as she and Maggie take some exercise by walking in the desert. Even from a distance, Maggie seems small and agile and Sandra lumbers slowly in a huge fur coat. We can easily tell

Maggie Van Allen (Bette Davis) tries to keep Sandra Kovak (Mary Astor) calm during the final months of Kovak's pregnancy with the baby of Van Allen's husband Peter (George Brent) in *The Great Lie* (1941), a Warner Bros. melodrama, in which we see one of the first obviously pregnant women on the large screen. When Sandra stands at the end of this scene, she is quite clearly too big for the ratty bathrobe she is wearing. Astor won an Academy Award for this performance.

when Sandra is beginning labor, because she is in bed, sweating, breathing heavily, and occasionally grabbing onto Maggie's hand. The door is closed to us when the doctor goes into Sandra's bedroom to deliver the baby, but we do hear a baby's cry in the next scene, while we wait outside with Maggie (who, interestingly, has the look of an expectant father: wearing a pair of slacks; pacing nervously back and forth; smoking a cigarette).[8]

The Great Lie includes all of the elements of a grand melodrama that American audiences expected: secrets among characters, visually cluttered, enclosed set, and the "celestial chiaroscurso" close-ups of women characters in pain. As Sandra gets closer to delivering her baby, we see more and more close-ups of both women's faces. In one of the most engaging scenes of the Arizona sequence, we watch an angry, huge Sandra crack under the pressure of "being a woman who must give up her glamorous life and career, however temporarily, and go to live in a cage with a keeper" (Basinger 412). Big as a house and bored to tears, Sandra has attempted to run away after sneaking a midnight snack. When Maggie busts her, Sandra begins to scream. Maggie smacks her across the face. As Sandra collapses, we see close-ups of both women's faces. They are both in high melodramatic agony.

Directed by Edmund Goulding, who had directed Davis in both *Dark Victory* and *The Old Maid* two years earlier, *The Great Lie* had enough star power and visual display to compensate for a plot that threatened at times to veer into the ridiculous, especially when the pregnancy ends. "After the male child is born ... the heart of the film is over. Its core is the long birth sequence in the Arizona shack" (Basinger 413). An American audience in 1941 knew better than to be surprised when Peter returns from the dead and the two women have to compete for him. Although the two women have negotiated every detail of the plot until now, the final sequence revolves around Peter, who will be the final judge of the situation that the women have created. In his position as benevolent patriarch, Peter chooses in a way that ensures that no Hollywood censor would interfere with this film: Sandra gets her career, Maggie gets her baby, and Peter gets his new son *and* two adoring women whom he has forgiven.

The Great Lie represents perhaps the first mainstream American film in which a woman's pregnant profile moves across the movie screen clearly—and the only such Hollywood film to reveal pregnancy as a visual force for several years. For as many Hollywood movies during the war years in which women find themselves pregnant after the men have left the scene, few of them include scenes where we see actual pregnancy. One year before *The Great Lie*, Kitty Foyle (Ginger Rogers) endures pregnancy and subsequently a stillbirth in the film adaptation of the novel *Kitty Foyle*; the baby's father Wyn never knows about the baby's existence, and we never see an obviously pregnant Kitty.[9] In 1943 Rogers again starred in a film in which she discovers her pregnancy after her husband has left the scene: in *Tender Comrade*, she plays Jo Jones, whose husband Chris (Robert Ryan) is overseas when baby makes three. A "furlough wife," as the Hollywood advertisements for *Tender Comrade* told audiences at the time, Jo lives in a house with other furlough wives, and with their love and support, she safely delivers her son, just before she learns that Chris has died in action. We do see a glimpse of a stylish maternity ensemble on Jo at one point, but she turns her back before we can distinguish her profile.

The Miracle of Morgan's Creek

Censorship and modesty still characterized most Hollywood pregnancy narratives of the war years, until 1944, the year that everything changed for pregnancy in Hollywood movies. The most significant pregnancy movie of the 1940s was not a sympathetic and serious look at the tribulations of furlough wives, but was instead a comedy about a goofy single girl named Trudy Kockenlocker. In Preston Sturges's *The Miracle of Morgan's Creek*, Trudy (Betty Hutton) goes out one evening, gets drunk, "marries a soldier, and awakens the next morning unable to remember" anything more about her wild night (Leff and Simmons 127). Once she discovers that she is pregnant, from there we are on a wild course as Trudy tries to figure out how to negotiate her delicate condition among a cast of nutty characters that include her gun-slinging father (William Demarest); her smartass younger sister Emmy (Diana Lynn); and her devoted friend Norval Jones (Eddie Bracken). After a feature-length's span of shenanigans, sight gags, and slapstick, Trudy delivers sextuplets on Christmas Day.

The Production Code office had already struggled with Sturges over earlier films, and the problems that he had with the censors on *Miracle* delayed the release of the film for two years. Although the script, written by Sturges, reflected a very real phenomenon of wartime American life (Trudy suggests one of the "Victory girls," young women who "congregated near the gates of military posts, attaching themselves to young servicemen"), the Breen office insisted that he amend the screenplay several times, which he did (Leff and Simmons 126). As film scholar James L. Neibaur writes, "[I]t was not so easy for Sturges. The Breen Office … scrutinized his screenplay and a seven-page document of suggested revisions was submitted to Paramount Pictures. Sturges was left with only ten approved script pages" (http://sensesofcinema.com/2011/cteq/the-miracle-of-morgan percentE2 percent80 percent99s-creek/). When the movie finally opened in 1944, American audiences delighted in Trudy's delivery of six baby boys on Christmas Day. Paramount enjoyed high profits from the film, which has retained its prominence as one of the most distinguished of all American film comedies.[10]

The Miracle of Morgan's Creek not only represents a landmark achievement in pregnancy narrative during the studio years of Hollywood, but also suggests a real turning point for industry-wide censorship.[11] In the Code offices, even Breen himself seemed to understand that the war had caused a sea change in American attitudes and behaviors. He recognized that it "had unleashed forces that Hollywood could not ignore…. [T]he endless stream of movies about fearless warriors and faithful wives" now seemed irrelevant (126). *Miracle of Morgan's Creek* was an irreverent, edgy comedy that signaled real transformations in American filmmaking. These changes were subtle but profound, and had little to do with comedy, but once again, reveal how significant pregnancy narratives remain to our understanding of major transitions in American filmmaking. There is no better gauge to how narrative film changed in mid-century than to note the changes to onscreen pregnancy. And after *Miracle of Morgan's Creek*, pregnancy in American movies would not seem very funny for several decades.

Women's Noir: Melonoirique

Postwar pregnancy was being projected within the shadows of the dark, unstable, and profoundly disturbing film element *noir*. A film movement with roots in pre-war German film, and transplanted through the craft of many European filmmakers who emigrated to the United States before, during, and after World War II, noir's imprint in Hollywood began with adaptations of pulp fiction. *Double Indemnity* (1944), *Detour* (1945) and *Gilda* (1946) are iconic Hollywood films in which noir elements dominate. "Worldly, ambitious, and sophisticated," writes film scholar Thomas Leitch, "many of these European filmmakers managed to adapt to the big budget of Hollywood studios while maintaining their sense of expressive visual style and their fondness for literate dialogue" (33).

By the late 1940s, conventions of noir were becoming familiar to American moviegoers: noir "featured amateur criminals—people who did not think of themselves as criminals at all—trapped in ordinary situations gone wrong, using everyday drives for love and success as the basis for criminal nightmares" (33). These nightmares had especially distinctive visuals. Noir filmmakers often relied on contrasts in black and white to frame their narratives: "[T]he hallucinatory contrasts between glaring white faces and deep black skies, the lush orchestral scores ratcheting up moments of emotional intensity still further—all of these figures were familiar to film-noir audiences ... from a mythic world created mainly by other movies" (34).[12]

Until a film critic coined the term "film noir" in 1946, these dark films were often identified by writers, critics and studios as "melodramas," a misnomer that actually makes practical and critical sense. Like melodrama, noir is a shape-shifter, a reliably versatile set of tropes and emblems that can be transmuted and translated from one narrative to another. Many Hollywood films from the 1940s and 1950s include elements of both.[13] These interesting melodrama-noir films almost always include distinctive women characters, often those whom we understand to be damaged, displaced misfits.[14] These women are sometimes referred to as "femme fatales" or "spider women," yet also referred to as victims or martyrs. Their duality represents one of the most compelling characteristics of noir: women always embody opposites. When we see women in noir-melodramas, we are usually seeing double, and not just because these characters have both active and passive roles to play. Although sometime the women in these post-war films are sterile or childless (a characteristic noted by scholars of noir), some of the most compelling of these characters really *are* two people, because they are pregnant.[15] Their pregnancies represent the center of the noir melodramatic universe of these films.

Male Melonoirique

Between 1945 and 1950, besides the predictable weepies in which unwed mothers gave up their children, including *To Each His Own* (for which Olivia de Havilland won her second Academy Award in 1946), American audiences were exposed to some very different female characters than they had seen before. The days of romantic wartime women's films like the contrived and pleasant *Four Daughters, Four Wives*, and *Four Mothers* series were certainly over.[16] Modesty rules had changed significantly, and in some of these noir films we see obviously pregnant women, visuals that never would have slipped through an earlier Production Code era. Beyond the visuals, filmmakers were projecting pregnancy narratives that portended violence, evil, or disaster associated with pregnancy. Among these movies are one in which a violent train accident kills one very pregnant woman and sends her pregnant companion to the emergency room (Barbara Stanwyck and Phyllis Thaxter in *No Man of Her Own* in 1950); one in which a deaf woman is raped and becomes pregnant as a result (Jane Wyman in *Johnny Belinda* in 1948); two in which characters try to miscarry (Gene Tierney in *Leave Her to Heaven* in 1945; Bette Davis in *Beyond the Forest* in 1948); and two in which a character is murdered after—and because—she has announced her pregnancy (Laura Elliott in *Strangers on a Train*; Shelley Winters in *A Place in the Sun*; both in 1951).

In some of these movies, the male characters show us characteristics of noir that we recognize easily: they are innocent people going about their business when they become entrapped in circumstances in which they become criminals. Pregnancy functions in two ways in these films: it becomes part of the entrapment process, and also ensures that we see these innocent men as victims who also become, on some level, victimizers. In Alfred Hitchcock's *Strangers on a Train*, for example, professional tennis player Guy Haines (Farley Granger) must find a way to convince his prickly wife Miriam (Laura Elliott), from whom he is estranged, to consent to a quick divorce so that he can marry his new love Ann Morton (Ruth Roman).[17] Complicating Guy's task is that Miriam says that she is pregnant (but not with Guy's baby). When Guy travels by train to confront her about a divorce, Miriam tells him that she does not want a divorce, but instead wants to reconcile with him. We have almost no back story for Miriam, and we learn almost nothing about her from the scene in which she engages with Guy, except that she works in a record shop and she wears thick glasses. Miriam seems crass and obnoxious to Guy when he comes to discuss their divorce. In other words, she is the perfect pregnant noir woman.

Noir women "disturb the patriarchal system and provide a challenge to the world view" of the films because they appear as outsiders or misfits (Kaplan, 16). If noir women disrupt the narrative, then pregnant noir characters *really* mess things up. During the post-war era, besides the pesky Miriam in *Strangers on a Train*, pregnant characters provide plot complications in *Johnny Belinda* and *A Place in the Sun*, both of which suggest that the men are the victims of circumstances. In *Johnny Belinda*, the consequences for the men represent the center of Belinda's rape and subsequent pregnancy, and Belinda's fate is completely entwined with those of her doctor, her father, and her rapist. However, both Miriam in *Strangers* and Alice in *A Place in the Sun* present us with a different pregnancy narrative, one in which both women threaten to make their pregnancies public unless the fathers of their unborn babies marry them. Their pregnancies and subsequent deaths initiate a downward noir cycle for both Guy Haines and George Eastman.[18] These menacing pregnancies threaten to deny both men the women they love, and also threaten to keep them from upwardly mobile social tracks. We and both pregnant women recognize that they have no way to compete, and their pregnancies become bargaining power for them.

Both Miriam and Alice die in ways that Guy and George cannot control in these films. From the time they both die, the circumstances of their deaths become the center around which each plot pivots. For audiences who have met both Miriam and Alice, however, their deaths represent even more than unfortunate accidents or misunderstandings. In both films, we are the only people besides Guy and George who understand that these women are not just in the way, but that they are also the ticking time bombs that might explode the hopes and dreams of these men. Because of the nature of pregnancy itself, both women are twice as threatening to these men: they can talk about their pregnancies, and soon enough their bodies will reveal their unfortunately timed pregnancies to anyone who sees them (a point not lost on either Miriam or Alice). The audience becomes familiar with both Miriam and Alice just enough that when they die, we understand that however annoying, malicious, or obnoxious they have been, they are two *pregnant* women who have died. Their deaths become doubly heinous, and haunt both films long after both women are dead.

Beyond the Forest presents us with a different pregnancy narrative, one in which the pregnant woman herself represents the center of a film with an especially complicated melodramatic plot. Rosa Moline (Bette Davis), married to Dr. Lewis Moline (Joseph Cotten), leads a stultifying life; she feels bored, powerless, and caged. She discovers a way to escape when she meets Neil Latimer (David Brian), so she steals money and travels to Chicago to be with Latimer, who rejects her. She returns home and becomes pregnant by her husband. Latimer returns to tell her that he indeed wants to be with her. When Rosa tells Lewis that she is leaving him, he tells her that she must wait until his baby is born. Rosa, who earlier referred to her pregnancy as "the mark of death," threatens to kill herself. Hoping instead to abort, Rosa throws herself out of the passenger's side of a car and down the side of a hill. As a result of her injuries, she dies from infection.

Beyond the Forest has interested film scholars for many reasons, one of which is that the film reverses the gendered stereotypes of noir, allowing us to consider Rosa as the center of the film.[19] We learn early in the story that although talented and smart in many ways, Rosa has no interest in housekeeping (Davis says her famous line "What a dump!" in this film, referring to her own home) or in raising children. Rosa is the noir misfit, a woman who cannot channel her energy, "cannot maintain the repression" of her life, and cannot find a place in the world where she feels she belongs (Doane 64). Throughout the film she is rejected, abused, and dismissed by all of the men in her life; every time she thinks she has found a way to escape, she runs into obstacles. Rosa, who actually commits a murder in the film for which she is absolved, finally succumbs to "an even more atrocious crime against her own womanhood by a self-induced abortion—the crime for which she is punished by fever and death" (65). In *Beyond the Forest*, Rosa is condemned to die, like George Eastman in *A Place in the Sun* (and like Guy Haines's double Bruno Anthony in *Strangers on a Train*), for having murdered a pregnant woman.

At the beginning of *Beyond the Forest*, the calm, authoritarian male voiceover which introduces Rosa's tale delivers a clear statement in which he likens evil to a naked body—but not just any naked body: "This is the story of evil. Evil is headstrong—is *puffed up*. For our soul's sake, it is salutary for us to view it in all its naked ugliness once in a while" [my italics]. Who threatens to be "puffed up" in this film? Whose "naked body" does an audience project as "puffed up?" We might read *Beyond the Forest* in many ways: as an example of the engendered cruelties of noir film, as the narrative in which women's pathologies are revealed, etc. However we evaluate the film, pregnancy has to be a central element of our understanding of the story of Rosa Moline. *Beyond the Forest* stands as one of the most commanding of all melonoiresque pregnancy narratives, one with antecedents in the pregnancy tales of Hester Prynne and Sethe of Sweet Home. In this movie, pregnancy becomes the dark unruly element that cannot be controlled within the frame of the screen: we will project the puffed-up pregnancy that Rosa so dreads without having to see it.

No Man of Her Own

The remarkable cluster of pregnancy melodrama-noir films between 1948 and 1951 includes two Hollywood films in which we *do* see pregnant women who are puffed-up. In *No Man of Her Own*, Helen Ferguson (Barbara Stanwyck), eight months pregnant and unmarried, has been dumped by the baby's father Steve Morley (Lyle Bettger), who instead of marrying her, gives her a train ticket. We watch a very pregnant Helen negotiating the stairs, her suitcase, and the narrow aisle in the train car. She looks hot, tired, and uncomfortable. In true noir style, the world we watch in the film is a cruel and indifferent one: not one person on the train bothers to help Helen or offer her a seat. She sits down on her suitcase, and the camera then shows us a close-up of four feet. The high heels are nudging the wingtips, which move to stand. In the next shot, we see Hugh Harkness (Richard Denning) offer his seat to Helen. When Helen sits down, she is sitting next to Hugh's wife Patrice (Phyllis Thaxter), the high heels who had nudged her husband to give up his seat. And we see why Patrice was so quick to help Helen: Patrice looks to be about seven months along herself.

Helen is reticent to share her story with the couple, but they both tell Helen enough that she learns who they are, where they are going, and why. Patrice has never met Hugh's parents, so the couple is travelling to meet them before the baby is born. After chatting for a few more minutes, Patrice and Helen stand and make their way to the ladies' lounge.[20] Once inside the lounge, the two pregnant women stand side by side looking at themselves and each other in the mirror as they talk. We are behind them, and we see both them and their reflections as Patrice tells Helen more of her life story: she and Hugh have been living overseas since their marriage; her in-laws have never seen a picture of her; they do not know what she looks like. She shares some face crème with Helen that her mother-in-law had sent her; she says that she thinks that her in-laws are "well off." Patrice takes off her wedding ring so that she can put crème on her hands, and she asks Helen to wear her ring for a moment. "Isn't that bad luck?" Helen asks. "I couldn't have bad luck," Patrice answers, as a train whistle begins to blow in the background. Within seconds, the mirror is shattering, the ladies lounge is tipping over, and we are watching the two pregnant women roll around, screaming, grasping for something to steady them. The train car rotates all the way around, over and over. The screen goes dark and silent for a few seconds.

Patrice and Hugh die in the train wreck, but Helen and her unborn baby survive. She is wearing Patrice's wedding ring, and the hospital where she soon delivers her new son has assumed that Helen is Patrice Harkness. And so she becomes Patrice Harkness for the rest of the film, until Steve finds her and the baby, and tries to extort money. By then, Helen has an ally, Patrice's brother-in-law Bill Harkness (John Lund), who knows of her deceit, loves her anyway, and ultimately helps her. The film ends in a way that an earlier Production Code would never have allowed: the deceitful pair get away with their crimes when it becomes clear that Bill's mother killed Steve just before she died. Helen is now free to live with Bill. Unfortunately, he is no prize, as we can tell in the concluding scenes. When Bill tells Helen, "As far as I can tell, you were born the day I met you," we know that Helen will never have control of her own life. She has made a deal with the devil.

Scholars of noir often cite the use of the doppelganger in these films, and *No Man of Her Own* is exemplary of this use of doubles. Brothers Hugh and Bill; pregnant women Patrice and Helen; and finally sleazy misogynists Steve and Bill, all represent duplicity in this film. Of all of the pairs, the two pregnant women suggest the most interesting pairing because of how they look. The visual pregnancy shots in *No Man of Her Own*, particularly the sequence in which the two women bounce around helplessly in the rolling train car, heighten the horror of the accident, and draw special attention to the bodies of the women. In this film, pregnant bodies become victims before our eyes, indicating another duality that only pregnancy can expose: manipulation of the human body and its opposite, the uncontrollable power of the human body. Being heavy with child allows Helen to become someone else, and being heavy with child also necessitates that Helen be someone else. Looking pregnant makes Helen into two people, and so does being pregnant make her into two people. Her pregnancy makes *No Man of Her Own* an especially crowded melodrama, and one of the most unstable and unruly pregnancy narratives on the screen. But not the most unruly. That distinction belongs to *Leave Her to Heaven*.

Leave Her to Heaven

"*Leave Her to Heaven*," writes Jeanine Basinger, "is one of the greatest of all women's films ... superbly written, directed, and produced," it stands by itself as a cinematic triumph (96). Of all of the melonoiresque films made in post-war Hollywood, *Leave Her to Heaven* remains one of the most beautiful, and one of the most disturbing. Filmed in Technicolor, and starring some of the most camera-friendly faces in Hollywood, the film focuses on Ellen Berent (the always radiant Gene Tierney), an intense, stunningly beautiful woman who meets novelist Dick Harland on a train and quickly falls for him; dumps her fiancée; and marries him.[21] From this point on, we begin to suspect that all is not right with Ellen, who has especially difficult relationships with her own difficult family, and who seems to have an unhealthy attachment to her now deceased father. Although we see much about the Berent family to alarm us, the character of Ellen is "constructed as the source of the [Berent] family's troubles rather than as a participant in a structure into which she was born" (Renov 233). Ellen has issues, and we are the only ones who recognize this for much too long a time in the film.

From the first scene where Ellen meets Dick, the camera allows us to understand that she is potentially unstable. We see Ellen "reading Harland's book whose dust jacket—Harland's face—replaces her own face," writes Michael Renov (233). "This blocking of her visage is a startling sign of her emotional truncation, her desire to replace a portion of her identity and selfhood with that of another person, a male person" (233). Ellen becomes increasingly obsessive, jealous, and narcissistic, and the other people around her seem oblivious to what we see as alarming signs. By the time Ellen engineers the drowning of Danny, Dick's beloved younger brother, we know that we are watching the crime of a woman who is seriously ill. One of the most famous scenes of any Hollywood production, a scene so chilling that it is difficult to watch, this drowning scene defines Ellen for us: "[I]n what looks to be cold premeditation, Ellen lets Danny drown in the lake as she looks on from behind dark glasses" (235).

This horrifying scene is matched by the later scene in which Ellen, clearly several months pregnant, realizes that she can kill her unborn child. Like the early ladies' lounge-train wreck scene in *No Man of Her Own*, the scene of Ellen's miscarriage employs mirrors to help us understand the dynamic of the scene. As Ellen's sister Ruth (Jeanne Crain) folds a pile of baby clothes, a visibly pregnant Ellen, wearing an elegant dressing gown, begins questioning her in menacing tones: "What do you talk about when you go to town? Me?" Eventually, Ellen turns away and looks at herself in a full-length mirror. Disgusted at what she sees, she tells Ruth, "Look at me. I hate the little beast. I wish it would die." Although Ruth protests, we alone know that she means this, because she had hoped that Danny would die, also. Alarmed, Ruth leaves the room, but not before she accuses Ellen of being afraid. Alone at her dressing table, gazing at her own face in another mirror, Ellen sees her way out of the pregnancy. Once again, we are the only ones who understand her plan. And we probably wish that we didn't.

Ellen's face in close-up, her eyes wide, tells us that she has figured out how to make sure that the "little beast" inside her dies. She rises from the dressing table, goes to the closet, and pulls out first a beautiful blue negligee, and second, a pair of matching blue satin mules. The camera closes in on the shoes in Ellen's hands as the music grows more ominous, and then dissolves into a shot of Ellen standing in front of the closet door, wearing the blue ensemble. She once again looks at herself in the mirror, and applies perfume and lipstick. She then turns her back to the mirror, moves out of the room to the top of the stairs, carefully adjusts her slippery mules, and plunges down the stairs to rising music. We hear a scream as she plummets. She has successfully killed the little beast.

From the beginning of the film until Ellen's carefully premeditated suicide, her behavior becomes increasingly pathological. In a scene from early in her marriage to Dick, we see an attractive, competent, seemingly happy wife: "Ellen serves a perfect luncheon to Dick. Dressed in a pink peasant blouse with flounced sleeves, accompanied by soft, domestic music, Ellen expresses her obsessive desires" in a disturbing speech (Renov 234). "I have no intention of hiring a cook, a housekeeper, or any other servant," she tells Dick. And considering how we watch her get rid of both Dick's brother and her unborn child, we might recall this earlier domestic scene in which she tells Dick, "I don't want anyone else in the house besides us." As Robey, the male friend who narrates the story tells us, "jealousy is the most deadly" of the seven sins and also "the most stereotypically feminine ... Ellen's triad of homicides—of the crippled Danny Harland, her unborn son, and herself—are meant to be the actions of a jealous woman" (232). Ellen's profoundly disturbing story represents one of the clearest examples of the pregnancy narrative in Hollywood film in the post–World War II era. The seamless stylish beauty of the pregnant character is undercut by her dreadful and grim instability, which becomes a dark metaphor for what it meant to be female in post-war America.

Women characters were more sophisticated, more confident, and more articulate than before the war began, and pregnancy in these melodramatic-noir films highlights an anxiety over how to represent these changed characters on film. These women did not respond to earlier conventional Hollywood types. Sturdy enough to have defended the homefront while they grew babies and held down jobs in wartime films, women characters enjoyed a perverse kind of freedom of movement in

2. *The Weepies: Pregnancy, Melodrama and Noir*

Pregnant and crazy: Ellen Berent Harland (Gene Tierney, right) tells her sister Ruth (Jeanne Crain, left) how much she hates the baby she is carrying in *Leave Her to Heaven* (1945). Within minutes of this shot, Ellen will gaze into the mirror and decide to miscarry, and she will throw herself down a flight of stairs. Pregnant women are often framed in mirrors in melonoirique films, which does not just double them for us, but quadruples them.

the noir films of the late 1940s and early 1950s. They were lying, impersonating and murdering. They were rolling around in train cars and down the sides of hills with nothing to hold onto. They were endangering themselves and their unborn offspring by moving around and around. They were pathological, vulnerable, and especially duplicitous—literally. Whether they were liars, murderers, victims, or tramps, they were scary because they could not be controlled or prescribed. And they could all duplicate—they could all be pregnant.

The cluster of post-war melonoir pregnancy films parallels the early 1930s pre–Code melodramas in several ways. Both bodies of film escaped serious censorship, and both projected women who were complicated, challenging characters. These eras also share another legacy: Hollywood studios attempted to codify and regulate these women's films in the decades immediately following. In the late 1930s, the weepies would put on patriotic maternity wear and always include close-ups of crying women framed by light. In a similar way, the Hollywood studios of the 1950s also tried to fix these wild noir women, but good. In some mainstream 1950s Hollywood movies, women characters moved back into fixed stereotyped settings, as sweethearts, wives and mothers, often now safely situated in suburban settings. However, if women characters insisted on moving around instead of remaining static, if they did not conform to the Hollywood formula, then they were punished. In classic melodramatic style, their punishment involved rendering them powerless by taking away their most distinctive and potent characteristic: their ability to be pregnant.

1950s: Pregnancy Nightmares of Men

Nineteen fifty-one was a big year for Hollywood films in which pregnancy played a role. Besides *A Place in the Sun* and *Strangers on a Train*, studios also released *Father's Little Dividend*, Vincente Minnelli's sequel to *Father of the Bride*, about the trials and tribulations of Stanley Banks (Spencer Tracy) as he tries to cope with the pregnancy of his daughter Kay (Elizabeth Taylor). We watch Kay through three trimesters as she decorates her lovely nursery, and as her maternity wear becomes more and more stylish. With the post-war baby boom at full throttle in 1951, *Father's Little Dividend* enjoyed special popularity, especially for a sequel. The movie projected and advertised a particular American fantasy: that of the prosperous WASP home in the suburbs. This dream world included "a professional father and a homemaking mother living in a comfortable single-family house" where "fathers ruled with firm, if bemused, authority" while their wives watched over their harmonious homes in smart style (Hatch 46).

Stanley Banks was not the only character named Stanley on the screen in 1951, and probably not the one we remember best. Also released that year was the film adaptation of Tennessee Williams's stage play *A Streetcar Named Desire*, starring Marlon Brando as Stanley Kowalski, Vivien Leigh as his sister-in-law Blanche DuBois, and Kim Hunter as his pregnant wife Stella. *Streetcar*, along with *A Place in the Sun* and *Strangers on a Train*, represent films in which the men—handsome, virile, sensuous—become the objects of our gaze. In *Streetcar* the women characters do not compel us visually. We watch Blanche struggle "to produce the illusion of youth through lighting and costume," and we see her as an aging, faded beauty (Hatch 58). Stella is "routinely dressed in oversized clothes that deemphasize her pregnant body" (58). However, close-ups of Stanley's face replace the earlier female Madonnas that audiences had come to expect in Hollywood dramas: "Brando's face in *A Streetcar Named Desire* is rendered beautiful" (58).[22]

Director Elia Kazan created a film narrative which is ultimately a celebration of Stanley's beauty most pointedly through his visual choices. He reversed the gaze structure in the film so that Stanley becomes "the object of the gaze ... of Stella, Blanche, and the film spectator" (56). If all eyes are on Stanley's muscular beauty, then Stella's pregnancy reminds us that his wife is clearly among the women hot for him. Stella "quietly accepts" Stanley's shabby lifestyle, and "willingly suffers the implicit abuse of a macho, working-class husband (Byars 103). Yet she loves this bully throughout the film in a way that even the film censorship board noticed: "Stella's desire for Stanley was palpable on the screen" (Hatch 60). Her pregnancy reminds us of their sexual attraction in every scene, especially the final scene, where although Stella leaves Stanley, "the audience has little faith that she will stay away" (60).

Except that they all include pregnancy narratives, the sunny story of the Banks family in *Father's Little Dividend*, and those dark narratives projected in *A Streetcar Named Desire*, *A Place in the Sun* and *Strangers on a Train*, might as well have been taking place on different planets in 1951. That they all include pregnancy narratives suggests another characteristic they share: they are all films in which the male characters' roles are unstable or disruptive. Even Stanley Banks, although often a buffoon, assumes that he ought to be in charge even as he "feels his authority is fading" (48). These "male melodramas" reflected changes in American demographics—and also changes in the power structure of Hollywood—during the 1950s.[23]

No longer were the stereotypes of the strong, stable bread-winner and the male hero reliable types, and Hollywood studios reacted by trying to tailor movies to the tastes of professional men, those who might need some reassurance. Women were increasingly independent in every way, including financially, and many critics of the day noticed a "perceived shift in the balance of power" in all traditional American institutions, including the family (48). This "increased anxiety" over the role of men in American society certainly contributed to how Hollywood studios were projecting pregnancy in these male melodramas (48). For every fertile Miriam, Alice, Kay, or Stella, 1950s Hollywood also provided audiences with women characters whose pregnancies ensured that they would be barren or childless. And in the 1950s, it would be their own damn fault.

In *Come Back, Little Sheba* (1953), we learn from Lola Delaney (Shirley Booth) that her husband Doc (Burt Lancaster) sacrificed his

Stanley Kowalski (Marlon Brando) and his pregnant wife Stella (Kim Hunter) in *A Streetcar Named Desire* (1951). Director Elia Kazan privileges Brando's visage in the film, often framing the couple so that Stanley faces us and we see Stella's pregnant profile.

chance to finish medical school and instead married Lola, pregnant with his child at the time. After suffering a miscarriage that left her unable to conceive again, Lola and Doc, now an alcoholic, live miserable lives. Lola suffers from chronic depression, which we understand from her listlessness, her slovenly look and her unkempt house. When explaining to her potential boarder Marie (Terry Moore) that their little dog Sheba is missing, Lola also confides openly about their childlessness: "We haven't any children, you know." After Doc attempts AA, falls off the wagon twice, and returns home to dry out near the end of the film, Lola straightens up: "She has changed visibly, now wearing a crisp, pastel shirtwaist dress. She has replaced kitchen curtains, has painted the ice-box, and is now prepared to make Doc a 'nice, hot breakfast'" (Byars 119). Still lonely and damaged, sadder but tidier, Lola has transformed herself. *Come Back, Little Sheba* "teaches women how to keep their men and teaches men what women *should* be" (119). Lola's unintended tragic pregnancy has made her life a series of continuing losses which have punished her husband, and we see her total contrition at the end of the film.

Georgie (Grace Kelly) tries to make the best of living in poverty in a dingy hotel suite with her alcoholic husband Frank (Bing Crosby) in *The Country Girl* (1955), but she cannot affect much happiness into the flat. We learn in flashback that Georgie and Frank did have a son who died in a traffic accident. Frank has always blamed himself for neglecting to notice that his little boy was playing in traffic, and as a result, Frank "makes the decision to have no more children, rendering Georgie child-less and, therefore, marginal" (119). Frank's career as a popular enter-tainer is in peril, and throughout the film we watch him struggle to regain his sobriety and his integrity. Like Lola in *Come Back, Little Sheba*, Georgie becomes the anchor of her damaged 1950s family. Also like Lola, who considers leaving Doc, Georgie "rejects independence, realizing that the solution, for her too, lies in the re-creation of the familial insti-tution" (121). Both characters do the right thing, but both of them pay the price that their pregnancies demanded: they remain freakish, aber-rant, and punished in the 1950s paradigm of the nuclear family.

Karen (Deborah Kerr) in *From Here to Eternity* (1953) presents us with the most tortured of the 1950s pregnancy narratives in mainstream Hollywood fare. As she begins her affair with Sergeant Milt Warden

(Burt Lancaster, again), Karen explains to him why her marriage is a sham: her husband, (Warden's commanding office on the Pearl Harbor base) went out philandering one night, and arrived home too drunk to help his pregnant wife get to the hospital. As a result, Karen hemorrhaged, miscarried, and became sterile. Now, she has herself become a lost and heartbroken philanderer, which seems to suggest that the film "encourages its audience to believe that she wants—like *all women*—to have a 'normal' happy family" (104). Karen, like Lola and Georgie, is the tragic freak of nature, a married woman who cannot be pregnant.[24]

From Here to Eternity looks backwards melodramatically at World War II from 1953, and as such, represents the plight of women during the war in ways that actually reflects the shifting values of the 1950s. As Rebecca Bell-Metereau points out, the film places the famous love scene between Karen and Milt on the beach as a counterpoint to the military scenes on either side of it. The "beach scene, which symbolizes the power of passion, female sexuality, and heterosexual intimacy," remains the movie's most memorable scene because it contrasts to the "regimented masculine domain of hierarchy, devotion to duty, alcoholic escape, and repressed homoerotic attachment to one's fellow soldiers" represented in the scenes around it (103). The movement of the natural world around the lovers stops when the Japanese attack Pearl Harbor, and Karen retreats to the mainland. Like all of these other male melodramas of the decade, *From Here to Eternity* "tried to put a lid on women's freedom and independence, placing them back in a position of dependence and subservience" (104).

Authentic Victory Girl Trudy Kockenlocker, whose healthy "sexual liberation" represented a "boon to departing soldiers" in the world of wartime cinema, would not have been welcome in the 1953 version of World War II. In the 1950s, her stamina and female vitality would have been too threatening to a studio system that already felt threatened from all sides. Indeed, the studio system, long a bastion of male privilege and strict codified formula and profit, was being forced to react to outside changes, and would never seem as securely institutional as it had before the 1950s. Among the threats to Hollywood studios in the 1950s: antitrust lawsuits that eventually busted up the studio-theater monopolies; more and more studio actors leaving the ranks to act independently; the House on Un-American Activity hearings, which rocked the world of entertainment and damaged careers and reputations among thousands of workers in the Hollywood industry. But perhaps the two most significant threats to the Old Guard in Hollywood were the Supreme Court's decisions to allow foreign films to be shown in the United States in their uncensored entireties, and the rising power of television.

The influx of foreign films had a lasting impact on American cinema. In 1948 (the same year that the monopolies of the Big Five studios were challenged in the U.S. courts), Roberto Rossellini's *The Miracle*, starring Anna Magnani, caused near riots when it opened in New York.[25] "A spiritual allegory to its admirers and a shocking blasphemy to its detractors," the movie involved "a dim-witted peasant girl (Magnani) seduced and impregnated by a man she believes to be St. Joseph" (Doherty, *Censor*, 302). The story is archetypal: "Driven from her village, taken in at no inn, she gives birth alone in an empty church in the mountains" (302). After the film was confiscated and banned, the promoters sued, and the case came before the Supreme Court in 1952, which ruled that motion pictures were afforded First Amendment protections because they represented "a significant medium for the communication of ideas" (302). The Hollywood Production Code, although not affected directly by this ruling, was certainly in jeopardy, since Hollywood films would now be in direct competition with films from elsewhere—and the studios could no longer control which movies played in which theaters. Now inspired and engaged by narratives from other parts of the world, American filmmakers of the 1950s enjoyed a higher level of independence and better access to theater screens, than they had enjoyed since before World War I.

Lucy Ricardo

The growing popularity of television also posed a new test for Hollywood studios, which had not faced a direct competitive challenge to their strength before. Studios were losing money and audience numbers in direct relation to the growing number of television stations on the air, especially in metropolitan areas. Despite efforts to lure audiences with upgraded technological developments and gimmicks, mainstream movies struggled to compete with television dramas and comedies that enjoyed both artistic and technological innovations. Television, for example, could present live performances of dramas, and could project realistic portrayals of subjects not allowed in studio productions, such as drug addiction or kidnapping.[26] Although subject to a production code of its own (based loosely on the Film Production Code), television did prohibit profanity, graphic sexual content, and graphic violence. The use of the word "pregnant" was prohibited on air, but as in 1950s film productions, women could look pregnant on television shows, and characters could talk about their pregnancies through the usual euphemisms. That especially turned out to be a good thing for both American television and American movies in 1953, when Lucy Ricardo became pregnant.

In the 1950s, the television industry offered opportunities for women that film studios did not, and Lucille Ball represents one of the most successful of all television performers and entrepreneurs. She was the first woman in American television to run her own production company, initially with her husband Desi Arnaz and later on her own. Desilu was also the first production company to film its shows, particularly Ball's own *I Love Lucy*, with audiences in attendance, and the first studio to use multiple cameras and sets for one show. Also among the distinctions for *I Love Lucy*: Lucy Ricardo was the first television character whose pregnancy became part of the fabric of the show itself, and Ball was the first television actor to use her own pregnancy as part of the narrative of the series. Over seven episodes that season, audiences watched Lucy get into all of her usual trouble, including her attempt to work her way into show business by taking on the identity of a man in a barbershop quartet.

What made all of this even more unusual was that audiences knew that they were watching a pregnant actor, and they loved her for it. When Ball delivered her healthy son by Caesarean section on the same day that Lucy Ricardo delivered her son (off-screen, of course) on the show, the news made happy headlines everywhere. These double births seem more culturally significant than 1950s America might have imagined at the time. Lucy-Lucille's pregnancy, complete with morning sickness, maternity wear, jitters and fears, and great expectations, came into audiences' living rooms in ways that many adults already recognized, but had never seen performed as drama or comedy. Lucy normalized on-screen pregnancy for audiences, and made pregnancy accessible not just to television narrative, but to film narrative as well. From 1953 on, pregnancy would never again be hidden, silent or static, nor would the pregnancy narrative be delegated almost exclusively to the melodramatic mode. Lucy Ricardo brought pregnancy to life, in front of our eyes.[27]

In many ways, however, pregnancy narratives remained at home in the weepies, especially those American melodramas that had nourished pregnancy on film, almost exclusively, for the first sixty years of American cinema. As the Hollywood studios lost their grip on where and how audiences watched films, and as television became more popular, however, the restrictions and modesty of the film community would look stilted and old-fashioned. Pregnancy would begin to show in every kind of narrative film: from the Big Five studios to the small B studios; from melodramas to comedies; from the beginning of pregnancy to labor and birth. Sturdy pregnancy narratives would survive and thrive. The weepies, and the complicated fusion of melodrama and noir that had eventually embraced pregnancy on the screen, would become part of a rich and useful legacy of pregnancy narratives in subsequent decades.

The Production Code had not smothered the pregnancy narrative after all, but had merely moved it temporarily out of sight. Along with other subversive or questionable film conventions, pregnancy narratives were temporarily "run underground" (305). One of the first genres to reveal the organic growth of the pregnancy narrative *above* ground was the "alien and aberrant cinema" that had been suppressed or ignored during the Code years, the B movies. Among the Bs that featured spaceships, werewolves, pods, and aliens, audiences also began to see unusual and sometimes spectacular pregnancies on movies screens. Some of the earliest and most interesting aliens of the late 1950s and early 1960s were a scary group who looked as if they were just like you and me, but were really from somewhere else: teenagers. Thanks to the weepies, film noir, and Lucy Ricardo, the teenage pregnancy narrative was orbiting, and about to land. American movies would never be the same.

3

Pregnant Teenagers and Other Monsters

Peyton Place

In 1954, New Hampshire housewife Grace Metalious sent the manuscript of her first novel, a potboiler that she had entitled *The Tree and the Blossom,* to New York publishers. Several turned her down, but one, Julian Messner, Inc., decided to publish. First, however, the publisher told Metalious's agent that the title of the book needed to be changed to the name of the little New England town in the book: Peyton Place.

Peyton Place was immediately popular with American reading audiences, and made Metalious suddenly rich, famous and miserable. For many Americans, however, the novel provided a pleasurable and saucy read. The novel "indicted 1950s morality, and recast the soap opera, all in one big, purple-prosed book" (Callahan). "It would spawn a sequel, a smash film nominated for nine Academy Awards, and television's first prime-time serial" (Callahan). At a time when most first novels might sell a total of 3,000 copies in the first year, Metalious's sold 100,000 copies. One week before the novel was released in 1956, it was already on the best-seller list, where it would remain for six months (Callahan).[1]

The now-famous opening lines of *Peyton Place* suggest why it might have captured readers: "Indian summer is like a woman. Ripe, hotly passionate, but fickle, she comes and goes as she pleases so that one is never sure whether she will come at all, nor for how long she will stay" (1). The novel is well-written, the narrative voice is consistent and clever, and the characters seem familiar to many readers. More importantly, the narrator, although not explicitly graphic, tells us a great deal about the private lives and secrets of the main characters, including generous detail about their private musings. And what are they thinking about? Themselves, mostly. And sex.

Like all well-crafted melodramas, *Peyton Place* includes plenty of secrets, and strands of several stories that eventually braid together, several of which can be characterized as pregnancy narratives. The very first story we read in the novel is the secret pregnancy narrative of Constance MacKenzie, thirty-five-year-old widow and mother of thirteen-year-old Allison MacKenzie. By the time we have read the first fifteen pages, we know more about Allison than she knows about herself, and we understand a great deal about how her mother thinks. The narrator spills the story immediately and all at once: Constance moved to New York City when she was nineteen, and became a secretary to a wealthy shop owner named Allison MacKenzie. The narrator continues, allowing us to hear how Constance thinks of Allison:

> Within three weeks he and Constance became lovers and during the next year a child was born to them whom Constance immediately named for its father. Allison MacKenzie and Constance Standish were never married, for he already had a wife and two children "up in Scarsdale," as he always put it. He said these words as if he were saying, "up at the North Pole," but Constance never forgot that Allison's first family was painfully, frighteningly near [15].

The narrator continues: Constance took great pains to "plan for herself and her unborn child," and she created a fiction about her marriage and her daughter, whose birth certificate she altered by using "a little ink eradicator" and substituting "a different number for the last digit of her daughter's year of birth" (16). When Constance's lover died in an automobile accident, she moved back to Peyton Place with three-year-old Allison and opened a dress shop with money she had inherited from her lover, who "was a good man, in his fashion, with a strict sense of responsibility" (16). From that time on, no one "ever questioned the fact that Constance was the widow of a man named Allison MacKenzie. She kept a large, framed photograph of him on the mantelpiece in her living room, and the town sympathized with her" (17).

Throughout the novel, Constance worries about her daughter Allison in a way that only a mother with secrets can worry. The nature of her worries helps us understand Constance's priorities and value system better. For example, at Allison's thirteenth birthday party, Constance notices that the guests are playing post office. "For the first time since Allison's birth," the narrator tells us, "Constance felt the finger of fear which is always ready to prod at the minds of women who have made what they considered to be 'A Mistake'" (50). Then Constance projects her nightmare: "A quick picture of her daughter Allison, lying in bed with a man, flashed through her mind, and Constance put a shaking hand against the wall to steady herself" (50). Constance's greatest fear, our narrator tells us, is not that Allison will get hurt, or even that she will get in trouble. Her greatest fear is that Allison will 'GET HERSELF TALKED ABOUT!'" (50).

Eventually, Constance meets Michael Rossi, the hot new principal of the high school, who takes her breath away. They become lovers and eventually marry in the novel, but not before the very wise Michael schools Constance on how to think about sex, her daughter, and the idea that her daughter might think about sex. The conversation comes up because a teenage girl in Allison's high school class, Betty Anderson, has become pregnant. Constance argues that Betty had "been thinking too much about sex," and she becomes cranky when Michael reminds her that all teenagers think about sex. Constance, stammering and stuttering, argues that teenagers should not have sex. She cannot bring herself to say the word "intercourse," to which Michael reacts:

> What the hell have you got against the word intercourse? ... It's a good, serviceable word. Yet you'd rather rack your brain for fifteen minutes to find a substitute rather than use it.... I'm not going around advocating fornication on every street corner and an illegitimate child in every home ... a kid at fifteen or sixteen, and oftentimes younger, is physically ready for sex ... [and] he feels a tremendous, basic drive for sex [217].

Of course, Michael is talking to a woman who *does* have an illegitimate child living in her home (although he does not yet know Constance's secret), so at this point, he cannot fully understand her skittishness on the subject. But we understand, because we know Constance's own pregnancy story, and we understand something about how it informs her behavior and how she relates to other characters. Until she falls in love with Michael, Constance behaves like a stiff board. She is brittle, and especially frightened by the fruit of her unintended pregnancy, Allison. Throughout the novel, she worries incessantly about the very thing that the narrator had told us Constance's mother had worried about: how her daughter's behavior might reflect back on her.

Constance needn't worry, however, because Allison, who will not become sexually active until she is nearly grown, seems to be the most accessible and accurately drawn of all of the characters in *Peyton Place*. An adolescent when the novel begins, Allison worries about what adolescent girls in America are always worrying about: what she looks like. She tries to understand changes in her own body. She compares herself to her best friend Selena, who has started menstruating. Allison decides that she wants nothing to do with having a period.

> But as far as she was concerned, "periods" were something that happened to other girls. She decided that she would never tolerate such things in herself… She thought of "It" [menstruation] as a large bat, with wings outspread, and when she woke up on the morning of her thirteenth birthday to discover that "It" was nothing of the kind, she was disappointed, disgusted and more than a little frightened [49].

Allison MacKenzie becomes our most clear-eyed guide through *Peyton Place* as she matures. She and her mother, whose intertwined stories put the plot into motion, represent a dominant strand of the melodramatic braid of the novel. But they are not the only ones. Among the other plotlines are those of Selena Cross, Allison MacKenzie's best childhood friend, and Betty Anderson and her boyfriend Rodney Harrington. Betty, Rodney, and Selena represent a rogue's gallery of troubled teenagers in *Peyton Place*. What unites them, of course, is pregnancy.

Selena Cross, a smart girl from the wrong side of the tracks in Peyton Place, lives with her mother, younger brother and alcoholic stepfather in a shack outside of town. When she is seventeen, Selena becomes pregnant by her stepfather, who, we discover, has been abusing her for several years. She imagines what would happen to her if anyone—including her employer, Constance—were to find out about her pregnancy: "If you knew, she thought. If you knew what the matter is, you wouldn't talk so gently to me. You'd tell me to get out of your sight" (138). She "knew her town, and its many voices. 'A girl in trouble.' 'She got in Dutch.' 'She's knocked up.' 'The tramp. The dirty little tramp'" (138).

Selena confides in Dr. Swain who admits her to the hospital and terminates her pregnancy. We hear about this from Dr. Swain's nurse, Mary Kelley. Dr. Swain tells her to prep Selena for an appendectomy, and Mary asks, "Doc, what're you doing?" "I'm removing her appendix," he replies, "Do you understand that, Mary?" Nurse Kelley understands, and she assists, but not before she struggles with the ethics of the situation. Mary Kelley might surprise readers with her especially thoughtful questions about ethical behavior and hypocrisy. Readers in the 1950s might have fully engaged with her here:

> Talk was cheap. It cost nothing to give voice to what you wanted people to think you believed. Mary wondered if medical ethics could be compared to the question of tolerance. When you talked, you said that Negroes were as good as anybody. You said that Negroes should never be discriminated against, and that if you ever fell in love with one, you'd marry him proudly. But all the while you were talking, you wondered what you would *really* do.... When you talked, you declared that if you fell in love with a Protestant ... you would marry him anyway.... You knew you were safe in saying these things ... [152–53].

After Dr. Swain finishes operating (he indeed removes Selena's appendix as well), Mary realizes that her actions provided the answers to her questions about ethics. Admitting to herself that by assisting and helping perpetuate the story of the appendectomy, she is troubled, but sturdy. "Resolutely," the narrator tells us, "she picked up the detective novel that she had started the night before. She forced her eyes to concentrate on the printed page..." (155).

Betty Anderson, another poor girl from the wrong side of town, has a sexual relationship with Rodney Harrington, the amoral son of the town's wealthiest factory owner. We know that she and Rodney have sex in his car regularly, and one night their tryst ends with Betty's hissing voice: "Smart guy who knew all about it. So smart he doesn't even know enough to wear a safe. Get me home, you dumb jackass. Quick!" (203). The narrator continues: "But unfortunately, Rodney did not get her home quickly enough, or her douche was not strong enough, or, as Rodney was inclined to believe, the Fates were out to foul him up good" (203). When Betty tells Rodney that she wants them to marry, he arranges with his father Leslie for Betty and her family to be paid $500 instead. Betty confronts Leslie, who will not be bullied by some pregnant working-class girl. To punish her, he halves the money, warning her that he will keep halving the money if she continues to insist that his son marry her.

3. Pregnant Teenagers and Other Monsters

Rodney and his father celebrate by driving around in Rodney's convertible. Betty, after incurring a beating from her immigrant father, leaves Peyton Place to "visit a maiden aunt in Vermont" (211). The narrator tells us that the townspeople eat Betty's story up, serving it, "along with meat and potatoes, at every supper table in Peyton Place" (211). Among those who devour the story were Allison and Constance, who "used [the story] as a sort of hammer with which to drive home her reasons for chastity in young girls" (211). "You see what happens," Constance tells Allison, "when a girl lets some fellow paw her. The result is what happened to Betty Anderson" (211).

Why *Peyton Place* was such a popular novel has often been more interesting to literary scholars and critics than the novel itself.[2] Some attribute its popularity to its purple prose and lurid content; others dismiss it for its contrived melodramatic plotlines and conventional middle-class characteristics. Those can only be partial answers to why this novel was a bestseller. Readers who wanted to read lurid prose in the 1950s had other dirty novels from which to choose, and there were other contrived melodramatic novels in bookstores as well. *Peyton Place* appealed to reading audiences because, like *Uncle Tom's Cabin* a century earlier, it represented a social melodrama that mirrored its times, one that "at its heart … is a manifesto, a blistering indictment of small-town values, classism, and racism" of the post-war era (Callahan). However, *Peyton Place* represented more than a mirror of the times: it was also a clear and frank articulation of the experiences of women as sexual beings.

Peyton Place is a female coming-of-age novel that documents the ways in which teenage girls learn to live with the complications of their reproductive selves. Allison MacKenzie's understanding of her period suggests both *Incidents in the Life of a Slave Girl*, and anticipates later coming-of-age literature, including *The Bluest Eye*, in which we read about characters' periods. Among the most striking characteristics of *Peyton Place*—certainly a characteristic that would have drawn readers in the baby-crazy 1950s—is that it presents various stories of pregnancy. Like pregnancy fiction before it, *Peyton Place* includes elements of the melodramatic (*Incidents in the Life of a Slave Girl*), characters whose secret pregnancies have informed their world views in isolation (*The Scarlet Letter*), and pregnant characters who force us to see them as both

victims and victimizers (*The Old Maid*). Unlike earlier pregnancy narratives, however, the narrator in *Peyton Place* does not mince words.

In 1954, readers of the novel could recognize familiar life experiences that nobody ever talked about: Allison getting her first period;
Rodney forgetting to wear a condom; Selena pleading with the doctor
to help her. *Peyton Place* enjoyed great popularity because it provided
refreshingly candid depictions of women's sexuality and subsequent
complicated lives. By the time Betty Anderson leaves town near the end
of the novel, we have been exposed to an entire spectrum of stories about
female sexuality and pregnancy issues: from Constance's secret pregnancy, to Allison's period, to Selena's rape and abortion, to Nurse Kelley's
ethical insights about pregnancy, and finally back to Betty's pregnancy.
In *Peyton Place*, we must consider any number of female-centered issues,
including pre-marital sex, violence against women, abortion, birth control, and teenage sexuality.

Grace Metalious sold the rights to *Peyton Place* to Hollywood in
1956, and the film adaptation was released in 1957. Although popular at
the time, the film, like the novel, has often been dismissed as typical
1950s melodrama: a "sanitized sequence of slamming doors, wayward
glances, and A-line skirts" (Callahan). Bending to the Production Code,
the adaptation included "no abortions, no moonlit swims, and certainly
no Betty asking Rodney if it was up and hard" (Callahan). The film does
include elements that qualify it as a "social melodrama" (in fact, the film
adaptation is faithful to the Selena-rape-Dr. Swain-abortion plotline).
It also represents a "female-oriented melodrama," in which a "young
and virile male" intrudes on a "community of women and children" and
sets them all straight (Byars 148–49). *Peyton Place* indeed includes elements of this kind of melodrama, where a healthy man "identifies the
problem—the female protagonist's lack of connectedness to a male—
and enables its solution: their coupling and integration' into a larger
community/family framework" (149).

Yet the film *Peyton Place* does not represent just any 1950s melodrama, because the "virile male" (Michael Rossi) and "female protagonist" (Constance MacKenzie) are not our primary focus. Its teenagers
represent its vitality and its central focus. "*Peyton Place* is the first American film where middle-class adolescent sexuality is portrayed openly
onscreen" (Pomerance, *Movies*, 183). In 1957, Metalious's book and the

Hollywood adaptation were hitting a collective nerve in America: the "sexually bounded narrative of this coming-of-age tale replicates a broader, deeply pervasive irony or proportion" that characterized American culture. The teenagers' sexual longings and freedoms are "pitted against repressive bourgeois decency and modesty; the secret life of darkness and fear" of the grownups looks petty and cowardly, compared to the daring and lively teenagers (184).

Peyton Place, filmed in beautiful pastel blue interiors and lush autumn gold exteriors, reveals that beyond the repressed and authoritarian world of their parents, Allison, Selena, Betty, and the other teenage characters are growing and moving in ways that their adult counterparts cannot. We see the adults in the film most often confined in small cluttered spaces: Constance's (Lana Turner) overly tasteful living room; the Cross family's tiny one-room shack where Selena (Hope Lange) endures her stepfather's violence; or Dr. Swain's (Lloyd Nolan) cramped office. In contrast, the teenagers frolic outdoors, amid the trees and lush New England vegetation. The grown men in their suits and ties, women corseted and pinned up, look static and staid compared to the teens with their flowing hair and graceful movements. The teenagers in *Peyton Place* move around the screen in a fluid, natural choreography that becomes the graceful counterpoint to the adult world of stymied longings. Sexuality becomes part of their dance, and for a fleeting moment, the teenagers appear to us to be a dream, the opposite of the "dark and cold emptiness" of their parents' vision (181).

Lolita

A year after *Peyton Place* projected a group of frustrated teenagers on American movie screens, we met another adolescent girl in another controversial novel. This was no homegrown, lurid melodrama, however. This was Vladimir Nabokov's *Lolita,* first published in France in 1955. Among the novels that Americans could have chosen to read in the 1950s, on first glance, no two seem more dissimilar than *Peyton Place* and *Lolita.* Yet they actually share a great deal. As Ruth Pirsig Wood points out, "the novels have much in common. Both are stories of a pubescent girl's matriculation to womanhood" (3). *Peyton Place* includes the stories of *several* adolescent girls who, like Dolores Haze in *Lolita,* are exposed to "the hazards" of growing up female: these teenagers experience "abandonment, rejection, overprotection, underprotection, victimization" (3). They also share another trait: *Lolita*, like *Peyton Place*, is haunted by pregnancy.

The novel *Lolita* has always been controversial, but never out of print. In a contemporary American culture in which we "have, for the past 200 or so years, progressively eroticized, put at the very heart of our constructions of the desirable, the young body, the innocent, the unspoiled," the novel continues to engage readers (Kincaid, *Lolita*, B19). However, how we read *Lolita* is informed by our own times, of course, and violence against children gets much more public attention than it did in the 1950s. In her best-selling memoir *Reading* Lolita *in Tehran*, Azar Nafisi described Nabokov's protagonist Humbert Humbert's narration style: "[H]is ability as a poet, his own fancy prose style, exposes him for what he is," which is, as James R. Kincaid describes Humbert, "a vile, if fancy-talking, Humbert of a monster," and the novel in which he talks like a highbrow is "clearly about pedophilia, rape, and destruction of innocence" (B18).

Humbert is educated, smooth, and makes us laugh as he tells his sick story. He is a classic pervert, one who can hide among the cluttered allusions he includes in his tale, and can play on our sympathies when he needs to. His clever manipulation of his audiences—within his story and outside of it—defines him as a deviant. Humbert has many strategies for convincing us that his is a love story, and that he is a victim, and most of them seem plausible (another characteristic of a child molester). Occasionally, however, Humbert slips, and tells us something that reveals the pervert in him. One of the slips that suggests just how pervy he is, has to do with how he thinks about pregnancy.[3]

Lolita is actually framed by suggestions of pregnancy. Early in Nabokov's foreword, blowhard John Ray, Jr., PhD, who has consented to edit the memoirs of now-deceased Humbert Humbert, tells us of a *"Mrs. 'Richard F. Schiller,' who died in childbed, giving birth to a stillborn girl, on Christmas Day, 1952, in Gray Star, a settlement in the remotest Northwest"* (4). And in his final chapter, Humbert, writing to us from prison, reminds us that Lolita is expecting a child at the time of his writing: "I hope you will love your baby. I hope it will be a boy" (309). Within this frame of pregnancy, Humbert confesses his story of love for Lolita.

3. Pregnant Teenagers and Other Monsters

After telling us all about his background, his parents (picnic, lightning), his divorce, he tells us how he came to meet widow Charlotte Haze and her daughter Dolores. When he first sees twelve-year-old Dolores, she is sunbathing. He lapses into the language of delight: "Then, without the least warning, a blue sea-wave swelled under my heart and, from a mat in a pool of sun, half-naked, kneeling, turning about on her knees, there was my Riviera love peering at me over dark glasses" (39).

From that point on, Humbert's tale revolves around his obsession with Dolores, whom he privately refers to as "Lolita." In order to be near her, he marries Charlotte, a woman he finds fatuous and vulgar. He tells us that he has done Charlotte a favor by marrying her: the marriage "improved her looks" and gave her the "radiance of utter adoration" (76). As he gets to know Charlotte, he begins to recognize "a resemblance to the lovely, inane, lost look" of Lolita in her mother, which helps him when he makes love to his bride. After drinking a highball, Humbert gets through the lovemaking by imagining. He begins by imagining Lolita as a fetus inside her mother:

> ... I would manage to evoke the child while caressing the mother. This was the white stomach within which my nymphet had been a little curved fish in 1934. This carefully dyed hair, so sterile to my sense of smell and touch, acquired at certain lamplit moments in the poster bed the tinge, if not the texture, of Lolita's curls.... [A]t Lolita's age, Lotte had been as desirable a schoolgirl as her daughter was, and as Lolita's daughter would be some day ... Lottelita, Lolitchen [76].

He continues: During "the fifty days of our cohabitation," Humbert day-dreams about having Lolita all to himself. In one of his projections, he has impregnated Charlotte, and "a prolonged confinement, with a nice Caesarean operation and other complications in a safe maternity ward" might give him the chance to "be alone with my Lolita for weeks, per-haps" (80).

Humbert no longer has to imagine Lolita as a zygote when Providence smiles on him. Charlotte dies and his dreams come true: he alone will tend to Lolita. Through much of the rest of the novel, he travels through the American heartland with his "nymphette." "On the American highways with Dolores," writes Sofia Ahlberg, "Humbert is a bumbling, pathetic tourist of popular culture, his mental faculties muffled by his enormous desire" (71). The more time he spends travelling with and abusing this teenager, the more he insists to us that she has the power in the relationship; hence the construction of Lolita as seductress, temptress, maneater.

Along the way, Nabokov allows us the chance to see Dolores as an abused girl, if only for a few fleeting moments, when, for example, she cannot stop crying at the news of her mother's death. Nabokov also reveals Dolores as a normal girl whose sexual awakening is typical, despite Humbert's fantasies about her. Humbert tries "to make Lolita's experience decidedly sinful, casting her as the fallen woman," but Nabokov will not allow it (Goldman 101). By the end of the novel, we are onto Humbert's scam, for many reasons that Nabokov has provided. Among them is our knowledge of how Humbert perceives pregnancy.

From his obsessive—and especially twisted—projection of Dolores as an unborn baby inside of Charlotte, to his daydreams about impregnating Charlotte in order to get her out of the way, Humbert identifies pregnancy as a tool and a weapon for his own use. Pregnancy becomes all about him and for him, something he can control and conjure in order to quench his endless thirst for Lolita. His focus on "the little curved fish" of Lolita inside Charlotte, or his idea to keep Charlotte out of the house with a Caesarean, reaffirm our understanding of Humbert as a sick, narcissistic rapist, one who knows that his body can provide the seed for his domination of Lolita. All of this is confirmed to us in the last chapter of Humbert's memoir, the last time he sees Lolita. She is seven months pregnant.

In the final scene between Humbert and Lolita, Nabokov shows us an inverted image of an earlier scene in which he had told Lolita about her mother's death, and she had not been able to stop crying. Here, it is Humbert who cannot stop crying, and by this point, we understand why. After receiving a letter from Dolly-Lolita in which she tells him that she is married, expecting a baby, and needs money, Humbert immediately gets on the road again, "at the wheel of the old blue sedan" that had carried him and Lolita through the country. He fantasizes about killing Lolita's husband; when he gets to where she and her new husband live, he puts his gun in his pocket and knocks on the door. He looks at Lolita, and his plan to do away with Mr. Lolita dissipates: "The moment, the death I had kept conjuring up for three years was as simple as a bit of dry wood. She was frankly and hugely pregnant" (269). When Lolita invites him in to sit down, he moves in carefully, noting Lolita's likeness to a martyr: "Dolly Schiller flattened herself as best she could ... to let me pass, and was crucified for a moment, looking down, smiling down ... her watered-milk-white arms outspread on the wood. I passed without touching her bulging babe" (270).

Throughout the novel, Humbert has expressed only contempt for the middle-class values and tastes of the people around him, especially those of Charlotte Haze and her daughter. His "sabotage and perversion of the family unit, and the housewife in particular," has taken his whole energy thus far (Ahlberg 71). To see his Lolita in her present circumstances upsets him beyond anything he can imagine. "The picture of homely domesticity in the new Schiller household is unsettling to Humbert," writes Eric Goldman. "Why isn't Lolita reaping the ruin of the fallen, deviant woman rather than leading a stereotypically 'decent' life?" (100). Nabokov allows us to understand in this final scene that Humbert cannot abide what he sees in Dolly Schiller. And what he sees in her is not just a conventional married woman, but a pregnant one. Since we know that Humbert values pregnancy as a weapon, we also know that he feels victimized and wounded by Lolita's pregnancy. He cries out to us, just before he asks Lolita to run away with him, "I will shout my poor truth. I insist the world know how much I loved my Lolita, *this* Lolita, pale and polluted, and big with another's child, but still ... mine..." (278). When she refuses to leave with him, Humbert is unable to control his tears.

First-time readers of *Lolita* most likely understand from the beginning that we are reading the memoirs of a recently deceased Humbert. We come to understand, in Humbert's final pages, that we are reading these memoirs only after he and Lolita have *both* died. We will not recognize the name "Mrs. Richard Schiller" in the foreword of the novel, except in retrospect, however. Only by turning to the beginning of the book once more, will we find Dolores, who, we are told, died in childbirth. In an inversion of the Christian birth story, Dolores died after delivering a dead daughter on Christmas Day. The final cruelty of Humbert's abuse has been that the life of Dolores Schiller, which looked promising after her abuse at the hands of Humbert Humbert, has become a story of loss and indifferent waste.

How are we to recognize her in the first pages of the foreword? We cannot, so her death and stillbirth do not resonate very deeply before we read Humbert's story. Only after we have travelled through Humbert's story, and are forced back to the beginning, do we realize how profoundly victimized this young woman has been. Throughout the book, Dolores is called by many different names (Lo, Dolly, etc.), all given to her by others, especially by Humbert, whose name for her becomes the title of the book. Called by any number of shifting, unstable signifiers, Dolores Schiller led a life in which she never defined herself at all, but was defined instead by all the adults around her. Her chief abuser, a madman who equated pregnancy with control, used his ultimate weapon—his language—to define her as Lolita.

As difficult as Nabokov makes all of this for us, he also helps us understand Dolores Haze more clearly by giving her the doubleness of pregnancy. Her happiness at the end of the novel, and her normal pregnancy make Humbert's earlier ideas about pregnancy seem especially craven and twisted, and his many shifting names for this girl more obscene. That her pregnancy kills both her and her baby girl, and that we cannot understand that until we return through Humbert's story, makes her the most heart-wrenching victim of Nabokov's novel. Dolly and her stillborn baby become nameless casualties. Only Lolita endures.

Lolita endured, of course, beyond Nabokov and through cinema. When Stanley Kubrick secured the film rights to *Lolita*, he got independent financing, moved to England from Hollywood, and began working on the screenplay with Nabokov.[4] In a 1973 interview conducted by Gene Phillips, Kubrick recalled that when he received Nabokov's first draft, he "discovered that it would run for several hours if all of its four hundred pages were filmed as they stood" (146). After major revisions, Kubrick had a shooting script; Nabokov "speculates that Kubrick used about twenty percent" of his original draft (146). Kubrick was able to incorporate that twenty percent, however, in a way that would allow the film to avoid censorship battles. "I wasn't able to give any weight at all to the erotic aspect of Humbert's relationship with Lolita in the film," Kubrick told Phillips (147). Instead, he chose other cinematic tools by which to tell Humbert's story, some of which Humbert (James Mason), who sees himself as the central and ultimate victim of *Lolita*, might have approved: Kubrick appropriates the characteristics of melodrama into *Lolita*.[5]

3. Pregnant Teenagers and Other Monsters

The sets, including Charlotte Haze's (Shelley Winters) home, Clare Quilty's (Peter Sellers) decadent hideout, and married Lolita's (Sue Lyon) rundown house, all have the cluttered, cramped look of melodrama. The beautiful musical score, with lush piano and strings, also suggests melodrama, beginning with the opening credits, where we hear the *Lolita* theme while we watch a close-up of a man's hands as he slowly paints the toenails of a female. Here, Humbert transforms Dolores into Lolita before the film begins and before our eyes, accompanied by an especially lyrical love theme. The opening credits also represent an example of how Kubrick translates Humbert's clever puns and twisted narration into physical choreography, which he does often. When Charlotte shows Humbert around her house, for example, she glides gracefully from room to room: "[S]he leans in the doorway, barring his departure, while her well-preserved body assumes a provocative posture almost as a reflexive action" (Walker 64).

Kubrick frames the entire narrative between two deaths: a prologue in which Humbert confronts and murders Quilty in his bizarre castle, gives the film an immediate "peculiar tone … a mood of brilliantly organized black comedy, happening in a world that is realistic enough to contain terror, pain, and death, yet fantastic enough to surprise and amuse" (59). This opening sequence (after which the caption "4 years earlier" appears on the screen and we are off), is balanced at the end with another caption, informing us that Humbert Humbert died of "coronary thrombosis in prison awaiting trial for the murder of Clare Quilty."

None of the deaths are Lolita or her baby, however. Kubrick's *Lolita* is alive and hugely pregnant the last time we see her in the movie. Six months pregnant, "married, and beginning to assume her mother's blowsy vulgarity, she has a commonplaceness totally appropriate for Mason's flood of grief, guilt, and remorse" (64). Our larger-than-life, pregnant Lolita reminds us that she is multiple people: she may have been a precocious teenage girl, but she is now a housewife and a woman with a baby inside her. Lolita's thriving pregnancy in the movie helps us to understand that which her multiple names tell us in the novel: that she is much more than the Lolita that Humbert defines. His sorrow, ultimately, is that he can no longer control her. Her pregnancy makes her vital, and locates her beyond Humbert at the end of the film.

Dolores Schiller née Haze (Sue Lyon), otherwise known as Lolita, turns down the chance to run away with Humbert Humbert (James Mason) in the final scene of *Lolita* (1962). Kubrick translated Nabokov's Humbert faithfully and in a variety of ways, including Humbert's complete freakout at Dolores's marriage and pregnancy at the end of his tale.

An earlier scene in which Lolita, Humbert, and Charlotte watch a horror movie at the drive-in represents another of Kubrick's adept translations of the novel, and also provides us with an example of his rendering of Lolita's character.[6] As they watch Christopher Lee and Peter Cushing battling for evil in *The Curse of Frankenstein*, we watch a close-up of their hands. Humbert, sitting in the middle between the two women, grabs Lolita's hand when she screams, Charlotte then grabs Humbert's same hand, and the three of them play handsies until Charlotte realizes that she is holding Lolita's hand.[7] One of the funniest, most telling, and memorable of all of the sequences in the film, the drive-in movie scene suggests a horror: we are watching the title character scream in a horror movie called *Lolita*. This scene also reminds us that Lolita has the tastes of a typical American teenager. She is doing what all teenagers wanted to do at the time: She is watching a cheesy B movie at a drive-in.

Teenpics

Although *Peyton Place* and *Lolita* include plots in which teenagers play significant roles, both movies were marketed to adult viewers, and would have had marginal appeal to American teens in the 1950s. Mainstream Hollywood fare represented just another American institution in which "teenagers" had become not a group of people, but consumers and consumables. The Big Five studios attended to teens by presenting beautiful melodramas in which teenagers figured prominently, often starring popular young stars. Sandra Dee and Troy Donahue were both featured in two high-profile movies in 1959: *Imitation of Life* and *A Summer Place*, the latter an especially lush pregnancy narrative in which Dee's teenage character Molly becomes pregnant with Johnny's (Donahue) baby near the end of the film. Donahue later starred with Connie Stevens in the 1961 melodrama *Susan Slade*, in which Stevens copes with an unintentional pregnancy. These films were targeted toward adult audiences, and did not fully engage American teens, who were not that excited to see backlit shots of Lana Turner and Lloyd Nolan. Teen viewers seemed to understand that the popular young stars were being used as "youth insurance" (Doherty, *Teen*, 216). Teens knew that these films were not for them. They had other choices, and they had the means to make those choices.

As a result of the convergence of several factors after World War II, American teenagers "became a group" (47). As consumers and as citizens, as children and as students, "the teenager was counted a special animal requiring special handling" (46). Thomas Doherty explains:

> Sheer numbers and the group proximity born of the population shift from rural to urban and suburban areas encouraged a collective and standardized response; the very nature of a complex bureaucratic society assured it…. At once socially special and specially socialized, '50s teenagers experienced the same things together—through their assigned place in the burgeoning consumer economy, in the increasing uniformity of public school education throughout the states, and in national media that doted on their idiosyncrasies [46].

American teenagers in the 1950s and early 1960s had more money, freedom and attention than any other teens had ever had. They had access to cars, televisions, and radios, where they could hear music that thrilled them. "Because musical tastes and radio airwaves were not as easily segregated as public facilities" in the United States, teenagers everywhere began to notice rock 'n' roll (55). Teenage popular tastes— in music, magazines, and movies—now had the attention of the money of their parents' generation. The lesser studios, especially, were on it. Filmmakers "had both to *recognize* that the teen audience was crucial to their economic future and to *court* it successfully" (66). They learned quickly how to cater to teens, which made those Hollywood producers who had always been marginal—the B studios—relevant and vital. Always more experimental and less concerned with the Production Code police, during the late 1950s and early 1960s, B film companies delivered an especially compelling offspring: the teenpic.

A "product of the decline of the classical Hollywood cinema and the rise of the privileged American teenager," the body of teenpic film is substantial, and includes multiple genres (14). Often theaters would show two teenpics as a double feature, choosing them by genre to appeal to both teen boys and teen girls. Doherty describes some of these winning pairs:

> Thus Howco paired Jacques Marquette's dragpic *Teenage Thunder* (1957) with "rock 'n' roll quickie *Carnival Rock* (1957)"; *Young and Dangerous* (1957) paired with *Rockabilly Baby* (1957); Allied Artists' *Unwed Mother* (1958)/*Joy Ride* (1958) and AIP's *Sorority Girl* (1957)/*Motorcycle Gang* (1957) and *Diary of a High School Bride* (1959)/*Ghost of Dragstrip Hollow* (1959) [113].

At the same time that studios and movie exhibitors began cashing in on teenpics, the teenpics themselves became more and more elaborate, sometimes mixing "rock 'n' roll, drag racing, high school vice" and other categories into one film. Often teen pregnancy showed up in these films as part of the mix. *Unwed Mother* (tagline: "Over twenty thousand girls a year live this bitter story!") is a crime-pregnancy movie about a teenager whose boyfriend lies to her, involves her in a robbery, and then goes to prison, leaving her pregnant and ashamed. *Because They're Young* (1960) combines a rock 'n' roll plotline with teen pregnancy (and stars a young Dick Clark as the most understanding high school teacher ever).

One of the most thoughtful and well-crafted pregnancy teenpics, *Blue Denim* (1959), produced by a major studio, Twentieth Century-Fox, features Carol Lynley and Brandon DeWilde, with music by distinguished composer Bernard Herrmann. Adapted for the screen from a stage play by James Leo Herlihy (who also wrote the novels *All Fall Down* and *Midnight Cowboy*), *Blue Denim* embeds the teen pregnancy narrative within the construct of a larger teen rebellion–experimentation plot. The movie ends with a sequence in which Lynley's character Janet, along with her boyfriend Arthur, have arranged for an illegal abortion for Janet. We see her get into a waiting car, where a woman sitting next to her puts a blindfold over her eyes, so that she will not know where she is going. Just before the car moves, Janet's parents intervene, and she and Arthur agree to marry and move to another town.[8]

American teens had serious issues with which they grappled during these years, including how to negotiate with their parents' generation, and *Blue Denim* reflected many of these issues well. Teens were certainly getting mixed signals from their parents' generation about sex and about gender issues. As one of the "barriers of equality and independence" that "broke down" for American teenagers during the post-war years, the sexual barrier was perhaps the most difficult because older generations were not talking to teens about sex. Like teenagers before them, however, American teens were sexually active. During the 1950s and 1960s "it became increasingly common among those who had no plans to marry. For women born after 1949, the odds were that they would have sex before they reached age twenty" (Fessler, 7). Between 1945 and 1973, "one and a half million babies were relinquished for non-family or unrelated adoptions' in the U.S (8). Young women would pay an especially high price for their sexual freedoms. Like the characters in many of these teenpics, real pregnant teenage girls represented a "social stigma" to their parents' generation.

Blue Denim distinguishes itself, with high-profile teen movies *Rebel Without a Cause* (1955) and *Splendor in the Grass* (1961), as films that treat teenagers—both the characters and the teen audience watching them—with respect.[9] In all three of these movies, directors Philip Dunne, Nicholas Ray and Elia Kazan (respectively) present teenagers not just as goofy or scary stereotypes, but as people with conflicted interests, trying to read a confusing world around them. Their parents are hopeless losers. Worried about how their teens' behavior reflects on them more than anything else, they react with anger, indignation, or silence. Especially regarding sex, post-war parents seemed helpless.

"Fearing that sex education would promote or encourage sexual relations, parents and schools thought it best to leave young people uninformed" (8).[10]

Teens' moviegoing habits reflected the uneasy status between childhood and adulthood that American teens projected: in search of themselves, they watched everything. They watched movies from every genre made by small studios and large. "As the decade's most dedicated class of theater patrons, '50s teenagers supported the whole range of popular movies," writes Doherty (196). But they loved the films that they knew were made especially for them. Teens "could be counted on to support virtually any film format reworked to teenage tastes: the Hollywood musical (*Rock Around the Clock*), the crime melodrama (*Crime in the Streets*), the horror film (*I Was a Teenage Werewolf*), and so on" (196). *I Was a Teenage Werewolf*, in fact, was one of the most popular low-budget films of the era, spawning a slew of teen horror movies "People bug me," troubled teen (and future werewolf) Tony (Michael Landon) says to his shrink. Every teenager got it.

Perhaps among all teenpics, horror movies engaged teens because they "showcased the underside of teenage life, portraying a reckless, rebellious, and troubled generation.... Whether imperial and negative or indigenous and affirmative, they accentuated subcultural differences, resistance, and alternatives to parent cultural values" (Doherty, *Teen*, 196). Horror movies might have appealed to "the male half of the target audience," but teenage girls watched horror, too, and might have noticed that horror teenpics had something in common with other movies that they were watching, especially the unwed-pregnancy B movies. Some of those teen viewers knew too much about pregnancy as horror. This sense of pregnancy as horror was not new, of course. Mary Shelley, whose life as an unwed, pregnant teenager fueled her rich imagination in monstrous ways, had already told us all about it.

Frankenstein

Pregnancy narratives have always thrived within horror literature and film, probably because real pregnancy stories can sometimes suggest the horrible. Nathaniel Hawthorne had read enough history by the time he wrote *The Scarlet Letter*, for example, to know the pregnancy story of Anne Hutchinson, a historical figure whose name he invokes in the third paragraph of the novel. Hutchinson went on trial for heresy in Boston in 1640, when she was forty-six years old and pregnant for the sixteenth time. During her trial, she went into premature labor in her seventh month of pregnancy, and delivered "a strange mass of tissue nothing like an infant" (LaPlante 217). The Puritan clergy, already threatened by Hutchinson's intellectual prowess, took every opportunity to make the details of her unfortunate pregnancy public. Hutchinson's own minister, John Cotton, described the birth to his congregation as "[s]everal lumps of man's seed, without any alteration, or mixture of any thing from the woman" (217). Hutchinson's miscarriage, which almost killed her, became "the talk of Boston" (218). The learned clergy and governor made sure to point out that "the deformed birth" proved that Hutchinson was at least suspect. "Women who bore such babies were, like witches, possessed by the Devil" (218).[11]

The Puritan fathers would have had fits, then, if they had known about Mary Shelley. Mary Wollstonecraft Godwin Shelley had an unconventional upbringing, and many judged her to be heretical. Her early life and teen years were defined not just by pregnancy, but by pregnancy gone wrong. By the time she published *Frankenstein; or, The Modern Prometheus* in 1818, Mary was quite familiar with versions of "the horror story of Maternity" that the Puritan fathers had publicized (Gilbert, 222). She knew that her own mother had died as a result of *her* birth in 1797. She was herself an unwed teen who had already experienced the death of a premature daughter by the time she had finished the novel; she was a "nineteen-year-old girl who ... was no ordinary nineteen-year-old" girl (221). During the years that she was writing and publishing *Frankenstein*, when she was between seventeen and twenty-one years old, Mary "was almost continuously pregnant, 'confined,' or nursing" (224).[12] *Frankenstein* is saturated with the language and imagery of pregnancy. How could it not have been?

Victor Frankenstein creates "an artificial womb without light," and denies himself sustenance while he is pregnant with the monster. He does not take care of himself, but works in his "filthy creation" without rest.[13] "Small wonder," writes Clare Hanson, "that when the monster is 'born' it has the waxy appearance and 'dull yellow eye' of a sickly, undernourished baby" (49). The night that his monster is born remains seared into his memory. "It was on a dreary night of November that I beheld the accomplishment of my toils" (42). He gets ready for the procedure: "I collected the instruments of life around me, that I might infuse a spark of being into the lifeless thing" (42). His creation moves and opens his eyes: "I saw the dull yellow eye of the creature open; it breathed hard, and a convulsive motion agitated its limbs" (42).

Frankenstein is stunned by how horrible his creation looks; he had hoped for a creation that looked like a human. Although the monster's limbs were in proportion, "his hair was of a lustrous black ... his teeth of a pearly whiteness"; his creation is hideous in his sight (42). Having endured a two-year pregnancy of "such infinite pains and care" with the "wretch," Frankenstein, exhausted and overwhelmed, cannot look at his creation any longer, so he tries to sleep. He has nightmares, one about his fiancée Elizabeth, and one about his mother: "I thought that I held the corpse of my dead mother in my arms: a shroud enveloped her form, and I saw the grave-worms crawling in the folds of the flannel" (43).

As if nightmares are not enough, Frankenstein is awakened with a start, in a cold sweat and shaking, by his creation, who is staring at him. The "miserable monster whom I had created" cried and made noises, reaching for him. Frankenstein runs out of the house, where he paces until morning. But Frankenstein has mother's ears. He listens for his monster's cries all night, "attentively, catching and fearing each sound as if it were to announce the approach of the demonical corpse to which I had so miserably given life" (43). During this first sleepless night, Frankenstein thinks back to before his monster was born. Back then, the creature was understandably ugly, but now that the creature has been born and is alive, "when those muscles and joints were rendered capable of motion, it became a thing such as even Dante could not have conceived" (43). Frankenstein is heartbroken, and suffers from postpartum depression: "Mingled with this horror, I felt the bitterness of disappointment; dreams that had been my food and pleasant rest for so long a space were now become a hell to me" (43).

Frankenstein, like all new mothers, feels a sense of loss after he births his monster. He had high hopes about this creation, and his "fantasy baby, who has existed entirely as a psychic projection of its parent, is inevitable and violently lost" (Lucas 62). The new monster forces Frankenstein, like other new parents, to realize the "stark discrepancy between the dream baby and the demanding emergent subjectivity that breathes, moves and perceives the world from a distinct, separate point of view" (62). As the monster begins to move around and perceive, Frankenstein must not only confront the emerging point of view of his monster but, like a good parent, he must speak for his monster. In Shelley's novel, the monster never narrates his own story. But we get the picture anyway, and if we do not, we have only to wait until 1931, when *Frankenstein* "went Hollywood." Perhaps because the film adaptation privileges the monster's perspective, *Frankenstein* has become "the most famous horror film of all time" (Jones 96).

The 1931 Universal film made a star of Boris Karloff, whose "sensitive portrayal" and "range of emotion ... beautifully conveyed without dialogue," made the horror of the film especially pointed.[14] The birth scene remains one of the most famous scenes in all of Hollywood history: Frankenstein (Colin Clive) in "his spectacularly elaborate art-deco laboratory animating his creation with lightning flashes," screams "It's alive! It's alive!" (98). Karloff's monster has also become iconic. Designed by Universal studio artists and director James Whale, the tall square head "powerfully evokes the plight of an old consciousness forced to occupy a new paradigm, a round brain bolted uneasily into a machine-tooled skull" (Skal 132). The creation looms like "a modernist designer's nightmare: the seams show, the clamps and bolts stick out. Form follows function, but just barely" (132). Like "a battered hood ornament for a wrecked economy," the monster in *Frankenstein* was born to be knocked around and displaced, but to be respected nevertheless (133). He was so valued, in fact, that Universal convinced Whale to direct another film in which the monster met his mate. The Bride of Frankenstein was born in 1935.

Introducing a female into the Frankenstein story was not much of a stretch—the plot of *Bride of Frankenstein* is suggested by events in the latter half of Shelley's novel, in which Frankenstein aborts his second creation in his island laboratory, where "the soil was barren, scarcely affording pasture for a few miserable cows" (142). The nightmare vision of this abortion certainly suggests Shelley's own pregnancy history, and might also project a kind of "fear of maternal failure, fear of being the bearer of death while desiring to give life" (Hanson 50). Shelley's own mother had written about such fears in a letter before her untimely death in childbirth, a letter that her daughter had probably read by the time she wrote *Frankenstein*. Mary worried that being in a heightened state of fear might make her want to "torment ... a poor little animal, about whom I am grown anxious and tender" (50).

Shelley might have explored her fear of tormenting or killing the child *in utero*, but Universal Studios was not especially worried about Mary Shelley's fears. They had their own worries, mostly financial, and they worked diligently to bring the Bride to life. *Bride of Frankenstein* has become "a fixture in American popular culture" because it is especially well-crafted, and the Bride has such a distinctive look (Young 309). A "woman in a long white dress with a whacked-out, white-streaked Nefertiti hairdo and wild glazed eyes," the Bride (Elsa Lanchester) has become as iconic as her monstrous mate (309). Like her intended, the Bride is born on-screen in a spectacular display of light and sound. Lanchester based "her birdlike movements on the quick darting of swans," and she stood on 30-inch stilts in order to achieve the look of the newborn female monster (Jones 68). In the film, Frankenstein, once again played by Colin Clive, is persuaded by his crazy professor, Dr. Pretorius (Ernest Thesiger), to "create life," this time to give the lonely monster a female companion. When the Bride takes one look at the monster, however, she immediately shuns him, sending him into a violent, self-destructive rage. Needless to say, the wedding is off.

Audiences delighted in this kitschy Bride. Scholars have always attended to her as well. On a movie screen, the Bride turned Mary Shelley's anxiety about being pregnant into an opposing kind of fear: a projection of male anxiety and fear of women that had already been suggested by *Frankenstein* and other horror movies.[15] "At every level," scholar Anne Mellor wrote about the novel in *Mary Shelley: Her Life, Her Fiction, Her Monsters*, "Victor Frankenstein is engaged upon a rape of nature, a violent penetration and usurpation of the female's 'hiding places,' of the womb. Terrified of female sexuality and the power of human reproduction it enables ... [he uses science] to manipulate, control and repress women" (122). The movies *Frankenstein* and *Bride of Frankenstein* represent these anxieties as well. They are two of the best in a rich legacy of horror films in which monsters all suggest "'alternative' forms of reproduction" (Skal 159).

Indeed, the early 1930s saw the birth of the body of horror genre in Hollywood film. Along with Frankenstein and Mrs. Frankenstein, audiences saw advertisements for *Dracula* (1931), *Dr. Jekyll and Mr. Hyde* (1931), *Freaks* (1932), and others, all films which presented twisted dimensions to desire, sex, and reproduction: "Dracula eschewed conventional sex in favor of necks. Frankenstein pieced together the dead, the better to avoid his wedding night. Dr. Jekyll found a way to simply split in two" (159). As sterile as the genre might have seemed, ironically, horror films of the 1930s were fruitful. All of these films spawned entire industries and decades' worth of popular horror films. Among them, the *Frankenstein* films bore the most progeny: by the end of the 20th century, over fifty major *Frankenstein* movies had been produced, among them one directed by Andy Warhol (*Andy Warhol's Frankenstein*, 1973); one classic parody (*Young Frankenstein*, 1974); and one popular television sitcom (*The Munsters*, 1964–1966).

These films, especially popular with teenagers like fictional Dolores Haze in Kubrick's 1962 *Lolita* and many other real teens in the 1960s, were popular not just because they projected "transcendent resurrection figures" and "beings who couldn't die" (278). For teens, *I Was a Teenage Werewolf, The Curse of Frankenstein,* and other horror films included characters who could transform themselves. Horror characters always carry inside themselves the seeds to new identities, perhaps identities that will bring them happiness or relief. American teenagers delighted when horror characters transformed, often onscreen, sometimes in grotesque or violent ways. During the 1950s and 1960s, when their parents were preoccupied with who knows what, teens were learning how to transform themselves into the Other. "Monsters," writes David Skal, "provided an element of reassurance" (278). If monsters could birth themselves on-screen, then teenagers could birth themselves off-screen as well.

"All monsters are expressions or symbols of some kind of birth process, however distorted or bizarre" (287). Perhaps because teenagers are closer to their own births than their elders, they have always seemed to understand and appreciate the birth narratives of these monsters. Monsters reborn have power and depth, and they command respect. They are more complicated, perverse, and spectacular than any adult can imagine. Teenage fans of horror, some of whom grew up sitting in theaters in the 1950s and 1960s, who delighted and studied horror double features, were so engaged by these movies that they dreamed of becoming filmmakers. They left the theaters trying to figure out how best to frighten their parents when they went home after the movies. As they began to experiment with filmmaking, this new generation figured out that the best place to terrorize adults was at home. With years of B horror movies and teenpics as models, these young filmmakers often privileged pregnancy narratives. Their instincts were good ones, because pregnancy on film behaves like a lightning rod, one that electrifies the horror. American moviegoers were about to get a real jolt.

Horror at Home

If horror movies reflect our deepest fears, then our deepest fears since the 1960s have had to do with reproduction. It is no coincidence that horror movies moved into the domestic sphere around the same time that the birth control pill became accessible to women. To women, the pill represented a certain degree of control over their own bodies, and a certain amount of freedom for families who wanted to plan pregnancies. However, the pill also represented an entirely new set of fearful projections about the future of women's sexuality, sex roles between men and women, and basic reproductive facts. Nowhere were the insecurities and vulnerabilities of this new world, in which sex could be considered separate from reproduction, more profoundly identified than through narrative film. That women might have some power over how and when they reproduced seemed to encourage horror narratives in which men needed to assure themselves that they were still kings at home, however horrible their homes might be. The male characters in domestic horror movies in the final decades of the 20th century, unnerved by women's newfound freedoms, seem vulnerable, skittish, or sometimes just absent. Whatever else they were, the male characters in domestic horror were defined by paranoia. They had their reasons.

The research teams that worked on the pill were "all men, bent on 'improving' female biology" (288). When researchers realized that the first dosages in the early 1960s were too high and were responsible for blood clots and strokes among some women, they tried to adjust the dosages. About the same time that the pill was introduced, English doctors began prescribing a medication to combat morning sickness: thalidomide. "Taken during the first trimester of pregnancy, thalidomide could disrupt the formation of fetal limb buds, leading to babies born without arms or legs, or with stunted, flipper-like projections at the shoulders or hips" (289). Tampering with nature proved to be challenging for many pregnant women, for their families, and for the scientists involved. During these years, movies provided the clearest projections of the collective fears of a society destabilized by space-age pregnancy issues.

Perhaps the first domestic horror film during this time was the adaptation of William March's novel *The Bad Seed* (1956), in which we find out that the natural grandmother of bad seedling Rhoda Penmark was herself a serial killer. That this story takes place in contemporary times, and among decidedly middle-class characters, makes the horror real and deep to many in the audience. "*The Bad Seed* ... seems singular not only in bringing horror into the domestic sphere through a child, but also in suggesting that infants might be evil" (Sobchack 161). Through the decades that followed, American filmmakers gave us a series of families of bad seeds—many that we might have recognized, from homes that looked like our own. Besides Norman Bates, who seemed charming and devoted to his mother in *Psycho* (1960), there were countless others, including Damien Thorn in *The Omen* (1976); Michael Myers in *Halloween* (1978); Freddy Krueger in *Nightmare on Elm Street* (1984); Billy and Stu in *Scream* (1996); and Kevin Khatchadourian in *We Need to Talk About Kevin* (2011).

The bad seed movies, however, were only one of the subgenres of cinematic pregnancy narratives during the late 20th century, and probably not the most horrifying. Pregnancy itself became the heart of horror. David Skal describes the scene: "In the post–Pill age, 'normal' childbirth ceased to exist.... Reproduction crossed over into the realm of Gothic science fiction. Women would become pregnant by demons or computers, tinkered with by genetic engineers" (294). The movies in which women's wombs become dangerous places catapulted several young directors to fame, among them David Cronenberg, whose film *The Brood* (1976) presents the story of a mad psychotherapist whose fragile patient delivers a brood of "child-like homunculae, who act out her unconscious impulses" (299). David Lynch directed *7* (1976), which projects "human reproduction as a desolate freak show, an occupation fit only for the damned" (298).[16]

The many fears and anxieties of a society in which reproduction was no longer private, but was instead a subject in the public domain, were projected in a variety of ways by narrative film. Both B movies and mainstream Hollywood films began projecting nightmare children, born of mothers who were flawed or at least suspect. Among these horror pregnancy films, audiences were exposed to themes of "the madness of pregnancy, evil lurking inside the pregnant body, women's generative capacities out of control, anxieties about paternity and the paternal seed" (Oliver, 117). What made the mainstream Hollywood horror films especially frightening was that they had the seamless good looks of other genres. The mothers of bad seeds might frighten us, even as they wore great clothes and lived in nice townhouses. We watched the agony of one such mother—an attractive, professional one at that—as she saw her pre-pubescent daughter urinate on the expensive carpet during a cocktail party in her posh Georgetown home. We were immediately horrified: with *The Exorcist* (1973), reproductive horror took over even the most elegant dreams that Hollywood had given us on screens.

The Exorcist "proved to be one of the biggest boosts to the horror genre since the days of *Dracula* and *Frankenstein*" and also became one of the American movies to suggest that the demise of the nuclear family might have something to do with the horror (Skal 295). Among the movies produced during this time, *The Exorcist* and, three years later, *Carrie* (1976), involved mothers and daughters fighting the terror within fatherless homes. Besides their being domestic horror films involving only female family members, both films also represent pregnancy—or, more accurately, pre-pregnancy—narratives.[17] In *The Exorcist*, "a pubescent girl about to menstruate played the woman who is possessed—in one scene blood from her wounded genitals mingles with menstrual blood to provide one of the film's key images of horror" (Creed 44). *Carrie* also provides one of cinema's classic horror images, a female companion to all of the male puberty horrors of earlier decades: "[A]ll the hair-sprouting werewolves, rotting faces, and uncontrollable impulses of the horror tradition" become manifest in Carrie's story (Skal 356).

Like Pecola in *The Bluest Eye*, Carrie (Sissy Spacek) is completely ignorant of menstruation, and she becomes frightened when she discovers blood between her legs. Unfortunately for Carrie, she experiences her first period in a relatively public place: her high school PE shower room. Taunted by her classmates, who "begin pelting her with tampons and sanitary pads," Carrie's first period suggests not only violence and horror but also power—the telekinetic kind (Lindsey 282). Carrie is "a female monster [whose] monstrosity is explicitly associated with menstruation and female sexuality" (284). Her attraction to her classmate Tommy Ross (William Katt) also indicates that Carrie has mature, powerful feelings, which turn to violent rage in the most famous scene of the film. As Carrie and Tommy are crowned king and queen of the prom, we watch as other classmates make sure that a bucket of pig's blood pours over Carrie's head. Enraged and horrified, Carrie puts her newfound telekinetic powers to use in a spectacular sequence of graphic retributions against her classmates and teachers. Her telekinetic powers parallel her "emerging sexuality," and become "a literal inscription of the violence of her desire" (285). In *Carrie*, the female body, "its fluids, its sexuality, its reproductive power," becomes the locus of horror (285).

Carrie may have had the last dance at the prom, but the film, "through [Brian] De Palma's authorial camera movement and references to Hitchcock," represents "a woman's nightmare" where young women are ignorant, powerless to control their bodies, and therefore monstrous (292). Carrie was not just a nightmare for women, however. Everyone would have been horrified, and perhaps also relieved to know that Carrie would never live to reproduce. By 1976, American audiences were especially creeped out when they saw on-screen pregnancy. They had watched a different naïve victim, Rosemary Woodhouse, as she went through the various stages of her pregnancy. *Rosemary's Baby* had left an indelible imprint of pregnancy on the American movie audience. Rosemary's pregnancy has haunted American movie screens ever since.

Rosemary's Baby

The many bad seeds on screens during the late 20th century certainly represent a heavy "accumulated weight of birth-related horror imagery" and constitute an impressive body of horror (305). However, pregnancy itself became the locus for horror—and eventually the site of horror's antidote—during the late 20th century. Similar to the ways in which Linda's body in *Incidents in the Life of a Slave Girl* and Sethe's body in *Beloved* become the focus of their narratives, Roman Polanski's adaptation of Ira Levin's 1967 novel allows audiences to revel in Rosemary's pregnancy from beginning to end. We never take our eyes away from Rosemary (Mia Farrow), and we experience her pregnancy in ways that both horrify us and delight us. Rosemary may seem naïve and powerless to us initially, but by the time she sees her newborn son at the end of the film, Polanski has ensured that we understand Rosemary's potential for power. Significantly, *Rosemary's Baby* suggests our first glimpse of a mature pregnancy narrative in contemporary film: pregnancy reveals the power of the pregnant woman.

Rosemary's Baby gave birth to both Polanski's and Farrow's film careers. It was Polanski's first American film, and Farrow's first starring role in a movie; she had left the television series *Peyton Place*, where she had played Allison MacKenzie, shortly before filming began. The film was an immediate sensation with audiences, and delighted film critics. Through the years it has continued to garner respect from film scholars as well.[18] Polanski was able to transform a "Gothic coffee-table bestseller" into an attractive, taut, and suspenseful film (Jones 140). The film begins innocently enough: a young, energetic Midwesterner (Rosemary says that she is from Omaha), married to an ambitious but unknown actor names Guy (John Cassavettes), persuades him that since they want to start a family, they should move into a more substantial apartment. When we meet them, they are looking at as apartment in an old but charming building, the Bramford (filmed at the Dakota in Manhattan). We learn from the realtor that the last occupant was an old woman who had died, but whose furniture still remains.

As they tour the apartment, Polanski gives us our first subtle example of Rosemary's character. When the realtor tries to show the couple a linen closet located at the end of a long hall, all three realize that a large piece of furniture stands against the closet door. They are all puzzled, until Rosemary notices an imprint on the hallway floor, and points out that the late tenant must have moved the large wardrobe from another wall of the hallway in order to block the closet. The three of them move the furniture back to where Rosemary had pointed, and they look inside the closet, where they find a vacuum cleaner and a mop. Everybody laughs.

From that early scene and throughout the rest of the film, we get to know Rosemary Woodhouse, and we come to understand her gifts and strengths. As she and we negotiate our way through the slow but steady creeping terror of the plot, Rosemary helps us to decipher everything we see by questioning what she sees—and what others do not see. She is especially observant. For example, after she and Guy dine at the Castevets' apartment, she wonders, out loud to Guy, why the older couple has taken all of their pictures off their living room walls. Guy hadn't noticed, and he does not seem to care much. Later, Rosemary notices that Roman Castevet (Sidney Blackmer) has pierced ears; again, Guy has never noticed. Finally, Rosemary uses a Scrabble-like game of tiles to skillfully conjure up the anagram for Roman Castevet's other name, Steven Marcato.

As we get to know Rosemary, we understand her to be resourceful, watchful, and steadfast. She seems sensitive to her surroundings, to art, and to her own sensuality. She trusts her own judgment. Not only does she notice the "chalky undertaste" in Minnie Castevet's (Ruth Gordon) chocolate mousse, but she does not question her own judgment about it: she secretly and promptly throws most of it away in a napkin. In the sequence where Rosemary is being ritually impregnated by Satan, we understand her when she yells out, "This is no dream! This is really happening!" We know that she did not eat all of the mousse, and we know that she knows. Polanski allows us to be with Rosemary when no one else knows we are there, and we learn to trust her. Although she looks increasingly frail, a "wasted-looking" waif "dashing out against the light into midtown traffic," Rosemary is actually no shrinking violet (Skal 293). She and her pregnancy provide a sturdy frame by which we begin to understand her story.

Polanski frames *Rosemary's Baby* with Rosemary's voice: it is Farrow's voice that sings the haunting and beautiful wordless lullaby (composed by Krsysztof Komeda) that we hear during the opening and closing credits of the film. The framing continues with visuals throughout the film, especially those that require that we read structural and architectural frames. From the long hallway where Rosemary first sees the closet behind a piece of furniture, to the windows of her apartment that we watch her decorate with curtains, to the framed doorways that obstruct her (and our) view of Guy talking with Roman, we are guided by what Rosemary sees and does not see. During the first dinner party scene, for example, Polanski shows us a quick shot of Rosemary's profile as she tries to see into the living room where Guy sits with Roman. Then, we immediately see what she sees: the door frame, with cigarette smoke gently floating in the air. What are they doing in there, we all want to know. Rosemary wonders too, and she will remember, and the details that she remembers will eventually guide us through a series of framed doors.

Polanski frames Rosemary not only among door jambs and windows, but among people as well, helping us to see just how trapped this young woman really is. The most striking frame appears near the end of the film, when Rosemary, nine months pregnant, hot, and desperate, has spilled her story to Dr. Hill (Charles Grodin) and is waiting alone in an examining room for him to return, skimming a *Time* magazine (the cover reads "Is God Dead?"). She thinks that he is arranging for her to go to a hospital, but when he opens the door, Rosemary sees that he is not alone. She moves toward the door, and is blocked by three male figures: Dr. Hill, Guy, and the evil Dr. Sapirstein (Ralph Bellamy). We see all four of them standing still just long enough to notice that Rosemary is securely framed twice: surrounded by the three men who have all betrayed her, and by the frame of the narrow office door. Polanski and the three male figures all ensure that she will not escape.

The most significant frames of *Rosemary's Baby* include the frames of the different rooms in the apartment, and of the hallway and linen closet that Rosemary discovered in the first scene. We watch as Rosemary gradually transforms the apartment from a dark, uninviting space into a stylish gleaming home that functions smoothly. We are with her as she stands inside the frame of windows, hanging curtains in her tasteful white bedroom while watching her husband, framed and tiny in a small black-and-white television, as he performs in a silly commercial. We watch as she discovers the shelves for the mysterious linen closet, which she eventually restores. And we cannot help but notice that she has painted and cleaned that long narrow hallway that leads to the closet. Our final trip into that hallway, which Polanski has shown us several times, will be with Rosemary as she searches for the crying baby that she hears. Having constructed the frames of her closet, she knows exactly what to do, and she leads the way. She takes the shelves out and opens the portal to the baby. Almost without blinking, Rosemary leads us through the long birth canal of her closet, and we are all borne into the

Rosemary Woodhouse (Mia Farrow), nine months pregnant, reads an article entitled "Is God Dead?" in *Time* as she waits to see her doctor in *Rosemary's Baby* (1968). The film represents the first Hollywood production in which we experience an entire onscreen pregnancy from conception to birth, and in which the pregnant woman is the smartest man in the room.

final nativity scene with Rosemary, in her new role as mother of Satan's son.[19]

Rosemary—not the clever manipulative Castevets, not the gruff malevolent Dr. Sapirstein, and certainly not the weasely, spineless Guy—has exceeded our expectations. No weak-kneed, clumsy weakling, she. By trusting her good memory and her instincts, Rosemary guides us through the movie, teaching us to be observant and practical. When she figures out that her body is a battleground, she uses that information to control her defenses. When she does not trust the drink or the pills that Dr. Sapirstein gives her, she does not take them. When she no longer trusts Minnie Castevet, she drops the gifted amulet from Minnie through

123

a sidewalk grate. And when her husband tries to comfort her after she has seen her baby, she spits in his face, sending him reeling out of the room. Rosemary Woodhouse no longer will suffer fools. She becomes the mother-warrior and the most powerful character on the screen.

Without the restrictions of the Production Code, which had been replaced by a ratings system in 1966, Polanski was free to adapt the novel so that we can accompany Rosemary on every step of her journey toward motherhood. As such, *Rosemary's Baby* represents the first American movie of *any* genre in which the audience experiences an onscreen pregnancy from conception to birth, in chronological order. The pregnancy narrative represents the heart of the story, which suggests why we are still attracted and repelled by the film. Like *Peyton Place*, we experience a spectrum of women's sexuality issues and pregnancy details —from Rosemary's telling Minnie that she has menstrual cramps, to the trippy conception sequence, to the final scene of Rosemary, knife in hand, peering into her son's black bassinet. Unrestricted by outside forces, Polanski presents Rosemary's pregnancy narrative by using a language we already understand: pregnancy. We may not have babies with sulphur-colored eyes, but we all know something about morning sickness. Watching new mother Rosemary peering into her son's cradle may, in fact, give us all morning sickness.

Polanski's expert framing suggests that Rosemary "has 'un-shelved' the Maternal Macabre—has reclaimed its 'back rooms,' has forced it out of the cultural and cinematic 'closet'" (Fischer 427). *Rosemary's Baby* shines a brighter light on how women endure pregnancy than any film before it. That a horror movie can set a new standard for realism and openness in all subsequent pregnancy narratives might seem unlikely, but should actually make good sense. Like melodrama and noir, the horror genre has always been accommodating to changes in mores and tastes, and has rarely been hindered by set formulas or stock cinematic devices. And like Rosemary herself, the onscreen pregnancy narrative is especially resourceful and sturdy. Pregnancy stories can settle in and be at home anywhere.

We only need to look at the titles of other popular American movies released in 1968 to see how diverse and versatile the pregnancy narrative had become in mainstream cinema. That year, Barbra Streisand's Fanny Brice dressed as a pregnant woman as a sight gag in the musical comedy

Funny Girl. Joanne Woodward's shy schoolteacher Rachel had an abortion in the drama *Rachel, Rachel.* And Stanley Kubrick, *Lolita* eight years behind him, disoriented audiences with his epic adaptation of Arthur C. Clarke's *2001: A Space Odyssey,* in which the final image we see is a huge unborn baby, floating through space, looking at the Earth. Appearing the same year as Rosemary's baby boy, Kubrick's starchild suggests that the development of the pregnancy narrative was still moving and changing in ways that we could not yet imagine.[20] By 1968, American audiences knew what to expect when teenagers made accidental babies in cars, and mad scientists created them in laboratories. But giant babies floating among the stars? We were going to need a bigger spaceship.

4

The Mothership Arrives

Pregnancy in Science Fiction

Mary Shelley, Redux

Perhaps we are horrified by *Rosemary's Baby* not because Rosemary gives birth to Satan's baby, but because she embraces her newborn son. In an earlier decade of horror film, Rosemary might have taken one look at her newborn devil-baby, screamed, and run away. But this was 1968. Up was down; night was day; evil was good. Rosemary does not shy away from the infernal infant for more than a few seconds, and then she began to coo and sing to him. She looks the devil in the yellow eyes and then changes his diaper. Fragile-looking and dressed in cute little outfits, Rosemary still unsettles audiences at the conclusion of the film when we realize that she represents the slight but steadfast hero of an unstable narrative.[1] We have experienced Rosemary's entire pregnancy with her, however, and her investment seems clear: pregnancy is complicated, uncomfortable. Sometimes it can be risky, and often otherworldly and frightening. Being pregnant eventually demands superhuman powers, and sometimes defies real world physics and logic. In other words, pregnancy is science fiction.

That one human being can grow another inside her body seems especially fantastic even in the real world. For most of human history, pregnancy has been mysterious in many ways. By our own century, however, science and technology have made possible our understanding of almost every detail of pregnancy—and of reproduction—for almost every organism on earth. For our own species, we now have every available resource by which we can gauge even the tiniest detail of fertilization and gestation. Especially since Swedish photographer Lennart Nilsson's close-ups of a fetus appeared on the cover of *Life* magazine in 1965, how zygots, embryos, and viable fetuses look and grow before they are born has become part of our popular consciousness. Nilsson's remarkable photos were collected into a bestselling book entitled *A Child Is Born* in 1967. One of his captions should sound familiar to anyone who has seen Kubrick's *2001: A Space Odyssey*: "Like an astronaut in his capsule the fetus floats in its amniotic sac with the villa of the placenta around it like a radiant wreath" (86–87).

Kubrick's iconic star child—and *2001* itself—represent "a line of demarcation between the traditional and the modern" science fiction film (Doherty, "Genre," 182). In the second half of the 20th century, the genre that had once reflected the Cold War with "a static balance of terror, alien invasion, and human annihilation" transformed into a genre that was "mass-marketed, well-financed, state of the art, and intellectually challenging" (182). In the 1950s, American audiences had endured invasive pods from outer space (*Invasion of the Body Snatchers* in 1956); blobs of all sorts (*The Blob* in 1958); and insects run amok (*The Fly*, also in 1958); all of which represent speculative pregnancy narratives. By the time *2001* was released, however, the days of "pods and blobs, bug-eyed monsters and brain eaters, fifty-foot women and space bimbos" were behind us, and the era of the techno sci-fi blockbuster had dawned. Like the technological advances that made Nilsson's photographs possible, science fiction focused not on the skies, but in a new direction, turning "away from extraterrestrial menaces ... and toward the enemy within.... Don't watch the skies—watch the insides" (182).

That pregnancy, so dominant in other American film genres—melodrama, noir, horror—attached itself to the insides of science fiction during the final decades of the last century is not just a fluke, of course. Pregnancy has been part of science fiction since there has been science fiction. The pods, blobs and alien life forms of the 1950s were not even the first embryos in speculative film. For example, one of the mad science subplots of Fritz Lang's *Metropolis* (1927), often cited as the earliest post-apocalyptic narrative film, involves the creation of a dangerous robot that doubles for the heroine of the film, Maria. Writers have long created worlds in which reproduction happens outside of the body. In Charlotte Perkins Gilman's *Herland* (1915), for example, women have evolved so that they can reproduce multiple times without men. Other classic horror narratives (those of Frankenstein's monster and his Bride, for example) also project stories of beings who are born or reborn.[2]

In fact, Mary Shelley's *Frankenstein* is responsible for the birth of science fiction as well as modern horror. When she "wrote her novel of scientific experimentation and horror ... rather than magic or devilry ... the genre of science fiction was also born ... Victor Frankenstein's Promethean act is the appropriation of a power which resides not with the gods, but with women" (Cranny-Francis 220). Shelley demystified childbearing, allowing it to have scientific parameters, set in a laboratory and completely unattached from any female anatomy. Since the birth of Shelley's monster, and no longer constricted by the rules of anatomy or biology, pregnancy has gone rogue, often taking entire film genres along with it.

Since the late 1960s and *2001*, the genres of "horror and science fiction have tended to complement, rather than oppose, each other" (Sobchack, "Bringing," 146). Mainstream Hollywood filmmakers began frightening us half to death with domestic horror (*Rosemary's Baby*; *Poltergeist* in 1982; *Fatal Attraction* in 1987) and at the same time disorienting us with domestic science fiction (*Close Encounters of the Third Kind* in 1977; *E.T.* in 1982). Sometimes we cannot tell the difference, and eventually the difference seems inconsequential. For example: Is *Inception* (2010) a time-travel horror fantasy? A science fiction family melodrama? A futuristic crime thriller? Hollywood films have increasingly represented this fusion of "horror, science fiction, and family melodrama" where "the fantastic and the real pervade each other and insist on a closer and closer equivalence" (146).

What unites all of these seemingly distinct genres of film? Pregnancy, of course: that sneaky, insidious, and sturdy element that can invade any narrative by almost any means and without much reason. Pregnancy represents the common denominator of several American film genres that have been multiplying in our imaginations since the late 1960s. Of the invaded genres, science fiction—including dystopian and post-apocalyptic; space and time travel; and pure fantasy—projects pregnancy in myriad variations, and at its most spectacular. From *2001* to *Look Who's Talking* (1989); from adaptations of Margaret Atwood's dystopian *The Handmaid's Tale* (1990) to Kazuo Ishiguro's *Never Let Me Go* (2010); from *Total Recall* (1990) to *Children of Men* (2006); pregnancy has thrived and come alive in science fiction. Why? Perhaps because science fiction, which can steal so much away from humans—reason, intelligence, reproductive powers—can also appropriate those same gifts within boundaries that are especially expansive and fluid.[3] In other words, in a science fiction narrative, anything can happen. And anyone can be pregnant, whether he wants to be or not.

The Alien Trilogy

The original trilogy of Alien films—Alien (Ridley Scott,1979), Aliens (James Cameron, 1986), and Aliens 3 (David Fincher, 1992)—suggest "various representations of the primal scene" of birth (Creed 48).[4] Throughout the trilogy, but especially in Alien, the crew of the cargo ship Nostromo is haunted by "the figure of the archaic mother ... in her generative function—the mother as the origin of all life" (48). Mother is everywhere in Alien, beginning in the first sequence, in which the computer on the Nostromo, named "Mother," wakes the crew. As we watch "a long tracking shot down one of the corridors which leads to a womblike chamber," the seven crew members "emerge slowly from their sleep pods" (48). We are watching as Mother oversees the hatching of her seven eggs, in a "primal fantasy in which the human subject is born fully developed" (48).

Mother has awakened the crew to alert them to danger on the ship. Mother, inside her controlled, white "bland womb" of the Nostromo, nurtures the crew, who behave like a bunch of whiners. A crew of "equally bland techno-babies," they act unlike past B cinematic spacemen who had serious and boring military discipline. This team complains incessantly, pick on each other, and disobey orders regularly (Skal 301). When they begin investigating the trouble that Mother has warned them about, they have to enter another, darker womblike vessel comprised of "vagina-like portals," inside which the Nostromo crew discovers a cluster of sticky eggs. Crew member Kane (John Hurt) is the first crew member attacked by the alien mother of the eggs, his face covered by a many-armed "face-hugger" that shoves something down his throat (301). The others take him back to the Nostromo where, unbeknownst to any of us, Kane's body has been appropriated as the newly pregnant mother of a baby alien. This baby alien's birth will become one of the most famous scenes in all of cinema history, and certainly a milestone among pregnancy narratives.

In a nightmarish scene of pregnancy horror—and the creepiest dining scene in any movie—Kane gives birth to a baby alien through his stomach, but not before he writhes in pain, choking on blood, while his comrades hold him down on the dining room table. Inside their pristine corporate spacecraft, the blood and gore from this scene electrify the screen, making the "controlled environment" of this birthing place a "breeding ground for the Gothic-organic" birth (301). The crew never recovers from this violent birth-death nightmare, and neither does the audience. *Alien* is haunted by this newborn alien, a "fetus-bogeyman, an ever-growing, shape-shifting nightmare" (301). Not only does this alien eat its way out of its mother, but it continues to rebirth itself, torturing the crew to literal death, until only Ripley (Sigourney Weaver)

The creepiest dinner ever: in *Alien* (1979), the crew of the *Nostromo* thought they were going to eat, but instead have to deliver a baby alien gestating inside of Kane (John Hurt). Ripley (Sigourney Weaver, far left) will continue to combat alien pregnancy through three sequels, making her one of the most badass female warriors on film.

remains. The alien meets its match in the person of a female human, making *Alien*—and its sequels—the most significant of all pregnancy epics on film.

Ripley annoys the entire motley crew of the *Nostromo* for one reason or another, almost from the beginning of the film. She is brash, nonsense, humorless and demanding. She represents the deadly, ballbusting, spider-womanish bossman whom every male Hollywood character resented. In a different film from the same era, Ripley would have been wearing a severely cut business suit with big shoulder pads. Yet she also suggests the birth of a new movie type, one that indicates that "the natural order of things was upside down" (Doherty, "Genre," 194). Ripley thinks quickly, acts with courage, and behaves like a classic warrior; she is "the prettiest babe on board" yet "also the shrewdest operator" (194). By the conclusion of the film in which Ripley participates in yet *another* pregnancy sequence, she becomes "the dragon slayer who blows the beast into the vacuum of space" (194). In the finale, Ripley terminates the perpetual pregnancy of the alien by vacuuming it into outer space. After performing this elaborate abortion, she never looks back, but keeps moving through the franchise.

As many film scholars have pointed out, the character of Ripley reflects the anxiety of American men toward women of that era.[5] Ripley suggests a new type of hero, a female who can compete with men and triumph. Her skills and bravery never falter throughout the *Alien* films. "On the most overt level," writes Judith Newton in "Feminism and Anxiety in *Alien*," "the anxieties which this female hero resolves are those having to do with work.... [N]ow everyone is forced to be a company man or company woman, somebody whose work is neither controlled nor understood by them, and somebody who is finally expendable" (82). Yet there are also "more primitive" anxieties at work in the *Alien* trilogy, and they have to do with Ripley's having female reproductive organs (84).

We are reminded in many different ways that Ripley is not a man, and that even if she were, she would still be in danger—she could still be violated and knocked up like the unfortunate Kane in *Alien*. Being female gives Ripley no advantage, but instead seems to be a double danger in the trilogy. Kane is purely a victim of an alien life force, but Ripley, because she has a female anatomy, can be violated not just through her stomach, but through her reproductive organs as well. At the conclusion of *Alien*, Ripley strips down to her underwear. She looks starkly vulnerable. She looks female. At this point, she exposes not herself, but herself as Other to the "male need, demand, desire and fear" at work in the movie (Sobchack, "Virginity," 107). The alien that sneaks up behind Ripley in this scene is a rapist, "phallic and erect," ready to "destroy and consume the fearsome difference that Ripley has so suddenly exposed" (107). Ripley will never triumph, because Ripley is female.

The "male terror at female sexuality and at castrating females in general" in *Alien* becomes a deeper terror in *Aliens* and *Alien 3* (Newton 85). The dominant trope remains reproductive difference, and Ripley remains vulnerable because of her femaleness. Both *Aliens* and *Aliens 3* include landscapes and sets that "might be described as "abstract genital," a style that is "alternately penile and uterine, all sharp tumescent shafts, vaginal entrances, and fallopian interiors" (Doherty, "Genre," 196). In these films, Ripley takes on a more stereotypical female role. She behaves as caregiver, comforter, and mother figure to the girl Newt (Carrie Henn), and her more traditional role allows her "a culturally permissible way" to combat, "not for her own satisfaction or career advancement but for her children" (Doherty, "Genre," 195). According to Thomas Doherty, the genre of science fiction "may never have produced a more crowd-pleasing moment than [in *Aliens*] Ripley's imperative command to the killer queen: 'Get away from her, you bitch!'" (195).

All of Ripley's strengths come to naught in *Aliens 3*, which resembles a noir caged-woman film or a "bankable horror–science fiction series … where the killer-rapist ultimately achieves his goal, violating, impregnating, and destroying the too-adventurous female" (197). Ripley, pregnant with the offspring of the alien, destroys herself. This bleak ending "lays bare a piercing critique of a twentieth-century planet Earth inhospitable to independent female life" (198). Unlike Rosemary, whose rape by Satan leads to a final act in which Rosemary might negotiate a place for herself, the *Alien* trilogy offers no such recompense. There is no place for a female warrior in outer space, on Earth, or wherever, because she has this thing she can do, which seems alien and dangerous: she can reproduce, which is too scary, powerful, and uncontrollable. She can be pregnant. Better that she kill herself.

Sigourney Weaver consented to play Ripley in a fourth *Alien* film,

Alien Resurrection (1997), directed by French director Jean-Pierre Jeunot, because she liked the script.[6] Two hundred years have passed since Ripley's death, but scientists still have her DNA. Dead, pregnant Ripley is cloned, and the embryonic alien she was carrying is surgically removed for study by scientists, who mix alien DNA with human DNA to see how a hybrid alien-human race behaves. They misbehave terribly, and cloned Ripley must help rid the spacecraft of all of the aliens before they invade Earth. This time, Ripley has a different investment, however. The alien queen is her offspring, and has inherited from Ripley a set of female reproductive organs. This alien has a womb, and can reproduce like a mammal—no eggs needed. Earth is in trouble if aliens can gestate babies like human women. And Ripley is also in trouble, because she has some alien DNA and an alien daughter with whom she sympathizes in subtle ways throughout the film. After much conflict, including scenes of aliens popping out of human bodies that suggest the birth scene in *Alien*, clone Ripley destroys her offspring in order to save the Earth.

Like other science fiction narratives, the *Alien* films, especially *Alien Resurrection*, play with conventional margins of all kinds; they pass "across know and marked boundaries ... as Earth and space, as inside and outside, as self and other, as male and female" (Sobchack, "Virginity," 113). In *Alien Resurrection*, Ripley and the Alien Queen share characteristics in ways that make them both sympathetic characters and also both suspect. This hybrid development provides the fourth *Alien* film with a perspective on the nature of good and evil that harkens back to mythology as it projects into the future. Ripley has been raped by an alien, and like "all those fascinating sexual unions between humans and beasts," including "Leda and the swan; Zeus as a bull ravaging Europa; Demeter as a mare ... composite figures like minotaurs and centaurs," Ripley and her Alien Queen daughter are a new breed that no one could foresee (Dervin 98). By the edge of the 21st century, not only can a female Ripley be raped and humiliated by pregnancy, but she reproduces in ways that cannot be controlled. We might hope that after centuries of scientific experiments gone wrong, and monster-creatures created only to be destroyed, those scientists who cloned Ripley might have known better. But no. Clone Ellen Ripley represents just the beginning of another science fiction nightmare that has to do with pregnancy and reproduction.

Replicants and Clones

Three years after *Alien*, Ridley Scott directed another science fiction film that was also destined to be considered classic, *Blade Runner*.[7] Based on a Philip K. Dick story, the film is set in 2019 post-apocalyptic Los Angeles, and centers on policeman Deckard (Harrison Ford), whose mission is to find and destroy four pesky replicants who have rebelled again their corporate maker, the Tyrell Corporation. A stunning blend of noir, romance, and post–A bomb nightmare, *Blade Runner* continues to distinguish itself as a haunting portrait of longing and indifference in a bleak urban landscape. As Deckard searches for the four wayward replicants, he does the thing that detectives should never do but always end up doing: he becomes emotionally invested in the replicant world when he falls in love with Rachael (Sean Young), "one of Tyrell's most advanced replicants" (Ryan and Kellner 62).

Blade Runner does not represent an obvious pregnancy narrative. It does represent one of the late–20th century films that projects the fears of a world in which humans can create, but cannot control life outside of a womb. Born in a laboratory not unlike Victor Frankenstein's, the replicants of *Blade Runner* look and act human. The female replicants are sex toys as well—without the worrisome female reproductive organs that get so many people, including Ellen Ripley, into trouble. The Tyrell Corporation has even provided them with back stories, including photographs. When Deckard questions Rachael about her past—he is testing her—she shows him a picture of her "mother." When a police interrogator questions Leon (Brion James), a man suspected of being one of the errant replicants, Leon loses control of himself when asked about his mother. "My mother," he seethes, "I'll tell you about my mother." With that, Leon kills the interrogator.

Like Rachael and Leon, the replicants have been given such detailed backgrounds that they are hungry for more. Their "assurance of a future relies on the possibility of acquiring a past.... [T]he replicants search for their origins. They want to know who 'conceived' them" (Bruno 190). The replicants want to know who their mothers are. Unfortunately for them, when they realize that they were conceived and incubated elsewhere, and that their mothers are photographs, they get angry and start killing people. Because they can feel pain, love, remorse, anguish, and fury, they lash out—at their father, the Tyrell Corporation. They still want to know about their mothers, and they still want to live. When they know that both are impossible, some of them, like Roy (Rutger Hauer), die gracefully, releasing doves into the air as "a symbol of charity and forgiveness" (Ryan and Kellner 64). Sometimes the replicants behave more humanely than the humans do, which divides our sympathies and doubles their profiles. For audiences of science fiction nearing the turn of the millennium, the world of replicants, androids, and clones seems especially unstable, frightening, and exhilarating.

Louise Brown, the first real-world test-tube baby, was delivered in England in 1978, and Elizabeth Jordan Carr, the first American test tube baby, arrived in 1981. The advent of in vitro fertilization, and the ethical and moral issues suggested by the real world of genetic engineering have engaged narrative film ever since. Like *Blade Runner* and *Alien*, most science fiction films have focused on the clash of science and corporate profits, and suggest that institutional flaws of cloning can lead to chaos, evil, or destruction. In addition to the replicants of *Blade Runner*, Hollywood provided a nightmare vision of 94 adolescent Hitler clones in *The Boys from Brazil* (1978), based on the novel by Ira Levin of *Rosemary's Baby* fame. In 1993, *Jurassic Park* presented us with living dinosaurs who were not supposed to reproduce. We see their eggs in the final shot of the movie, ensuring not only that the scientists were wrong, but that we could expect a sequel. In 1996, Harold Ramis's fantasy *Multiplicity* did offer some relief from the nightmare aspects of cloning, although ultimately Michael Keaton's clones in the film become especially problematic for him. In 2005, *The Island* projected a dystopian world of 2019 in which two young clones (Scarlett Johanssen and Ewan McGregor) discover who they are and why they have been cloned: for organ harvesting. They eventually escape their fates. Other cloned characters in other dystopian worlds are not so fortunate.

Never Let Me Go

Alien Resurrection and *Blade Runner*, with their unstable narratives and our ambivalent sympathies, both anticipate the most remarkable of the recent clone films, one in which our voiceover narrator and the other characters we know best are the clones themselves. In *Never Let Me Go*, a British production adapted faithfully from the 2005 Kazuo Ishiguro novel of the same name, we experience Kathy's story. We first see a title card that explains that "the breakthrough in medical science came in 1952. Doctors could now cure the previously incurable. By 1967, life expectancy passed 100 years." Then, framed as a flashback and told to us by an adult Kathy H. (Carrey Mulligan), we meet adolescent Kathy and her two best friends Ruth (Keira Knightley) and Tommy D. (Andrew Garfield). We see no adults interacting with these children, except for their teachers and nurses, who treat them indifferently. Clearly, none of these characters have parents or families or know anything of their infancies. We probably figure out quickly that these children are clones, especially after we see their stern headmistress (Charlotte Rampling) tell them at an assembly how special they are. In mute tones and with minimal flourish, we see that the entire short lives of these clones have been orchestrated and prescribed by some unknown and unnamed institutional or corporate entity.[8]

We grow to like these characters, especially Kathy H., the narrator of her own short life story, whose tale is divided into three acts. In the first, dated 1981, we watch youngsters Kathy, Ruth and Tommy as they spend their school days at a boarding school called Hailsham. They seem to have typical adolescent experiences: they play sports, attend assemblies, and eat together. As they grow, we see them bicker with each other, whisper to each other at night in their dormitory beds, and buy each other little gifts at the school's irregularly scheduled "sales," where they pay for their purchases with tokens. We should feel very uncomfortable immediately, because of the look of the film. In all of the Hailsham scenes, everything that we see is distinctly monochromatic. All of the children's nondescript clothes, especially when they are indoors, have a gray-blue tint to them that makes them blend into the coloring of the walls around them. When they draw or paint (artistic endeavors seem to be encouraged among them), we still do not see colors beyond dull blues and grays. The interiors of the school—dining hall, assembly hall, dormitory, school rooms—look dingy and singularly generic. When the children play outdoors, the contrast between the green grass and their bland sport uniforms seems clear. But the weather is often dreary, and we most often watch the children interacting indoors.

When the excited children rummage through the "car boot" sale, the camera lingers on the wares: broken toys, dolls without eyes and legs, single pieces of board games. These "unspectacular items are treasured and traded," writes Keith McDonald about the same scene in the novel (78). We see these small tokens, like Ruth's tiny horse, displayed in the children's rooms throughout the film. They represent "part of the collections that the students see as linking them to a sophisticated outside world" (78). For us, these tokens become portentous visual reminders of the "poverty of experience" that we see before us (78). Eventually in the film, we will see a cloned human walking without a leg, and a woman wearing a patch where her eye used to be. Even later in the film, Kathy and we will notice Ruth's tiny horse sitting by her bedside as she waits to be rolled into the operating room for her final "donation."

In an early schoolroom scene, teacher Miss Lucy (Sally Hawkins), who has seemed uncomfortable among the children, stands in front of their attentive class. She suddenly and calmly explains to the children who they are and why they are together at Hailsham. All of our fears are realized when we hear Miss Lucy use a special vocabulary to adorn the truth. These children have been created to be harvested:

> The problem is you've been told and not told. That's what I've seen while I've been here. You've been told but none of you really understand. So I've decided I'll talk to you in a way that you will understand. Do you know what happens to children when they grow up? No, you don't, because nobody knows. They might grow up to become actors, move to America. Or they might work in supermarkets. Or teach in schools. They might become sportsmen or bus conductors or racing car drivers. They might do almost anything. But with you, we do know. None of you will go to America. None of you will work in supermarkets. None of you will do anything except live the life that has already been set out for you. You will become adults, but only briefly. Before you are old, before you are even middle-aged, you will start to donate your vital organs. That's what you were created to do. And sometime around your third or fourth donation, your short life will be complete.

Since these youngsters were described earlier by their headmistress as "special children," we might wonder that they do not question Miss Lucy. But they do not. They sit passively, perhaps glazed, at their desks. The rain continues. We see a close-up shot of a dead flower in a vase. The scene concludes with this grim vision. In the next assembly hall scene, the headmistress announces that Miss Lucy no longer teaches at Hailsham.

In the second act (dated 1991), Kathy, Ruth and Tommy have turned eighteen. They leave Hailsham and move to "the cottages," a group of run-down rural houses where they pass the time waiting to begin their "donations." They all continue to behave like adolescents, although their bodies have matured; Ruth and Tommy, now a pair, make love regularly with their door open. However, they all "remain trapped in a state of adolescence ... unable, unschooled, and unprepared for any semblance of an adult or free existence" (79). We see adults and outsiders infrequently during this act, but we know they are out there somewhere, and that our threesome will get the call. When they do, in Act 3, we will have to bear with them while they come to terms with their donations and completion. Kathy, who among the three has become a "carer," or one of the Hailsham students who works as a post-op nurse, also helps us through the horrific nightmare that is the lives of these three cloned humans.

In the final act of the film (1994), we watch Kathy as she takes on her role as carer, tending to other young people who have begun to give donations. She does her job well, with calm assurance and competence. She encounters Ruth by coincidence in a "caring center," and she arranges for a reunion for herself, Ruth (whose health is especially precarious after two surgeries), and Tommy, who has also had two surgeries. The three friends take a day trip to the sea, where they reminisce and laugh. In the next scene, we are back in the caring center with Kathy and Ruth, who is about to make her third donation. We attend her surgery, watching from behind a glass partition as she lies on an operating table under lamps. Her only remaining lung is removed from her lifeless body, and she has "completed." We will watch a similar scene of Tommy, after which Kathy will end her voiceover narrative with one final, elegant soliloquy:

It's been two weeks since I lost him. I've been given my notice now. My first donation is in a month's time. I come here and imagine that this is the spot where everything I've lost since my childhood has washed out. I tell myself, if that were true, and I waited long enough, then a tiny figure would appear on the horizon across the field, and gradually get larger until I'd see it was Tommy. He'd wave and maybe call. I don't let the fantasy go beyond that. I can't let it. I remind myself I was lucky to have had any time with him at all. What I'm not sure about is if our lives have been so different from the lives of the people we save. We all complete. Maybe none of us really understand what we've lived through, or feel we've had enough time.

Those of us watching Kathy's story bear "witness to trauma and loss" in *Never Let Me Go*, and we are doubly traumatized because the world of Kathy, Ruth, and Tommy looks "disturbingly similar to our own" (76). Like other effective horror–science fiction narratives, *Never Let Me Go* represents aspects of our own times, in which "the practice of harvesting" organs "has become a largely unspoken but widely recognized fact of life" (76). Both the novel and the film versions also suggest other familiar sequences to us: the operating room deaths in *Never Let Me Go* provide a nightmare version of the monster's birth on a table in *Frankenstein*; the dining hall scenes look like perverse and discolored versions of any number of dining hall scenes from the *Harry Potter* films, six of which had been released by 2010.

Beyond its similarity to the *Harry Potter* series, *Never Let Me Go* also suggests a current narrative preoccupation with institutional and corporate control and dysfunction, especially about the ethics of reproductive regulation. The cluster of dystopian pregnancy texts and movies of the early 21st century seems remarkable, all of them characterized by representations of pregnancy and childbearing as part of nightmarish descents into cannibalism and human depravity. In *The Road* (2009), an adaptation of Cormac McCarthy's 2006 dystopian novel, anarchy and chaos reign in a post-war former United States. An unnamed man (Viggo Mortensen) and his young son (Kodi Smit-McPhee) spend the entire film trying to avoid gangs of dirty, hungry people who roam around, sleeping in abandoned cars and scavenging for anything to eat, including other humans. Women are impregnated like cattle, and newborn babies are roasted for dinner. In *Children of Men* (2006), adapted faithfully from the 1992 novel by P.D. James, English women have become infertile in 2021 England, and when one pregnant immigrant shows up, hero Theo (Clive Owen) must try to save her and her unborn baby.

Never Let Me Go also shares a legacy with earlier dystopian classics. Besides *Frankenstein*, the novel and film adaptation resemble Aldous Huxley's *Brave New World* in which unintended pregnancy and genetic engineering engage the characters from London to New Mexico and back again in AD 2540; and *1984*, George Orwell's definitive portrait of the invisible institutional hand that powers and controls every aspect of every life. Like these and other science fiction classics, *Never Let Me Go* introduces us to characters in whom we invest our trust and loyalties. In order to understand these characters' stories, we must learn new languages—or at least we must learn to appropriate new definitions to old words in order to negotiate the unfamiliar dystopian landscape ("donation" and "complete" may never seem the same after *Never Let Me Go*).

The powerful may co-opt certain words and phrases in *Never Let Me Go* and other dystopian pregnancy narratives, but like Winston Smith in *1984*, the characters have a certain grace, especially when they tell their stories themselves. Kathy H. breaks our hearts by her "ability to recount her experiences in a world that goes so far as to disenfranchise her from the human mass, where she is reduced to a cog in a bioconsumerist culture" not unlike Frankenstein's creature, who does not even have a name (81). At least, we might think, the craven and ruthless institutions that created Kathy H. never took away her name. Because when a character loses her name to captors, and is then renamed in their image, we are into some deep dystopian trouble. Just ask Offred, the renamed narrator of her own living nightmare, whose frightening tale has become the most powerful of all the modern dystopian pregnancy narratives: Margaret Atwood's *The Handmaid's Tale*.

The Handmaid's Tale

Margaret Atwood created her masterwork *The Handmaid's Tale* in 1984, "the year in which pundits looked back on George Orwell's dystopia to assess how much of his vision we had escaped" (Neuman 858).[9] To anyone who was paying attention to women during the middle of the 20th century—and Atwood was paying attention—the real world reflected a series of confusing signals for women that might suggest that most people had not escaped Orwell's dystopia. Although some saw improving conditions for women, for other observers, "the world seemed to be getting a little too free for women" (858). Around the world, the 1980s especially saw a backlash against the progress that women had achieved, as Shirley Neuman outlines in her excellent essay "Just a Backlash."[10] By 1984 in Iran, the radical Islamist regime "had forced women out of Iranian universities, out of their jobs, and back into their burqas and their homes" (859). In Afghanistan, women were being "encouraged" not to read or write. And in Romania, the government "monitored women monthly for pregnancy, outlawed birth control, and abortion, and linked women's wages to childbearing" (859).

Atwood did not need to travel from her home in Canada to Romania, Iran or Afghanistan to find hostility toward women in 1984, however. She could look to her immediate south and find American reactions to women's increasingly public presence in Ronald Reagan's United States that might have troubled her. Although American women enjoyed a higher standard of living and freedoms than many women in other parts of the world (they were, for example, attending college and working outside their homes in record numbers), their numbers in "the lowest-paid occupations" were growing steadily, and "they made no gains or lost ground in the better-paid trades and professions" (859). Fewer and fewer women participated in government and public service. The Reagan years saw major cuts to programs that served women, and his "government defeated bills to fund shelters for battered women" (860). Those groups who opposed the legal right of American women to terminate their pregnancies increased their activities, often resorting to violence. By the end of Reagan's second term in 1988, the federal government "ceased to fund legal abortions, effectively eliminating freedom of choice for most teenage girls and poor women; several states passed laws restricting not only legal abortion but even the provision of information about abortion" (860).[11]

Besides all of this, Atwood also saw something else if she scanned American television: popular chat shows in which fundamentalist Christians sat around talking, preaching the Gospel, and occasionally asking their viewers for donations. By the 1980s, when cable television was reaching more and more households, this group (some of whom could boast that they were welcome any time in Reagan's White House) had its own generic name: televangelists. During the Reagan years, Jimmy Swaggart, Oral Roberts, Jerry Falwell, Pat Robertson, and the husband-and-wife team of Jim and Tammy Faye Bakker became so popular and successful that they could boast, among other things, several universities devoted to their causes; a chain of amusement parks; and their own cable television network. They believed in traditional values which they had gleaned from their interpretations of the Bible, and they had many followers. Many of these televangelists warned their congregations of the dangers of feminism, as Pat Robertson indicated in a letter to his church members. Feminists, he wrote, "encourage women to leave their husbands, kill their children, practice witchcraft, destroy capitalism and become lesbians" (861).

Much of what Atwood must have noticed about American culture during these backlash years appears in thin disguise in the Republic of Gilead, the patriarchic theocracy in what seems to have been Cambridge, Massachusetts, in *The Handmaid's Tale*. It is set in the early 21st century; the handmaid who narrates her own story is named Offred (Of-fred), a name that identifies her as handmaiden to a Commander Fred _____, a "Commander of the Faith," and his wife Serena Joy, whom Offred recognizes almost immediately "from before" as a popular televangelist for a children's Gospel show. "She was the lead soprano," Offred tells us very early in the novel. "She was ash blond, petite, with a snub nose and huge blue eyes which she'd turn upwards during hymns" (16).[12] After the television show, Offred continues wryly, Serena Joy "went on to other things" (16).

The "other things" were, of course, her husband's paramilitary Christian revolution, in which the entire federal government of the United States was destroyed, and the white supremacist, fundamentalist Republic of Gilead was established along the East Coast. Since then, women, including Serena Joy, no longer enjoy professional careers; many of them are just lucky to be alive. People of color, the aged, and the disabled have been trucked off to the nuclear wastelands, and the remaining white women have taken the roles of subservient goodwives or helpers. Their sole charge is to serve the men and to bear them children. Unfortunately for Serena Joy, she and most other women are unable to conceive. (Nuclear war? Environmental poisoning? Both?) Young women like Offred, found to be fertile in this radioactive world, have the choice of living in enslaved pregnant surrogacy, or dying in ditches somewhere. Offred, an especially clever and observant narrator, has chosen to live as a baby incubator and sex slave to the Commander. She seems to understand that her addition to the Commander's household strains everyone, especially Serena Joy, who looks as if she is paying a dear price for the new Manpublic. "The woman sitting in front of me was Serena Joy. Or had been once. So it was worse than I thought" (16).

Offred tells her story in pieces, moving leisurely between the "time before" to her present circumstances in the home of the Commander. "There's time to spare," she tells us (69). Because her primary function in the household is to be impregnated (in a creepy ritual where the Commander reads a Bible passage, then has intercourse with a blindfolded Offred on his wife's bed while Serena Joy sits behind them, fully clothed, cradling Offred's head), Offred has a great deal of time to remember the details of everything. She then tries to make some sense of all of it for us. "Her commentary is often ironic, often analytic, often critical of herself and of her peers," but Offred has great insightful and hawk eyes (Neuman 861). She has no illusions about the negotiation she has made. She knows why she and her handmaiden sisters remain alive in Gilead while so many others, including her own activist-feminist mother, are either dead, consigned as "unwomen" or sent to work camps amid nuclear waste. Her explanation of the "Ceremony" reveals a woman who understands herself: "Copulating would be inaccurate, because it would imply two people and only one is involved. Nor does rape cover it; nothing is going on here that I haven't signed up for" (94).

Unlike Kathy H., whose reality we recognize as artificial and contrived in *Never Let Me Go*, Offred's world looks like our own. Offred takes great care to help us with those aspects of Gilead that we might not understand. She describes clearly how the new society works: reading and writing are forbidden; nonconformity of any kind results in death or disappearance. She is especially adept at explaining the significance of new rituals, and their relationships to old ones. Often she weaves her memories of the time before into her narrative of her present world as a handmaiden. For example, she tells us about a "Birth Day" celebrated by the Wives and the Handmaids: that rare holiday when a Handmaiden delivers a baby. On this occasion, Ofwarren is about to deliver, and all the women ride in a "Birthmobile" to the delivery, which Offred describes. The delivery scene reminds Offred of her own birthing experiences, in which we might hear echoes of Chopin's Edna, after having watched Adele's delivery in *The Awakening*:

> Ofwarren is in the master bedroom, a good name for it; where this Commander and his Wife nightly bed down.... Two women I don't know stand

143

on either side of her, gripping her hands, or she theirs.... She's grunting now, with the effort.... We're with her, we're the same as her, we're drunk ... here's the crowning, the glory, the head ... and it slithers out ... oh praise.... Our happiness is part memory.... The Wives are here to bear witness to the naming. It's the Wives who do the naming, around here.... We ache. Each of us holds in her lap a phantom, a ghost baby.... Mother, I think. Wherever you may be. Can you hear me? You wanted a women's culture. Well, now there is one. It isn't what you meant, but it exists. Be thankful for small mercies [126–27].

Most of Offred's memories throughout the novel have to do with her family from before Gilead: her husband Luke and her young daughter. Offred knows nothing of what happened to either of them. When the family tried to escape to Canada, Luke was shot, and Offred's daughter taken from her as she herself was taken away. But she brings both Luke and her daughter to life for us often, remembering how she used to bathe her daughter, or remembering conversations with her husband. While she watches Ofwarren giving birth, she tells us about her daughter's birth. "What I remember," she tells us, "is Luke, with me in the hospital, standing beside my head, holding my hand.... Oh, he said, oh Jesus, breath coming out in wonder. That night he couldn't go to sleep at all, he said, he was so high" (126).

The Birth Day ceremony represents the matrix of the Republic of Gilead, and Offred gives us ample detail so that we understand the terminology and significance of this ritual of birthing. (Later, Offred will learn that Ofwarren's baby was not a normal infant, but was instead a "shredder" that will disappear.) But during Birth Day itself, Offred seems especially alert and vital. As the day ends and she gets ready to go back to the Commander and Serena Joy, however, she becomes more subdued. She explains one last aspect of Birth Day, and her tone is stoic, chilling, heartbreaking: Ofwarren, after giving birth, will "be allowed to nurse the baby, for a few months, they believe in mother's milk. After that she'll be transferred, to see if she can do it again, with someone else who needs a turn. But she'll never be sent to the Colonies, she'll never be declared Unwoman. That is her reward" (127). Offred returns to her solitary room, where she tells us that she is "too tired to go on with this story" (129).

The Commander breaks his own rules regularly to sneak Offred into his private study, and he also takes her to a brothel called Jezebel's (which Offred recognizes as a hotel from before times) for an awkward sexual tryst. Near the end of her tale, Offred reveals that she thinks she is pregnant, and she also indicates that the father is not the Commander (who is most likely sterile). The father is probably Nick, the Commander's chauffeur, with whom she has been sleeping, with Serena Joy's covert consent. Fortunately for Offred, Nick also belongs to the underground movement. On the final pages of her tale, Offred is arrested and whisked into a waiting van, and we suspect that she is being spirited away by Nick's associates. "It's all right," Nick tells her, "go with them" (293). When Nick calls her by her given name (one we never learn), she does what he says. She takes the risk of getting into the waiting van, telling us that she knows she is gambling: "Whether this is my end or a new beginning I have no way of knowing" (293).

But Atwood ensures that we have a way of knowing something of Offred's fate. Her novel ends with an addendum, "Historical Notes on the Handmaid's Tale." In the same way that Hawthorne's "Custom House" establishes a fictional authenticity for *The Scarlet Letter*, this coda verifies Atwood's tale. Presented as "a partial transcript of the proceedings of the Twelfth Symposium on Gileadean Studies" in June 2195, this document represents both a funny send-up of an academic conference paper, and a fascinating perspective on the Gilead we already know from Offred (299). In the transcript, we learn from Professor James Darcy Pieixoto of Cambridge University, England, that the title of the tale was "an homage to the great Geoffrey Chaucer," and that the tale was transcribed from old cassettes, not from a manuscript (301). Dr. Pieixoto also tells us that the cassettes were discovered in "a metal footlocker" in Bangor, Maine, on the "Underground Femaleroad" by which enslaved women in Gilead escaped (301). So, in 2195, Gilead is no longer a republic, but has become instead an area of scholarly interest to historians and anthropologists.

The scholarly presentation tells us nothing about Offred herself. Almost as a final indignity, Offred's Gilead—the one she pain-stakingly described for us—becomes instead all about the powerful men who controlled Offred. No matter how much we might want to know whether or not our storyteller survived and escaped, we will never know any of it from this presentation, which focuses instead on the identity of Commanders who might have enslaved Offred, not on Offred's narrative. Was Offred's Commander Waterford? Judd? Who might have been responsible for particular practices in Gilead? Whose big idea was it to use women to control other women? It might have been "Judd's, but the implementation has the mark of Waterford upon it" (308). "The evidence," the professor tells us, "favors Waterford" (309). What do we care? What happened to Offred?

Atwood has explained that she chose to set *The Handmaid's Tale* in New England, where the first settlements were defined by Christian fundamentalism. "Countries continue the way they began; they rearrange the symbols and structures but something remains of their origins" (quoted in Neuman, 867).[13] With the concluding scholarly conference, Atwood provides us with the specter of the patriarchy; in the subsequent centuries, Offred's tale has been subsumed by the stories of the Commanders in the same way that Anne Hutchinson's pregnancy was appropriated by John Winthrop and Cotton Mather, and Hester Prynne's pregnancy tale was manipulated by Hawthorne's smitten narrator. Offred herself places her story in the margins of a larger narrative early in her tale: "We lived in the blank white spaces at the edges of print. It gave us more freedom. We lived in the gaps between the stories" (57). Yet in these gaps between the stories of the institutions and people who enslaved her, we will find hints of Offred's freedom, and the seeds of hope. As Shirley Neuman points out, "implicit in every dystopia is a Utopia" (866).

Never Let Me Go suggests that human cloning reflects the worst, most selfish, most greedy of human instincts, and that all humans have dignity. *The Handmaid's Tale* parallels the hell of American institutionalized slavery, suggesting that attempting to regulate reproduction requires that a society obliterate every shred of integrity it ever had. But neither narrative reads simply as cautionary. These dystopias both engage our most complex reactions. We must consider the fates of everyone in these dystopian worlds, which are such complete creations that they appear as nightmares for *every* character in them. For example, the England in which Kathy H. lives looks disappointing and decidedly unhealthy (cloning has not done much for Kathy's former headmistress, for example, who sits disabled in a wheelchair by the end of Kathy's story). In *The Handmaid's Tale*, both "men and women are ruthlessly entangled in the powerful political structure of the state" (Chadha 33). All dystopian characters are pathetic, from the hack physicians who remove Ruth's remaining lung, to the clueless Commander who sneaks sex with his surrogate an hour after he reads a sacred passage from the Bible to his household. In these narratives, the boundaries between victim and victimizer are espe-cially unstable, allowing for Offred's "blank white pages" of freedom and hope, not just for her, but for the world in which she lives.

What provides relief and hope in dystopian narratives is the glim-mer of rebirth embedded in each. Just as any character, male or female, can become pregnant in science fiction, so too can anyone be reborn. In *Alien Resurrection*, a cloned Ripley becomes much more able to nego-tiate the world because she has blended DNA: she is stronger and more perceptive for her encounter with an alien. By the end of *Blade Runner*, hardened detective Deckard has learned to think of replicants as beings with feelings and integrity. Kathy H.'s story of grace and dignity forces us to question the values and ethics by which we decide whether any human beings should be treated as consumable goods and profit centers. Offred, by telling us everything, writes her way out of the margins and into the center of her own tale. Her story of powerlessness, terror, and loss becomes a shield for her, a tale of courage and hope that endures beyond her own life.

All of these dissonant narratives have imbedded within them healthy seeds of harmony, all planted by an element they share: preg-nancy. As in melodrama, noir, and horror, pregnancy invades dystopian science fiction in ways that ultimately challenge us to move from horror or fear to wonder and hope. Pregnancy in these dystopian texts pulls us along from wherever we think we are to a new place where we must imagine the lives and feelings of aliens, religious fanatics, and pregnant women. Science fiction has the capacity to make us all feel pregnant or sometimes reborn. After the grim excesses of dystopia, we might have difficulty imagining that science fiction can make any of us smile, maybe even laugh, or leave us awestruck with wonder. But even Offred had a wry sense of humor. She knew that humor always counters fear, which may explain cinematic fantasies about pregnant men. Better to be preg-nant and laugh about it than to be afraid of pregnancy. Or something.

Pregnant Men and Talking Fetuses

Science fiction may allow men to be pregnant, but as we know, some of them pay for their pregnancies with their lives. Besides the unfortunate Kane in *Alien*—possibly the most famous pregnant man in film history—other male characters carry beings inside their bodies in science fiction cinema. Most notable among them is George (Marshall Bell), a member of the Resistance movement on Mars in *Total Recall* (1990). George's twin brother Kuato, a powerful clairvoyant mutant, lives and hides from the authorities inside George's abdomen, only bearing himself out to see the future for Resistance leader Hauser (Arnold Schwarzenegger). Like Kane, both George and Kuato die in violent circumstances, both shot by traitors to their cause. Just before he dies, Kuato tells Quaid how to defeat greedy bastard Cohaagen (Ronny Cox), who controls the entire air supply for the Martian colony. Hauser follows his instructions.

Hollywood movies in which we follow men's pregnancies have almost exclusively been marketed as comedies, often using pregnancy as a sight gag or a punchline. In *Rabbit Test* (1978), Lionel Carpenter (Billy Crystal, in his first film role) becomes pregnant in some way (we are never told how; just as well), and he delivers a baby girl at the conclusion. Four years after making *Total Recall*, Arnold Schwarzenegger starred with Danny DeVito and Emma Thompson in *Junior* (1994), in which Schwarzenegger plays Dr. Alex Hesse, a gynecologist who experiments with a fertility drug on himself, imbeds an embryo into his abdomen, and becomes pregnant. After some typical romance and comedy hijinks, Dr. Hesse delivers a baby girl by Caesarean section, and names her "Junior."

Thanks to the real researchers who worked on IVF technologies, and to the increasing technological advances in film arts and sciences, late 20th-century pregnancy on film looked more sophisticated and spectacular. In the romantic comedy *Look Who's Talking* (1989), single accountant Mollie (Kirstie Alley) has an unfortunately timed fling with her boss Albert (George Segal) and becomes pregnant. We know she is pregnant before she does, because not only do we watch Albert's sperm penetrate Mollie's egg, but we hear it. The fertilized egg begins to talk to us in a voice that sounds just like Bruce Willis. We follow this voice as he grows in utero, and we journey through the birth canal with him ("Put me back in! Put me back in!" he pleads). As Mikey, he talks to us throughout the rest of the movie, and throughout two sequels, *Look Who's Talking Too* (1990) and *Look Who's Talking Now* (1993). That we can actually watch a fetus grow into Mikey before he is born makes

Mikey a very special character. But even Mikey might admit that watching him is not nearly as exciting as watching another wide-eyed little boy on the big screen. Barry Guiler of Indiana gets to do what Mikey wanted: he gets to be put back in. Barry is one of the lucky people who has been invited into the mother of all motherships in *Close Encounters of the Third Kind*.

Close Encounters of the Third Kind

Until Stanley Kubrick's *Dr. Strangelove* (1964) and *2001*, science fiction films had traditionally garnered little respect from Hollywood. Rarely did they win major awards beyond the technical. Since then, however, many science fiction movies, including *Close Encounters of the Third Kind*, have been "nominated for best picture or director awards" (Perkowitz 197).[14] Science fiction movies often win "lesser Oscars for musical score, cinematography or ... special or visual effects," but many are now considered to be classics, including *Close Encounters*, which was added to the Library of Congress National Film Registry in 2007, ensuring its preservation (197). The American Film Institute also includes *Close Encounters* on several of its lists of Great American movies.[15]

For all of the distinguished attention *Close Encounters* has received from moviegoers and institutions, film scholars have been especially hard on Steven Spielberg's 1977 film through the years.[16] Although they credit *Close Encounters* as being part of a cluster of science fiction movies from the late 1970s and 1980s that led to a "resurgence of the genre's popularity" and "commercial success," the movie itself raises a number of issues for scholars (Sobchack, *Screening*, 12). Among them: the plot is predictably male-oriented. It represents one of the late 20th-century Hollywood films in which American men try to restore themselves as The Man: "patriarchy and paternity seek to happily resolve their relationship" (Sobchack, "Bringing," 156). The cinematic resolution "is as ingenious as it is predictable ... the good-weak father of the family melodrama attempts to regain his political power and patriarchal strength by moving *outside* or *beyond* the space of his natural family" (156). Instead, this father figure is "born again as an adorable child with the special power to again affect both familial and global events" (156–57).

Although he "abandons his familial responsibilities to go off in search of a pipe dream" Roy (Richard Dreyfuss) seems to be rewarded for being a deserter (Booker 136). The movie "privileges the male role in a rather traditional way," allowing Roy to be the character we know best and with whom we sympathize most (136). "Misunderstood by his humorless wife and unappreciated by his conventional kids," Roy's "playfulness and curiosity are viewed as threatening and contemptible by his family" (Sobchack, "Bringing," 158). Roy eventually sheds his earthly civilian life as hopeless loser, and dons a spacesuit, thereby transforming into another American type: an astronaut. Astronauts "are clearly those figures who centralize and visually represent the values and virtues common to all the male protagonists of [science fiction] in a single archetypal presence" (Sobchack, "Virginity," 107).

Close Encounters also includes some especially "offensive stereotypes," among them "the use of Indian mysticism as an emblem of spirituality," by 1977 a "cliché of Western popular culture" (Booker 135). The film associates "spiritual openness with childlike innocence," which implies that "a greater Indian spirituality is also a suggestion of Indian childishness" (135). This perpetuates "any number of Western racist and colonialist stereotypes about the simplicity of the non–Western mind" (135). Beyond the Indian stereotype, the "depiction of women is troubling" (135). Both Ronnie Neary (Teri Garr) and Jillian Guiler (Melinda Dillon) seem to be types: Ronnie behaves like a shrew. By contrast, the more sympathetic Jillian is the sensitive, marginal artist who "understands Neary's need to follow the call he has heard," and who also "has no husband to abandon" when she travels to Devil's Tower (136). She goes to "retrieve her son, rather than to leave him behind" (136). Like "a good soccer mom, Jillian simply comes to pick up her child" (136). If "Jillian wants to regain her child," then "Roy wants to regain his childhood" (Sobchack, "Bringing," 158).

To be fair: Ronnie initially tries to understand her husband Roy when his behavior becomes erratic, eventually fears him, and rushes away with their children in the station wagon. She has more patience and understanding than most partners would have under the circumstances. Also, we should not assume that Roy is the only one among the characters who might be abandoning someone. We see many men and women suited up and waiting to board the mothership with Roy, and they may also have left their families behind. But all right, fine. The film scholars are all correct. *Close Encounters of the Third Kind* presents us with offensive stereotypes of American women; valorizes the errant father figure; and celebrates the dominion of an entitled Western culture over the childish belief systems from elsewhere. The movie has been doing all sort of things wrong since 1977. Why then is *Close Encounters* considered such a remarkable film by so many? The answer, of course, has to do with pregnancy.

Nineteen seventy-seven introduced several movies destined to become classics: *Close Encounters of the Third Kind, Star Wars, Annie Hall, Saturday Night Fever, Eraserhead, Julia, The Turning Point,* and *The Deep.* Americans could also watch great films from around the world: Luis Buñuel's *That Obscure Object of Desire,* Paul Verhoeven's *Soldier of Orange,* and Peter Weir's *The Last Wave* were all released that year. Among these sophisticated films, several included spectacular special effects—especially *Star Wars,* directed by Steven Spielberg's friend George Lucas, who along with Francis Ford Coppola and Martin Scorsese were considered to be the most innovative of the "film school generation" of filmmakers.[17] These directors and others, including Woody Allen, had been teen moviegoers during the years when raunchy B movies and cheesy science fiction films were popular. Clearly this group of teens had been paying attention.

As the film school generation became successful, they used their almost unlimited resources and understanding of advanced technology to make movies that suggested their affinity with European art films and low-budget B films of their youth. Although many of the early films of Lucas and Spielberg hark "back to early film serials, comic books, and '50s sci-fi and horror movies," they often twisted film conventions and predictable types in ways that audiences could not predict (Lewis 374). For example, their heroes are regular nobodies or children, undistinguished guys who live in the suburbs. Characterized by "constant locomotion ... a child's world composed of brief and seemingly meaningless bursts of activity," they "leave behind a mess they have no intention of ever cleaning up" (374). In *Close Encounters,* a crazed Roy breaks windows, uproots shrubs, and plays with mud inside the house. American movie audiences had never seen a guy in a tract house go quite so crazy before.

However juvenile Roy and *Close Encounters* might seem, the movie's success had much to do with a refreshingly new vision of American life and of unrestricted, imaginative filmmaking. Spielberg and his peers became so successful so early in their careers that they could afford to ignore old Hollywood rules, earning "the right to make their films without studio interference" (374). *Close Encounters,* with a screenplay written by Spielberg himself, reveals the vision of a young filmmaker who is clearly not old Hollywood. Like other films from this era of experimentation—*Bonnie and Clyde* (1967), *Easy Rider* (1969), *MASH* (1970), and others—mainstream Hollywood appeared to have lost its mind.[18] *Close Encounters* presents itself as a conventional movie in many ways, but it includes a deceptively subversive streak. The film challenges old stereotypes and "disavows alliance with traditional patriarchal institutions and traditional paternal behavior" (Sobchack, "Bringing," 157). "The government and the military are viewed as deceitful and stupid, lacking in imagination and vision, and contemptuous of those they profess to protect" (157).

From an early scene in which a police car runs off a cliff in pursuit of an alien ship, the authorities look comical and inept. The military seems unethical and petty. Used to authoritarian military types in sleek space uniforms, 1977 audiences delighted in the motley international crew of *Close Encounters.* The scientists work in chaos; they all talk at the same time. The lead scientist, Claude Lacombe (François Truffaut), does not run an especially tight ship. He does not even speak English, but keeps his long-haired translator David Laughlin (Bob Balaban) close.[19] Lacombe approaches his work with dreamy romanticism, and the other scientists, scruffy and geeky, behave humanely. As we get to know the scientific crew, we realize that they are the only people who have any understanding not only of the alien encounter, but of Roy and Jillian's plight. Lacombe, in fact, recognizes Roy after Roy has snuck onto the landing site at Devil's Tower. Does Lacombe turn Roy in, as he would have in a 1950s space adventure? No, he does the opposite: He invites Roy to join the journey. To the delight of an audience conditioned to watch stiff, disciplined spacemen and rigorous uniformed watchmen, Lacombe surprises us. Roy, he reminds the military police, has been invited to this alien party. Forget the paperwork nonsense. He has a right to suit up.

And the aliens? They are also enlightened. Unlike earlier alien-invasion movies, the aliens of *Close Encounters* do not seem to want hurt humans or use us for fuel, but instead try to make peaceful contact. Their flights cause electrical disturbances on Earth, discord among families, and heartache for Jillian, who knows that they have taken her son. But these aliens do not destroy Washington D.C. with lasers or burn holes in the desert. Instead, they send messages to humans (including the anguished Jillian) explaining where and when they will arrive. The people who get the messages translate them into artistic expressions: drawings, movements, music. The aliens ask only that we use our imaginations and our heads. When they finally arrive, they bring their pregnant mother with them. She makes a spectacular entrance, providing us with a breathless display that weaves together light, music, close-ups of human faces craning toward the sky in wonder. In its beautifully choreographed splendor, the sequence in which the mothership finally reveals herself through the clouds above Devil's Tower untethers us from ourselves.

The language of space travel anticipates a correspondence to pregnancy: We "penetrate" atmospheres; we "abort" missions; we float freely in space tied to "umbilical hoses"; we return to the "mothership." From the moment Lacombe recognizes Roy on the landing field, *Close Encounters* becomes a pregnancy narrative. The mothership, after having been prepared for delivery by her smaller auxiliary vessels, delivers her offspring—among them men, women, and little Barry—and stays to be impregnated again with more humans. The aliens who disembark from the ship choose from among the waiting astronauts, and they choose Roy. Lacombe's last-minute instinctive move to include Roy suggests that Lacombe's tools are innovation and creativity. He knows that the aliens do not want trained astronauts. They want real people, like the ones they are returning: soldiers and Barry and a little girl with braids. They want to enclose Roy, a nutty but determined nobody from Indiana, into their mothership. They want to study and exchange with him, as they have with the returning humans.

The returning humans walk toward us down the gangway of the mothership, and they are stunned but not freaked out. They walk, talk, and behave in ways that suggest that they have not been hurt. The scientists on the ground who greet them accept and understand that these

153

The Mothership arrives at Devil's Tower in *Close Encounters of the Third Kind* (1977). The movie is well loved not just because of its spectacular effects, but because it projects the scientific community as a motley crew of progressive, unconventional and creative romantics who understand that space travel can induce rebirth.

travelers are special. Having gestated inside the mothership, these returning space veterans have grown and changed from whoever they were before. That among them are military personnel is no coincidence. An American audience both in 1977 and in the 21st century would easily see the parallel between these returning humans and military veterans: they are now different from the rest of us, having journeyed beyond us. The mating of the minds between aliens and humans inside the mothership transforms everyone involved. We know this when we watch Barry, now in his mother's arms, crying as he waves goodbye to the ship.

We really have no reason to assume that Roy will never return, or that his family will never know what happened to him. Instead, from what we see at the end of the film, we have every reason to believe that Roy's journey will enrich everyone involved. Spielberg makes sure that we see Roy's movement away from a place defined by the clutter of vapid television commercials, fast food chains and wasteful consumerism toward a place defined by music, light, and space. The others have returned—why not Roy? And who knows, after his rebirth, how he might express the changes he has experienced? Roy's and our experience with the mothership, graceful and powerful, might herald other rebirths. Perhaps exposing a regular little person to a new world will change more than just the little person. This might be a risky and dangerous kind of pregnancy, but gestating inside the mothership among aliens might enrich us all.

Space travel movies—especially those hopeful ones in which we are impregnated with new visions and ideas—have the power to move us "across known and marked boundaries that give identity to the world and to ourselves—as Earth and space, as inside and outside, as self and other, as male and female" (Sobchack, "Virginity," 113). *Close Encounters of the Third Kind*, along with other films of the late 20th century created by this new generation of filmmakers, reflect this significant shift of boundaries in American cultural values and tastes. For example, no longer did the film industry have the power to determine what was appropriate for audiences to watch; moviegoers decided for themselves. Nor did Hollywood films seem to define what we ought to look like or how we ought to talk any more; instead, they began to look like we looked. Movie characters now included a guy who thinks he saw a spacecraft, so he is too distracted to shave, and he looks strung-out. A mother whose son has disappeared into a spacecraft looks at us with red-rimmed eyes, a runny nose, and uncombed hair. Combing her hair was the least of Jillian's troubles in *Close Encounters*. We know her: a single mother, isolated in a little house by herself, trying to make sense of a world that does not make sense. Yes, we have met this woman before. She is Hester Prynne.

The Scarlet Letter, *Redux*

Our pregnant journey from Nathaniel Hawthorne's *The Scarlet Letter* to Steven Spielberg's *Close Encounters of the Third Kind* has moved us through many stages: from Harriet Jacobs's proactive pregnancies to those of Pecola and Sethe in the works of Toni Morrison; from Anna's tragic pregnancy in *Way Down East* to Rosemary's baby with sulphur eyes; from Trudy Kockenlocker's sextuplets to Kane's violent pregnancy in *Alien*; from Mary Shelley to *Peyton Place*. Our trusted guide has always been Hester Prynne, whose specter has appeared at almost every marker of our adventure. She haunts the American pregnancy narrative in many shapes: the ways in which others do her talking for her (*Way Down East*); her pride in having given birth (*Beloved, Push*); her understanding of loss and grief (*Never Let Me Go*); her ability to survive the Puritan fathers (*The Handmaid's Tale*); her projection of a new kind of future (*Close Encounters of the Third Kind*).

That we never actually encounter a pregnant Hester in Hawthorne's text seems just as well. Through the centuries, Hawthorne's silence on this point has become more and more powerful. Hester never needed to be pregnant in Hawthorne's tale; her story took on a life of its own long ago. In the same way that the scarlet letter on her chest had shifting meanings, Hester herself has become an American icon whose meaning shifts.[20] She has been projected as the symbol for everything from sinful sex to AIDS awareness to birth control, and more. She herself has been brought to life several times on film, beginning in 1908.[21] The extant American film adaptations begin with the 1926 production, directed by the Swedish Victor Seastrom. Hester was played by Lillian Gish, who had starred in *Way Down East* six years earlier. In 1935, the first talking adaptation was produced in Hollywood during the classics-to-film craze of the 1930s, and starred Colleen Moore as Hester. Both adaptations are

Hester Prynne (Lillian Gish) at her needle in *The Scarlet Letter* (1926). The novel and Hester have endured decades' worth of adaptations onscreen, including the 1995 revision starring Demi Moore, in which we see how Pearl happened.

respectable movies with cinematic integrity. Both try to be faithful to Hawthorne's text, which poses problems, of course, when the narrator of Hester's story keeps getting in the way.

Adapting Hawthorne's novel was not a problem for the 1995 production because this movie bears only a passing resemblance to Hawthorne's tale (the credits announce that the movie has been "freely adapted" from Hawthorne's *The Scarlet Letter*). After the film was released, we could have heard a collective howl from film critics and academics. The reviews were scathing—the film won the "Worst Remake or Sequel" Award at the annual Golden Raspberry Awards that year—and Hawthorne scholars were horrified. For those of us who have long since freed Hester Prynne from the text into which she had been bound, however, the 1995 *The Scarlet Letter* seemed promising. An adaptation that fills in Hawthorne's gaps and transgresses into unmentionable territory might give us some relief. We might find out what really happened. After decades of being hidden away, *finally* Hester Prynne might be pregnant. And we might even attend her when she gives birth to Pearl.[22]

The 1995 adaptation, directed by Roland Joffe, with a screenplay by Douglas Day Stewart, includes some real star power: Gary Oldman as Arthur Dimmesdale; Robert Duvall as Roger Chillingworth, and Demi Moore as Hester. In "part, a prequel to Hawthorne's text; in part, a historical contextualizing of the novel; and in part, a revisioning of its ending," this adaptation not only allows us to attend to Hester when she gives birth, but we also see scenes where Hester is bathing (and where she watches Arthur Dimmesdale as he is bathing), and we see a love scene in which Pearl is most likely conceived (Barlowe 81). The film fails not because the screenplay deviates from Hawthorne's text. The movie has other cinematic problems: the craftsmanship falters. Robert Duvall's accent, for example, is baffling and distracting. English? Irish? What? The pace of the narrative seems confusing and confused. However, the movie does some things very well. We see complex depictions of Native Americans, African slaves, and white settlers trying to negotiate the New World. We see some beautiful shots of 17th-century art. Sturdy Hester Prynne survives and endures this bad movie, thanks to a very vital Demi Moore.

Several Hollywood actresses were considered for the role of Hester before Moore was cast. She turned out to be an inspired choice, not only because she had the dark good looks of a fiery Hester, but because she had no problem showing some skin (she actually used a body double). In one scene, Hester "lifts up her dress to reveal her pregnant body" (Raw 130). When she does, it might occur to us that we have seen her before. Four years before, in fact. In August 1991, Moore had appeared in profile on the cover of *Vanity Fair* magazine, wearing only a ring on her right hand and a pair of earrings. Her face was turned toward us. She was seven months pregnant.

The cover, a color photograph taken by Annie Liebovitz, was a sensation and a shock in 1991. Some people loved it; others were offended. Whatever people thought at the time, we know now that Moore's naked pregnant body on the cover of a popular magazine upended how we present and consider pregnancy. The naked pregnant body at the newsstand became an American tipping point. From then on, pregnancy rocked. And rocked the world. Our pregnancy narrative, long just a predictable, conventional story we thought we all knew, had declared independence. Pregnancy had delivered, and pregnancy had arrived, looking big and clear and straight into the camera.

5

Ways of Seeing Pregnancy

The Gaze

The immediate controversy over Demi Moore's naked pregnant body on the cover of *Vanity Fair* eventually died down, but this cover did mark a change in how we address pregnancy in popular American culture.[1] Did the photo encourage us to think of pregnancy as a consumable good, one that encouraged pregnant women to buybuybuy in order to look like Demi Moore? Liebovitz's cover portrait, entitled *More on Moore*, "inaugurated an era in which the pregnant body began to be construed in terms of glamour and desirability" writes Clare Hanson in *A Cultural History of Pregnancy* (173). Film, television, and magazines celebrated pregnancy with images of attractive, form-fitting maternity wear and other pregnancy-related accessories, where a "pregnant woman is invited both to construct herself as eroticized object ... and to construct her foetus as the end and object of her pregnancy" (174).

Film scholars have attributed an entire subgenre of Hollywood movies to Liebovitz's *More on Moore* as well. "Since the appearance of Demi Moore's glistening, heavily pregnant belly," writes Kelly Oliver in *Knock Me Up, Knock Me Down*, "Hollywood screens have capitalized on images of cute and sexy mothers-to-be" (206). Beginning in the 1990s, American screens were covered with mainstream Hollywood's reaction to the high profile of celebrity pregnancy: romantic comedies focused on pregnancy—sometimes unintended, sometimes not. Near the turn of the century, we could watch glossy movies about beautiful, rich, white people having babies: *Father of the Bride II* (1995); *Nine Months* (1995); *Fools Rush In* (1997) and *Where the Heart Is* (2000). The 21st century provided even more romantic comedy pregnancy stories: *Knocked Up* (2007); *Baby Mama* (2008); *Labor Pains* (2009); *Baby on Board* (2009);

Away We Go (2009); and *The Back-Up Plan* (2010). These films provide a predictable formula where "pregnancy brings the couple together through a series of comic turns that revolve around a pregnant body and its various quirks" (70). Predictable or not, the pregnancy package continues to provide entertainment and consumer goods for the American film and television industries.

The pregnancy trends attributed to *More on Moore* were actually not new at all. Women's personal needs, including pregnancy, have been big sellers for a long time; Moore's pregnant body belongs to a century-long legacy of pregnancy as public property.[2] Menstruation, birth control, and pregnancy have long been the focus of advertisements circulated inside magazines. This cover merely moves the pregnancy narrative from the margins of advertising to the front page. Women have always attended to each other about their menstrual cycles and pregnancies in private networks of consultation, and have also understood that their pregnancies are their own private business for only so long—something Sylvia Plath attests to in her poetry in which a pregnant woman is reduced to a cliché. Rachel Cusk describes how this open secret about pregnancy feels to a pregnant woman in *A Life's Work*: "It is the population of my privacy, as if the door to my room were wide open and strangers were in there, rifling about…. [I]t is as if some spy is embedded within me…" (35). The baby, writes Cusk, does not cause "this watchful pressure; it is the baby's meaning for other people, the world's sense of ownership stating its claim" (35).

Pregnancy literature provides examples of the private ways that women help each other learn about their monthly cycles: in *Incidents in the Life of a Slave Girl*, Linda Brent tells us through code words that she has started menstruating. Grace Metalious is so clear about the periods of her characters in *Peyton Place* that we can almost time their menstrual cycles—or tell when they are late. The post-war women novelists (Lessing, Mortimer, and later Drabble, Byatt, Didion, Morrison, etc.) all include references to characters' periods or missing periods. We are with the adolescents Claudia and Frida in *The Bluest Eye* when they try to help Pecola with her first period. We can count the days between Offred's periods in *The Handmaid's Tale*. When Precious Jones tells us about her periods in *Push*, we do not even blink. Sethe's stories of how she gave birth in *Beloved* are both so awesome and spectacular that they hurt.

Yet pregnancy has been a public affair for at least a century in the United States, an experience shared by men and women who read magazines, listen to the radio, watch television, read novels. Since the late nineteenth century the marketplace has catered to women's most intimate needs in periodicals, first advertising with delicate euphemisms for menstruation ("napkins" or "towels"), underwear ("foundations"), and maternity wear. In the United States, Johnson & Johnson and Kimball & Clark began advertising "towels" in the 1890s, and by the 1920s, the many new women's magazines all included tasteful advertisements for sanitary products. "Women and retailers," writes Lara Freidenfields in *The Modern Period*, "created new practices around new menstrual technologies, carving out specific spaces in drug stores and bathrooms where menstrual products could acceptably be seen in public" (195). Offering off-the-rack clothing to pregnant women became standard in big department stores early in the 20th century as well, and mail order catalogues featured a variety of nursing brassieres, underwear, and outer clothing for pregnant women. For those women who sewed, *McCalls*, *Vogue*, and *Simplicity* were three of the hundreds of pattern companies that offered many maternity designs throughout the 20th century.

However, *More on Moore* represents more than just a consumer good, more than one of the pregnancy artifacts posing "as if they were works of art, images or signs and as part of the self-conscious creation of lifestyle" (Lury 77). The photograph represents the artistic vision of the artist, Annie Liebovitz. The bodies of pregnant women have always inspired works of art, and Liebovitz's stunning photograph distinguishes itself as part of a rich heritage of pregnancy art that dates back to ancient times. The most famous pregnant woman in all history, Jesus's mother Mary, has inspired countless sculptures, paintings, murals, and frescoes through the centuries. During the Middle Ages in Europe, pregnant Mary showed up in small churches and grand cathedrals, sometimes painted to show a small baby inside a translucent pane in her abdomen. Occasionally she and her sister Elizabeth, also pregnant with her son John the Baptist, appeared together, with the babies inside their bodies waving to each other. The Vatican withdrew many of these pregnant Mary likenesses during the Protestant Reformation and began closely regulating how Mary's image could be used. Images of pregnant Mary became especially rare.[3]

5. Ways of Seeing Pregnancy

The Vatican had little power to regulate paintings of other pregnant women, of course, and some of the most famous of all secular pregnancy portraits date from the 15th, 16th and 17th centuries, including Jan van Eyck's *Arnolfini Wedding* portrait in 1434, a beautiful formal portrait of the betrothal of Giovanni Arnolfini and his very pregnant bride, resplendent in green velvet. Two years earlier, van Eyck had painted *Figure of Eve*, showing an unsmiling Eve standing before us naked, holding an apple in her right hand, her left arm resting beside her pregnant belly. In the 17th century, Johannes Vermeer's paintings often focused on a pregnant form, perhaps his wife Catharina, who bore him fifteen children in twenty years of marriage. In *Woman in Blue Reading a Letter* we see the profile of a very pregnant woman, draped in an elegant blue smock, head bowed as she reads the letter she holds. In *Woman Weighing a Balance*, Vermeer's pregnant woman stands in profile, her belly almost touching the table before her, on which we see an empty jewelry box and pieces of gold and pearls. She holds a balance in one hand, as if she is getting ready to weigh the pieces. The shades on the window before her are pulled and the light is muted, but we can see that behind the woman hangs a painting of the Assumption. One of the figures in the painting is Mary, Queen of Heaven. [4]

The list of modern artists who painted pregnant women is impressive: Vincent van Gogh, Paul Gauguin, James Whistler, Gustav Klimt, Pablo Picasso, Lucien Freud, and Yao Lu. Some of these classic pregnancy paintings must have engaged and inspired artist-writer John Berger when he was studying how we look at images. In his groundbreaking *Ways of Seeing* (1972), Berger addresses the ways in which we frame whatever we see before us; our values, assumptions, and cultural contexts all contribute to how we contextualize works of art. One of the most significant factors that he describes has to do with gender difference. The "social presence of a woman is different in kind from that of a man," he writes. "A man's presence is dependent upon the promise of power which he embodies" (Corrigan 121). A woman, however, "confined into the keeping of men," has learned to survive by understanding that she is framed by men (122).

A woman, Berger writes, lives as two people, her "self being split into two" (122). Women project both themselves as they see themselves, and as men see them: a "woman must continually watch herself.

She is almost continually accompanied by her own image of herself.... From earliest childhood she has been taught and persuaded to survey herself continually" (122). As an example, Berger refers to Renaissance paintings of Adam and Eve, where Eve's shame "becomes a kind of display"; she "is naked as the spectator sees her" (123). Her nakedness has little to do with how she feels, but is "a sign of her submission" to whoever looks at her. We do not know who that might be, because the spectator is not in the painting, but watches outside the frame. And he is male. The spectator of "the average European oil painting is never painted ... and he is presumed to be a man. Everything is addressed to him" (124).

In famous artwork of women painted by men, the men provide the invisible frames within which the women see themselves as doubles. The "male gaze" represents the dominant way of seeing. But what about women spectators outside of the frame? How do women evaluate themselves within a male framework? Berger suggests that they evaluate themselves from the male perspective: "The surveyor of woman in herself is male: the surveyed female. Thus she turns herself into an object—and most particularly an object of vision: a sight" (122). If women evaluate themselves through a male lens when they see themselves in art created by men, then what happens when the artist is a woman? Women artists have also painted nude figures, many of them female, some of them pregnant. Mary Cassatt and Alice Neel each painted several series of pregnancy- and birth-related scenes. Do women frame their subjects differently? What if their subjects are pregnant women? (Annie Liebovitz's *More on Moore*). Perhaps we can get answers from an artist who confronted the male gaze, the female body, and pregnancy, and who expressed all of these in her work: Frida Kahlo.

Frida Kahlo

Frida Kahlo (1907–1954) began painting after a streetcar accident in Mexico City left her bedridden when she was eighteen years old. "She was literally impaled on a metal bar in the wreckage; her spine was fractured, her pelvis crushed, and one foot broken," writes biographer Hayden Herrera (xi). "From that day until her death ... she lived with pain....

5. Ways of Seeing Pregnancy

She lived as well with a yearning for a child she could never have—her smashed pelvis led only to miscarriages and at least three therapeutic abortions..." (xi). Though her marriage in 1929 to artist Diego Rivera looked from a distance to be glamourous and romantic, Kahlo's reality could be heartbreaking. She was "often deceived and occasionally abandoned by the man she loved," which contributed to her "deep sadness and inwardness, even self-obsession" (xi). Yet Kahlo did have lifelong professional encouragement and enthusiastic support from Rivera, who understood how extraordinary Kahlo's paintings were. "Frida began work [in the early 1930s] on a series of masterpieces," he wrote in his autobiography *My Art, My Life*, "which had no precedent in the history of art—paintings which exalted the feminine qualities of endurance of truth, reality, cruelty, and suffering" (quoted in Herrera, 144). "Never before had a woman put such agonized poetry on canvas as Frida did at this time..." (144).

Kahlo's "agonized poetry" had to do with one of her miscarriages, which occurred in 1932. Encouraged by Rivera and others to combat her depression through painting, Kahlo began "a series of bloody and terrifying self-portraits that were to make [her] one of the most original painters of her time" (143). In one of these works, a lithograph entitled *Frida and the Abortion*, Kahlo "stands naked and as passive as a paper doll, submitting to the various stages of her pregnancy" while tears "fall on her cheeks, and the hemorrhage that ended her pregnancy is depicted in droplets of blood that run down the inside of her leg" (146). Like so much of her work, *Frida and the Abortion* suggests "a kind of deadpan, reportorial directness" (151). Never sentimental or squeamish, this and others of her lost-pregnancy paintings fuse elements of Mexican folk art and Christian relic art. Composed as *retablos*, *Frida and the Abortion* shows great detail and planning: her body has three arms, the third "holds a palette shaped rather like the fetus" that floats beside her, "for Frida, making art must take the place of making children" (146).[5]

Among the most striking of the lost-pregnancy works is an oil painting entitled *Henry Ford Hospital*, named for the location of her miscarriage. The painting resembles a traditional *retablo* in many ways, but instead of floating saints or icons of the faith, Kahlo includes "floating symbols of maternal failure, including the fetus ... symbolic of her emotions at the time of the miscarriage" (144). Her stomach is still mis-shapen from the pregnancy, her body swimming in blood as she "lies naked in her hospital bed, hemorrhaging onto a single sheet..." (144). *Henry Ford Hospital* seems singularly dynamic in its attention to the effects of miscarriage on the female body, heart, and mind. Kahlo had studied enough classical Western art to understand the ways in which her work departed from the traditional. This self-portrait, with its floating uterus, fetus, and bloody sheets, would have stunned those spectators who expected to see framed portraits of glowing women with flowing hair. *Henry Ford Hospital*, writes Herrera, "is clearly a nude perceived by a woman, rather than one idealized by a man" (144). Kahlo's work represents a clear confrontation to the male gaze.

Most of Kahlo's paintings are self-portraits, and all of them challenge convention in several ways. She includes vivid images or suggestions of "procreation, and some directly reflect her despair at not having children" (148). She paints graphic likenesses of disembodied wombs, floating fetuses, and sometimes floating wombs with fetuses. She includes vegetation that resembles both male and female genitalia. In some paintings, she challenged the traditionally madonna-esque image of the mother. In *My Birth* we see "the infant's large head emerging between the mother's spread legs from the doctor's vantage point" (157). The birthing mother is rendered headless; a "sheet covering the woman's head and chest, as if she had died in childbirth, emphasizes the total exposure of delivery" (157). Where the woman's head ought to be hangs a painting of "the Virgin of Sorrows pierced by swords, bleeding and weeping" (157). In *Me and My Doll*, painted after another miscarriage in 1937, Kahlo sits solemnly on a small bed beside a naked baby doll. "Instead of a conventional image of a mother cooing over her infant, we see a woman sitting bolt upright, facing ... straight ahead. She is smoking and she is very much alone" (148). We are confronted by this grieving woman's direct stare.

Clearly Kahlo understood the dual nature of her position as a woman, and she was able to express that duality. In *The Two Fridas*, which she painted during an estrangement from Rivera in 1939, she identifies herself as two people in a way that anticipates John Berger's identification of women in *Ways of Seeing*.[6] Sitting side by side, the two Fridas are dressed differently: one in European dress—projecting the image by which other people see her—and one as a Mexican peasant—projecting how Frida sees Frida. They are holding hands. With her other hand, the Mexican Frida holds a small portrait of Rivera, shaped like an egg, from which "springs a long red vein that also resembles an umbilical cord emerging from a placenta" (278). The vein winds around the European Frida and onto her lap, where she stops the bleeding with a pair of sutures. Both Fridas wear their anatomically correct hearts outside their bodies. Both Fridas are looking directly at us without expression.

The Two Fridas is not the first painting in which Kahlo appears as twins, but it is certainly the most remarkable. Kahlo's understanding of her "two identities: the observer and the observed, the self as it is felt from within and the self as it appears from without" reveals her acknowledgment of herself as "both active artist and passive model … dispassionate investigator of what it feels like to be a woman and passionate repository of feminine emotion" (279). Both Fridas wear their most distinguishing features outside of their bodies: their hearts and their female reproductive apparatus. Kahlo insists that we consider her as an artist and as a woman; as Westernized and indigenous Mexican; and as wholehearted and heartbroken, all at the same time. Both Fridas gaze into our eyes, challenging us to accept them both, together. We can either turn away, or we can look them in the eyes.

One of the people who must have met Kahlo's gaze was the British scholar and filmmaker Laura Mulvey, whose documentary film *Frida Kahlo and Tina Modotti* (1983) explores the double vision of Kahlo's works. Several years before the documentary, Mulvey had published "Visual Pleasure and Narrative Cinema," in which she transmutes John Berger's ways of seeing into the "gaze" of the filmmaker's lens. Cinema, she explains, can be likened to "the moment when a child recognizes its own image in the mirror" (Corrigan 718). The "curiosity and the wish to look intermingle with a fascination with likeness and recognition … the "human face, the human body, the relationship between the human form and its surroundings" engage us when we watch film (718). When applied to narrative film—especially classic Hollywood film—the dominant gaze becomes decidedly male (almost always a white, privileged male perspective). Woman characters are always complicated and can be problematic on film. Mulvey describes women characters that could come out of our pregnancy narratives, including *The Scarlet Letter, Incidents in the Life of a Slave Girl, Way Down East,* and *The Handmaid's Tale.* Women in film, she writes, "must gracefully give way to the word, the Name of the Father and the Law, or else struggle to keep her child down with her in the half-light of the imaginary" (716).

In movies, Mulvey writes, the "man controls the film phantasy and also emerges as the representative of power" (720). Film audiences identify with the gaze of the "male protagonist as he controls events" (720). By allowing us to align within the frame of the male protagonist, the (male) director of the frame counteracts and defuses the effect that any female character might have on us. On film, the "determining male gaze projects its fantasy on to the female figure," keeping her profile within a narrative structure that he defines (719). Why must a female character be controlled? Frida Kahlo knew why: women are always doubles who can make us uncomfortable. A woman on-screen has the power to disrupt everything; not only "her visual presence tends to work against the development of a story line," but she has a power, hidden from the camera, that she—and we—already assume (719). What is the hidden power? Pregnancy, of course.

A classic male gaze frames women characters as doubles in the same way as an 18th-century painting of a nude woman frames her: as both an object of desire and a real female who knows we are watching her. A female character on film functions in the male narrative so that the male character can "live out his phantasies and obsessions through linguistic command by imposing them on the silent image of woman still tied to her place as bearer of meaning" (716). And the meaning to which a female character is "still tied?" She is tied to her female body, which can duplicate. When we see a female—any female—on film, we know without being told that if she is over twelve or thirteen years old, she has the capacity to grow another human being inside of her. She can double. Women do not have doubles; they *are* doubles. No matter how else they function within a film, no matter what they are or are not doing, if we are watching them through a conventional male lens, then we know what they can do. The male gaze tells us that they can always reproduce, and no one can stop them.

It is not a coincidence that Hollywood's studio system years were also the years when how we see women characters is most regulated (716). The horror and science fiction genres from the same years seem so vital and vivid because they are low-budget movies and therefore less scrutinized and controlled by the censors. Classic melodrama, noir, and even comedy provide examples of the opposite: the more attention from producers and censors, the stricter control over how women are framed. A woman needs to be in the frame, but she can screw everything up because she might get pregnant. The male gaze ensures that we are always projecting female characters through a lens of constant control, and ongoing fear. Women are simultaneously beautiful objects and potential hazards; the men with whose stories we are asked to identify both love and fear the women characters, whose secret power lies silently inside them.

These artists—Kahlo, Berger, and Mulvey—are representatives of the shock of the new during the 20th century. The shock came when they articulated the ways in which we are always manipulated when we are experiencing art. Self-consciousness allows us to consider how we evaluate paintings, photos, or moving pictures. We can experience our own manipulation, as if a curtain were pulled away to reveal the little humbug pulling all the levers. For film scholars, an understanding of the gaze now allowed for rereading of classic films from other perspectives. For example, what happens when we watch a noir film from a feminist perspective? Or a 1950s melodrama from the perspective of queer studies? How do the films of women filmmakers differ from those of men? What is a "woman's film?" From the 1970s on, scholars, artists, and filmmakers, inspired by the works of unconventional artists like Kahlo and innovative scholars like Berger and Mulvey, have considered all of these questions and more.

Mulvey also points out that Hollywood's seamless, beautiful and lucrative narrative films, all projected through this conventional male lens, began to change in the 1960s in reaction to "alternative cinema," a movement "that provides a space for a cinema to be born which ... challenges the basic assumptions of the mainstream film" (716). This new cinema shared much with mainstream Hollywood. Like all film art, it had been conceived the same way that old Hollywood had been conceived: through the fusion of art and science, and as a blend of international and domestic aesthetics. Independent filmmakers approached narrative film from perspectives that did not represent authoritarian or dominant cultures, and slowly, Hollywood itself began to change. If the male gaze had been dominant in American film through the middle of the century, then the gaze would be challenged by other ways of seeing during the second half, when we would have multiple gazes, multiple perspectives, multiple ways of seeing.[7] Pregnancy, of course, represents a most helpful guide to our understanding of alternative ways of evaluating movies.

Like Kahlo's *The Two Fridas*, both bodies—the mainstream and the independent—begin to look us in the eye in the 1960s and 1970s, and some of the most interesting films from this era include plots and images of pregnancy. For example, when actor-producer Salma Hayek began searching for a director for a production of the adaptation of Hayden Herrera's biography of Frida Kahlo in 2001, she turned to Julie Taymor, a talented director of films, opera and theater. The vision of Kahlo through a lens created by Herrera, Taymor, and Hayek challenges us to see women quite differently than it would have through the gaze of a pre–Code Hollywood camera. Through movies like *Frida* (2002), we must consider women as full human beings, as artists, and yes, as people who can grow other human beings inside them. We confront pregnancy from a different angle, one that privileges the pregnant woman's perspective. Kahlo would have recognized this shift in the collective gaze. In fact, she anticipated it.

Through both independent film and innovative Hollywood films, the pregnancy narrative began to reveal alternate ways of seeing women. Filmmakers, both independents and studio, began presenting women's pregnancy narratives that could not have been shown before, especially narratives of unintended pregnancies. Instead of suppressing or projecting formulaic and false narratives, these films suggest that the traditional male gaze cannot accommodate the pregnancy experience. The most effective pregnancy narratives of the modern age involve unconventional or experimental visions, like those of Frida Kahlo. Modern pregnancy narratives focus in unfiltered ways on women characters as human beings, some of whom are pregnant, and all of whom return our gaze. In one of the first great modern pregnancy narratives, we use a character's pregnancy almost in hindsight, to help us understand why she does the things she does—in Paris.

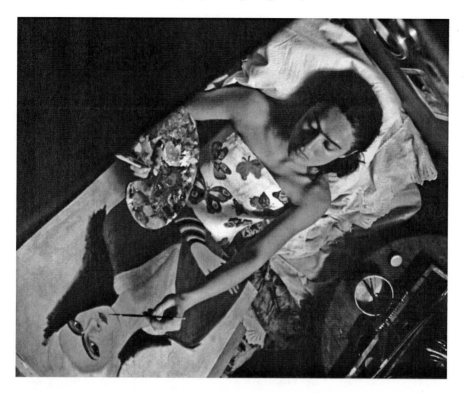

Frida Kahlo (Salma Hayek) begins a self-portrait from her hospital bed in *Frida* (2002). In most of Kahlo's miscarriage-abortion self-portraits, she is looking straight into our eyes. Like other recent collaborative films, *Frida* challenges us to confront our expectations, and to adjust the ways we see pregnancy.

Breathless

In 1960, Jean-Luc Godard's first feature film, *Breathless* (*À Bout de Souffle*) stunned and delighted American audiences. The plot is simple: a French bad boy Michel (Jean-Paul Belmondo) steals a car and then kills a cop. His American girlfriend Patricia (Jean Seberg), a student who aspires to be a journalist, first runs away with him but eventually turns him in. In the final scene, as Michel runs through the streets, he is shot in the back by an officer. Patricia approaches, and we see Michel in close-up, dying. He tells her that she is "dégueulasse." She doesn't appear to have heard him, and she asks the officer to repeat what Michel said. He repeats, and in the final shot of the film, Patricia is looking up at the officer, asking what "dégueulasse" means in English (loosely translated as "disgusting" or "bitch"). The screen goes black.[8]

Breathless represents one of the great French New Wave films, in which the characters look and behave like real people. They seem alternately confused, bored, or selfish; the dialogue sounds real; and the camera moves around Michel and Patricia in jerks (Godard insisted on a hand-held camera); this makes *Breathless* feel like a documentary film. Through the decades since 1960, the film has become iconic for many reasons. Scholars acknowledge its homage to film noir and other Hollywood genres, and they trace the influence *Breathless* has had on later filmmakers, including Stanley Kubrick, Robert Altman, Martin Scorsese, Quentin Tarantino, and Spike Lee. Critic Armond White likens *Breathless* to a classic Hollywood melodrama: "Godard deepens and elevates his protagonists into figures with the rich psychological compulsions of A-level melodramas like those of Minnelli, Nicholas Ray, and Otto Preminger" (White, *Cineaste*). White also notes that the film, not often noted for its romance, actually includes a love story defined by "innocence in the face of guilt." *Breathless* continues to resonate with "every new generation of college-student film lovers" because "no new film expresses political and cultural ambivalence as ingeniously as *Breathless* does" (*Cineaste*).

Breathless resonates with young viewers for many reasons, among them its pregnancy narrative.[9] Imbedded into the long sequence between Patricia and Michel in Patricia's room, Patricia tells Michel that she is pregnant. "You should have been more careful," he responds. We see a shot of Patricia's face, framed in a mirror, as she stares at him. In another subsequent sequence, we watch her stop on the street and look at herself in a mirror, smoothing her hands over her waist, as if she is looking for signs of a baby bump. Both pregnancy scenes are framed as reflections, identifying Patricia as a double—looking at herself and being looked at by herself. Beyond those two sequences, we neither see nor hear another reference to pregnancy in *Breathless*. But we need no more reminders. After Michel has died in the street and Patricia want to know what he said to her, the screen may go dark, but her pregnancy remains. It informs everything in the film.

Because no one mentions Patricia's pregnancy, and we alone know about it, we are insiders in their story. Having spent a long time in Patricia's room with this couple, we understand their attraction. We also might get why they appear so indifferent when they are in public. Michel needs money, and he needs to escape. Patricia needs to remain cool and stay in control. Because we see Patricia among other people, we know that she has dreams and plans to become a journalist. But she also has a secret: her pregnancy. When she learns that Michel is on the run, she eventually turns him in, which might seem confusing or inconsistent, unless we consider Patricia's secret. Patricia needs something soon— money, time, a doctor, an abortionist—*something*, because pregnancy does not hide for long. Turning Michel in becomes Patricia's way of moving her pregnancy narrative along. (The fact that she tells him about her call to the police is important; she is thinking about his welfare as well.) In *Breathless*, Patricia's silent pregnancy runs the show, in unconventional ways: without melodramatic fanfare, and through a rear-view mirror.

In interviews, Godard mentioned Nicholas Ray's films, especially *They Live by Night* (1948), as influential to his work. Like Ray, Godard uses film conventions in ways that expose them as conventions. In some other film, Patricia's pregnancy might have consumed us all through a melodramatic fever. However, in *Breathless*, Godard subverts the pregnancy narrative so that it behaves like a silent engine, running and informing Patricia's and Michel's actions. *They Live by Night,* in which Bowie Bowers (Farley Granger) is killed, but his pregnant wife Keechie (Cathy O'Donnell) lives, and French New Wave films like *Breathless* influenced many later American films in which a pregnancy narrative works quietly to nourish our understanding of characters without the melo of melodrama. In all of these films, pregnancy reflects the ways in which the characters are full human beings. Our understanding of the insecurities, strengths, talents, or fears of the main character relies on our understanding of pregnancy, which works its way through the narratives like a well-oiled machine.

In Richard Lester's *Petulia* (1968), the title character (Julie Christie) is about to give birth in an ambiguous final scene; we are not sure what will happen to her or to the baby she is carrying. The central character in Francis Ford Coppola's *The Rain People* (1969), young married Natalie (Shirley Knight), discovers that she is pregnant and hits the road, encountering a series of weirdos and creeps along the journey. In *Five Easy Pieces* (1970), Bobby Dupea (Jack Nicholson) ditches his pregnant girlfriend Rayette (Karen Black) at a gas station in the final scene of the film, leaving us and Rayette to fend for ourselves. Barbara (Kathryn Dowling) tells Bobby (Tim Daly) that she is pregnant in *Diner* (1982); we never know how or if they resolve anything about the pregnancy. And in Martin Scoresese's *The Departed* (2006), the only character left standing is Madolyn, who had told her boyfriend—police-mob snitch Colin Sullivan (Matt Damon)—that she was pregnant. We are the only ones who know that Madolyn (Vera Farmiga) had slept with dead hero Billy (Leonardo DiCaprio), and so when everyone else is dead at the end of the film, we can only hope that Madolyn is carrying Billy's child. We will never know. We get to decide for ourselves how Madolyn's story is resolved.

Pregnancy as an imbedded element in contemporary film represents a departure from earlier, more traditional uses of pregnancy, and speaks not only to the versatility of the pregnancy narrative, but to changes in the way we frame pregnancy on film. In contrast to classic Hollywood films where a formulaic pregnancy disrupts everything and contributes to the erosion of the hero, independent films offer a wide range of pregnancy narratives, including ones in which being pregnant does not define the women characters or the plots. Our interest in these characters has almost nothing to do with their being pregnant. Beginning with *Breathless* in 1960, a pregnant woman in a narrative film can be more character than pregnant character. Patricia in *Breathless*, Natalie in *The Rain People*, Rayette in *Five Easy Pieces*, Barbara in *Diner* and Madolyn in *The Departed* represent fully developed characters who just happen to be pregnant as well. As their narratives move, we assimilate their pregnancies as variables, but not determinants, in the value of their characters.

In addition to the embedded pregnancy, the ways in which we see abortion in film continues to change—but very gradually. We have examples of Hollywood films as far back as the 1930s that include abortion in their plots, but we only hear about terminated pregnancies vaguely until the 1950s, when *Peyton Place* hit the bookstores. Other Hollywood films from this time that include abortion in their plotlines are high melodramas: one character tells another that she should consider getting an abortion in *The Bachelor Party* (1957), and April Morrison (Diane

Baker) is almost tricked into having an abortion by her weasel of a boyfriend Dexter Key (Robert Evans) in *The Best of Everything* (1959). By the 1970s, however, the American pregnancy landscape had changed dramatically: birth control was legal and accessible to all women and, after 1973, so was abortion. As part of the unhinged madness of 1970s Hollywood, mainstream movies reflected these changes immediately.

Characters talk about and have abortions in a wide spectrum of films, from musicals (*Cabaret*, 1972) to epic dramas (*The Godfather Part II*, 1974) to quirky comedy-dramas (*Next Stop, Greenwich Village*, 1976). The abortions in all of these films are off-screen—we learn about them afterwards—and they all affect the plotlines. In each of these examples, the decision to have an abortion has been made by the pregnant woman alone: Sally Bowles (Liza Minnelli) in *Cabaret*; Kay Adams Corleone (Diane Keaton) in *The Godfather Part II*; Sarah (Ellen Greene) in *Next Stop, Greenwich Village*. Also in all three movies, the abortion precipitates the end of the relationship that produced the pregnancy, but does not end the female characters' roles in the film—we see all of them again, suffering the consequences of their decision to abort at the hands of their partners. Michael Corleone (Al Pacino), a look of sheer horror on his face, slaps Kay after she tells him that she aborted in *The Godfather Part II*. Sally stops sitting alone in her room and goes back to work in *Cabaret*. Sarah travels to Mexico with her new boyfriend in *Next Stop, Greenwich Village*.

That abortions have any role in these mainstream Hollywood films now seems remarkable until we remember that young blood had taken charge in 1970s Hollywood. The same producers who gave us *The Last Picture Show* (1971), *Mean Streets* (1973), and *The Deer Hunter* (1978)—all influenced by Godard's New Wave—incorporated stories of unwanted pregnancies into their films. These difficult pregnancies, especially the abortions, anticipate the various ways in which later pregnancy narratives behave on film. Recent abortion narratives reflect the real world, where women's "reproductive choices frequently involve vexed decisions in uncertain and complicated situations that are far from straightforward" (Oliver, *Knock*, 82). Before Roe v. Wade, abortions in movies were illegal and easier to stage, as in *Blue Denim*, where the pregnant girl gets into the back seat of the car and someone blindfolds her, or in *Love with the Proper Stranger* (1963), where Angie (Natalie Wood) climbs the narrow stairs of a tenement to meet the abortion provider, or in *The Carey Treatment* (1972), in which abortion is merely part of a crime scene. In films of the 1970s and on, abortion might have been legal, but it represented a complicated and lonely issue for everyone. Abortion became, in fact, difficult to integrate into stock Hollywood plots. Too singular, too private, the abortion narrative became also too hot for mainstream Hollywood studios to touch after the 1970s. One exception is now considered an American classic: *Fast Times at Ridgemont High*.

Fast Times at Ridgemont High

Cameron Crowe, a young writer working for *Rolling Stone*, had gone underground at a San Diego high school in order to write his book *Fast Times at Ridgemont High*, published in 1981. After the book's success, Crowe also wrote the screenplay, and the low-budget Hollywood film (just over $4 million) was released in 1982. Directed by Amy Heckerling (who later directed the *Look Who's Talking* series), the film introduced several actors to the screen whose names would become familiar to American moviegoers through the years, among them Sean Penn, Phoebe Cates, Judge Reinhold, Jennifer Jason Leigh, Forest Whitaker, Eric Stolz, and Nicolas Cage. At the time of its release, *Fast Times* impressed few critics, but did impress the young moviegoers who saw it. The young cast plays a group of Southern California teens living in the landscape of the suburban Valley, coping with various teen issues in subplots that sometimes intertwine. Although some of their problems seem funny—Brad Hamilton (Judge Reinhold) must wear a pirate suit when he works at a fast food restaurant, for example—there are other problems that are not funny at all. When fifteen-year-old Stacy Hamilton (Jennifer Jason Leigh) finds herself pregnant, we move from slapstick to serious quickly.

Stacy is a shy but bright girl who works in a pizza parlor in the Mall with her boy-crazy, precocious friend Linda (Phoebe Cates), who encourages Stacy to become sexually active. Stacy takes Linda's advice, first losing her virginity to one of her pizza customers, a 26-year-old salesman (she tells him that she is 19) with whom Stacy sneaks away at night. She climbs out of her bedroom window, gets into his car, and away they go, to "the point," where they have sex. After this first sexual encounter, Stacy has new confidence in herself as she continues to go to school and work. She is now sexually active, and we are with her for her second sexual experience, which takes place in her family's pool house with another character we know from a different plot line, Mike Damone (Robert Romanus). Mike is the Ridgemont High fixer: he makes a good living selling and scalping tickets and placing bets. When he walks Stacy home from school one afternoon, Stacy invites him to swim. They begin kissing. We see them undress, and we see a shot of their feet on a couch as they have sex. It is over quickly. Unfortunately for Stacy, the encounter is just long enough to ensure that she becomes pregnant.

Stacy tells Mike that she is pregnant while they are standing on the bleachers at the track field, and almost immediately, without any discussion to the contrary, they make a plan: he consents to take her to the clinic and to pay for the abortion. In the next scene, we see Mike in his bedroom. He is on the phone, and from over his shoulder we see that he is looking at a hand-drawn ledger: he is trying to call in some favors to help pay for the abortion. Immediately, we are back at Stacy's, where she is waiting in her driveway for Mike to pick her up. He never does. Instead, Stacy grabs a ride with her brother Brad, telling him that she is going bowling. He drops her off, and we watch Brad watching his sister as she runs across the street into the clinic. In the next scene, we are inside the clinic, watching Stacy as she dresses. A nurse comes in, asking about Stacy's ride home. Stacy tells the nurse that she is meeting her ride outside of the clinic. When she leaves, her brother is waiting for her. He promises not to tell their parents. With that promise, the abortion sequence of *Fast Times* ends.

Amy Heckerling has recounted the difficulties she and Crowe encountered when they were trying to get the movie released.[10] Universal had problems with male nudity, and with the abortion scene. Heckerling had filmed Stacy and Mike's sexual encounter with both actors naked, allowing us to watch them put their clothes back on. Although the studio allowed Leigh to be fully nude (and also allowed an earlier scene in which Stacy's friend Linda removes the top of her bathing suit, baring her breasts), it would not allow a shot of male frontal nudity. Why not? According to Heckerling, the studio decided that male nudity was "too aggressive" for the frame. As Crowe points out, this decision seems espe-

Teenager Stacy Hamilton (Jennifer Jason Leigh) has just had an abortion, and here she confides this to her brother Brad (Judge Reinhold), who has waited outside of the clinic to take her home. *Fast Times at Ridgemont High* (1982) represents the first mainstream American film to include a realistic sequence in which post–Roe v. Wade teens grapple with unintended pregnancy.

cially ironic because these teens are learning "to use sex as a weapon." We watch this scene from the perspective of the classic male gaze: naked woman, clothed man, clothed spectators. Like a spectator of a beautiful 18th-century painting, Hollywood assumed the gaze of *Fast Times* to be the dominant male gaze.

The studio also told Heckerling that in order to include the abortion sequence at all, the production would need to get permission "from the stockholders." Heckerling convinced the studio that the abortion sequence was essential because it pointed out that these teens are dealing "with problems bigger than they are ... they are little grownups with jobs, peer pressures, etc." They have big troubles, but are not yet equipped to handle them. *Fast Times* allows us to see, says Heckerling, how "everybody does it because that's what human beings do." Stacy's abortion does not stop action, but instead represents a coming-of-age experience that Stacy integrates into her life. After the abortion sequence, we see Stacy among her classmates, all on a field trip, watching a nursery full of newborn babies. Stacy is not the focus of the scene; her biology teacher Mr. Vargas (Vincent Schiavelli) becomes the butt of the joke here, like most adults in the film. However, we continue to follow Stacy beyond this scene. Eventually, she begins dating a guy who has pined for her throughout the movie. When captions tell us how these characters fared after the film ends, we are told that Stacy and Mark Ratner (Brian Backer) are dating, but that they still "have not gone all the way."

Fast Times at Ridgemont High represents the only American film in which we experience an entire pregnancy-abortion sequence from beginning to end, and in which that abortion sequence does not consume the entire focus of the film. Her abortion does not define Stacy. She continues to be a multi-faceted character whose story moves quickly beyond her abortion. Her abortion does not isolate her. In an amazing series of scenes, we see that after Stacy's abortion becomes common knowledge among her classmates (thanks to Linda), she is not ostracized. Mike is not as fortunate, however. His car is vandalized (someone paints "little prick" on the side), his locker is also defaced, and he must endure the wrath of Mark Ratner in a locker room brawl. Most remarkable: the other teens are upset with Mike not because he knocked up Stacy, but because he abandoned her, never even returning a phone call. Stacy's abortion tells us about these American teenagers. Like so many before them in Hollywood films, they live by a strong value system in which their code of honor seems clear. By 1982, they understand and accept abortion in their lives. They do not understand or accept cowardice.

Those teens could have written "little prick" across the Hollywood sign as well, because between this release and the time it was added to the Library of Congress National Film Registry in 2005, Hollywood had avoided the abortion narrative almost entirely. Most references to abortion since the 1980s are mere suggestions within dialogue, or are presented as cautionary tales: *Dirty Dancing* (1987), set in the 1960s, includes a subplot about a botched backstreet abortion; the HBO film *If These Walls Could Talk* (1996) "tells a tragic tale of three women who find themselves pregnant and must choose whether or not to have their babies" (Oliver, *Knock*, 87).[11] By the end of the film, two of the women have died and the third has changed her mind about the abortion. We hear superficial conversations about abortion in *Parenthood* (1988) and *The Opposite of Sex* (1998). We see what happens when a depressed woman tries to abort her fetus in *Revolutionary Road* (2008): April Wheeler (Kate Winslet) dies, slowly bleeding, remembering that her husband (Leonardo DiCaprio) thought that an abortion would be out of the question. In *The Ides of March* (2011), intern Molly Stearns (Evan Rachel Wood) has an abortion so that her pregnancy will not complicate or compromise the career of Mike Morris (George Clooney), governor of Pennsylvania and presidential candidate. She then commits suicide.

Hollywood studios were providing us with spectacular horror and science fiction pregnancy narratives during the same decades that they were avoiding abortion. At the same time that we could see aliens bursting through human chests in *Alien*, and replicants in *Blade Runner*, and when we could watch any number of *Demon Seed* pregnancy movies, we did not watch any narratives in which real people struggle with the abortion issue. Instead, merely the suggestion of abortion became a stale, predictable convention suggesting fear, separation, and death in American movies. The decision to have an abortion is made by the pregnant woman in anguished isolation; the abortion itself is off-screen; and the woman pays dearly for her decision—often with her life.[12] *Cider House Rules* (1999), a fine adaptation of John Irving's novel, provides some insight into the restrictions of abortion from a female perspective, but

180

ultimately tells us more about the male characters. Only a few thoughtful independent films have included abortion, among them *Citizen Ruth* (1996), in which characters have thoughtful conversations and complicated reactions to abortion rights, and *Greenberg* (2010), in which neurotic Roger (Ben Stiller) befriends housesitter Florence (Greta Gerwig), who has an abortion near the end of the film.[13] In the final scene of the movie, Roger is on his way to pick Florence up from the hospital.

Beyond these few films, and between 1982 and 2010, American movies have remained safely mute on this controversial issue, providing us instead with romantic comedies in which pregnancy can be cute and funny, or substituting spectacular intergalactic reproduction for human reproduction. In most American movies, the realities of abortion never show; in the same decades that saw the technologies of both filmmaking and women's health advancing, Hollywood films reacted by moving women's reproductive capacities into fantasy and science fiction. Although real American women and men have benefitted from years when reproductive options have become safer, and as the technology of pregnancy has improved (legal abortion, sonograms, many birth control options, IVF, disposable pregnancy tests, the "morning-after" pill, etc.), American movies have turned away. Why? Probably for the same sad reason that Mike Damone avoids Stacy Hamilton in *Fast Times at Ridgemont High*: too financially risky. "Thirty-seven years after the Supreme Court declared abortion legal in Roe v. Wade," film critic Stephen Farber wrote in 2012, "the subject is more polarizing than ever, as the rancorous Congressional debate over health care demonstrated. In this contentious atmosphere, Hollywood has chosen to play it safe and keep abortion invisible" (*The Daily Beast*).[14]

Abortion, Vera Drake, *and* The Story of Women

If we want to see how an abortion narrative behaves on film, we must abandon the Hollywood studios and look to Hollywood's twin: independent films. We will need to travel because the films that focus on real people dealing with abortion have been produced or financed outside of the United States.[15] *4 Months, 3 Weeks, and 2 Days*, a Romanian film which won the Palme d'Or at the 2007 Cannes Film Festival, is a sympathetic and graphic film in which college friends Otilia and Găbița arrange an illegal abortion for Găbiţa in pre–Revolutionary Romania. After much difficulty (both women must have sex with the abortion provider, for example), the abortionist gives Găbiţa a shot, and she aborts the fetus several hours later in a hotel room. We watch as Otilia wraps the fetus in a towel, puts it in her satchel, and wanders around the neighborhood. She climbs to the roof of a building, finds a trash chute, and shoves the bag into it. In the final scene, the roommates are sitting in the hotel restaurant. Găbiţa asks about the fetus, and Otilia replies: "You know what we're going to do? We're never going to talk about this, okay?" Găbiţa assents silently, and we watch the two women in profile, sitting at their booth in the restaurant, a wedding party silhouetted in a room behind them. Just before the screen goes black, and just after this long awkward silence, Otilia turns her head and looks straight into the camera, gazing directly at us. Frida Kahlo would get it.

Like *4 Months, Vera Drake* won acclaim and awards when it was released in 2004.[16] Like *4 Months*, it is set in the past, this time in post–World War II London, when abortion was illegal in England. Vera Drake (Imelda Staunton) is a middle-aged wife and mother who cleans houses for a living, takes care of her husband and two grown children, and regularly attends to a shut-in neighbor. Unbeknownst to any of her family, Vera is also an abortionist, providing the service when she gets a call from her business partner Lily (Ruth Sheen). Vera accepts no money for her services. She tells her patients that she knows that poor women especially need this help, and she can "put it right." We watch her perform several abortions during the course of the film, often enough that when we see her take her bag from the top shelf of her bedroom closet, we know she is going somewhere to attend to a pregnancy.

Vera, a smiling, cheerful woman, works quickly and competently. She always tries to calm her frightened patients, and explains to them what she is doing, and what they will need to do. When one of her patients becomes ill after the abortion, Vera is questioned and arrested, which shocks and confuses her family. She is sentenced to two years and six months in prison. In the final scene, Vera is welcomed to prison by two other women, both also doing time for providing illegal abortions. "My girl died," one of them explains. They have each been sentenced to four years, because this is their second offense. They both try to comfort poor Vera by telling her that she "will be back home in no time." We watch Vera walk slowly up the stairs of the prison, away from us. The final silent shot that we see in the film is of the rest of Vera's family, sitting at a table without her, drinking tea in silence.

Vera Drake and *4 Months, 3 Weeks, and 2 Days* both represent cautionary abortion tales, but unlike those produced in Hollywood, they caution us about a past in which women do not have access to safe abortion. *Vera Drake* also speaks to the hypocrisy of abortion access. Vera attends to a diverse group of working class women—some married, some not, one a Jamaican immigrant, another a mother with too many children. However, in a subplot that only we see, the daughter of Vera's wealthy employer becomes pregnant as the result of date rape. In contrast to Vera and the poor women to whom she attends, Susan (Sally Hawkins) has her pregnancy terminated in hospital by a physician who knows how to work around the legalities. (We have met this doctor: he is Dr. Swain from *Peyton Place*.) The contrast between Susan's expensive procedure and luxurious hospital room, and Vera's work in dark kitchens, is stunning. *Vera Drake* speaks to the indifference of institutions to women's singular capacity to be pregnant. Class, race, and privilege define these women, and their relationships to their own bodies remain fragile and dangerous. *Vera Drake* reminds us that abortion narratives, like all pregnancy narratives, are not really stories of abortion. They are the stories of women.

The Story of Women is, in fact, the English name of another European film about an abortionist, this one a true story. *Une Affaire de Femmes* (1988) tells us the story of Marie-Louise Giraud, the last woman to be executed by guillotine in France in 1943. Directed by Claude Chabrol, a New Wave director, *The Story of Women* relates how Giraud, a housewife and housekeeper like Vera Drake, provides abortion services for prostitutes and poor women in the years between the world wars in Cherbourg.[17] When she is arrested, the Vichy government decides to make an example of Giraud, and her appeals are turned down. In the final scene, we watch from above as Giraud is executed in a courtyard. Because we have gotten to know her and her family, the final execution sequence is shocking; it reminds us that Marie-Louise Giraud, a character we know well by then, was more substantial, vital, and fair than the institutions that condemned her. Like many pregnancy narratives, her story confronts us within a narrative frame that privileges her perspective; we are provided with a gaze that allows us to watch a woman whose actions make her not just human, but heroic.

Directors Claude Chabrol, Mike Leigh and Amy Heckerling are all filmmakers whose cinematic visions are particularly sympathetic to women and women's stories, and their work with abortion narratives reveals one of the most important aspects of pregnancy narratives: they transcend gender. Great pregnancy narratives come from everywhere and can be told by anyone. Some of the most significant pregnancy narratives on film have been envisioned by male writers or directors, some of whose work we have already explored. Preston Sturges thumbs his nose at Hollywood censors through his pregnant Victory Gal, Trudy Kockenlocker; François Truffaut provides a loving tribute to pregnancy in *Small Change* (1976); Woody Allen allows us to listen to a pregnant woman's fears and dreams in *Another Woman* (1988). These directors and others, including Joseph Losey, Tony Richardson, David Lynch, Martin Scorsese, Curtis Hanson, Mike Nichols, Roman Polanski (yes, Roman Polanski), Lasse Hallström and others, frame the stories of women in ways that feel genuine throughout their body of work. Like classic male authors—William Faulkner, John Steinbeck, Tennessee Williams—and contemporary writers Michael Chabon (*The Amazing Adventures of Kavalier & Clay*; *Wonder Boys*), Ian McEwan (*Atonement*), and Julian Barnes (*Talking It Over*; *The Sense of an Ending*), these film-makers frame their narratives, including pregnancy narratives, so that we can gauge how we see pregnant characters against how these pregnant characters see themselves. The best of these films are complicated and collaborative efforts.

Fargo

As the work of Amy Heckerling and Cameron Crowe on *Fast Times* attests, collaborations on film have produced some of the most powerful of all pregnancy narratives,. American collaborators Ethan and Joel Coen, whose films almost always make some reference to pregnancy in them, have relied on the talents of T Bone Burnett, George Clooney, John Turturro, Holly Hunter, and Frances McDormand in many of their films.[18] McDormand won several awards for her performance as Marge Gunderson in *Fargo* (1996), in which she plays the police chief of Brainerd, Minnesota. She must try to unravel two related crimes, a kidnapping and the murder of a state policeman. We know much more about the crimes that Marge does, but she quickly catches up, figuring everything out. Steady, practical, and unassuming, Gundersen solves the mystery that is plaguing sleepy rural Minnesota. Eventually, she apprehends the kidnappers—one of them, at least.

Fargo represents a remarkable pregnancy narrative, and Marge is a remarkable pregnant character throughout the film. We hear almost no references to Marge's pregnancy. Early on, she has a bout of morning sickness and throws up on the ice while investigating the murder of a state trooper, and later, she tells a former classmate about her pregnancy. But all we really know about Marge's pregnancy is what she wants us to know: nothing. We learn what we can by watching her. In one of the

"Two more months," Marge (Frances McDormand) and Norm Gunderson (John Carroll Lynch) tell each other as they get ready for a good night's sleep in *Fargo* (1996). Earlier in the day, seven-months-pregnant Police Chief Gunderson single-handedly apprehended a psycho killer as he was feeding his partner's leg into a wood chipper. The Coen Brothers are especially creative with pregnancy narratives in their movies.

most iconic scenes from any American film, Marge sneaks up to kidnapper Gaear (Peter Stormare) outside a remote hunting cabin in the woods. He cannot hear her; he is busy shoving a human leg (belonging to his unfortunate partner Carl, played by Steve Buscemi) into a wood chipper. Marge, arms together, points her gun at Geaer, gets his attention and arrests him. Alone with Geaer in the woods, seven months pregnant, Marge apprehends her man. In the next scene, we see Geaer sitting in the back of Marge's police car. She is watching him through the rear view mirror. She is scolding him as she drives.

Pregnancy in *Fargo* behaves like pregnancy in real life: the pregnant woman goes about her business, doing what she needs to do. Her pregnancy does not define her, and her pregnancy does not become the focus of her narrative. In *Fargo*, we get to know Marge well enough to understand that she is bright, trustworthy, and loyal, especially to her husband Norm (John Carroll Lynch). Norm, an artist who works at home painting bird stamps, takes care of their house and of Marge. In the final scene, after sequence after sequence of sudden murders and a bloody wood chipper, we are watching Marge and Norm cuddled in bed. "They announced it," Norm says. We might think that he is referring to any of the gruesome things we have just experienced with Marge, but no: Norm's mallard will now be on a three-cent stamp. Marge knows what he means, even as we do not. A consummate professional, Marge has left her ugly work behind her, and she is now in bed with her husband, warm and safe. Norm gently pats Marge's pregnant belly. "Two more months," he says. Marge says, "Two more months." With that lullaby, *Fargo* ends, a bloody mess transformed into a vision of comfort and hope, an unpredictable narrative grounded with images of a strong, smart pregnant police chief sleeping, somewhere in Minnesota. In a few years, movie audiences will see another smart pregnant female who lives in Minnesota. But this one will still be in high school.

Juno

A Canadian-American production, *Juno*, like *Fargo*, reflects how collaboration can provide us with a fresh perspective through pregnancy. *Juno* (2007) begins with sixteen-year-old Juno (Ellen Page) telling us in voiceover how she became pregnant by her friend Paulie Bleeker

(Michael Cera): "It started with a chair." We spend the next year with Juno, from autumn when she takes ten home pregnancy tests until the following summer, after she has delivered her baby. We watch her as she tries to decide whether or not to have the baby. She does go to the abortion clinic, but leaves almost immediately. She and her best friend Leah (Olivia Thirlby) discuss the options, and Juno decides that she is not ready to be a mother. She will find a nice couple and give them the baby. The two girls start looking through the want ads for couples, and they settle on Mark and Vanessa Loring (Jason Bateman and Jennifer Garner). In the meantime, in two subsequent scenes, Juno tells her parents and Paulie about her pregnancy. Juno tells them that she already has a plan. She wants to have the baby and "give it to someone who like totally needs it." Everyone copes.

Unlike pregnant teens in Hollywood films of the 1950s and 1960s, Juno can stay in high school, where we see her attending classes, going to Paulie's track meets, and talking about the prom. By spring, however, Juno might as well be somewhere else. She feels isolated and petty. She is huge and miserable, and even focusing on the prom seems problematic. Although Paulie has told Juno that he loves her, she distances herself from him. She does not know how she feels. By the end of her pregnancy, usually clear-eyed, clever Juno is a big mess. When she confronts Paulie at school about his date for the prom, she is crying, irrational and petulant. She tries to explain. She hates how she looks, she hates how she feels, and she knows that to those around her, she has become an object, something wild and spectacular to look at: "Look at me! I'm a planet!" she cries. Shortly after the prom incident, Juno apologizes to Paulie, and they resolve their differences. When Paulie notices that Juno is not in the stands during a track meet, he runs to the hospital, to find that Juno has delivered a healthy baby, now in Vanessa's arms. He gets to Juno's room, gets into bed with her. He is still wearing his high school track suit. They are both crying. When we see this couple next, it is summer, and they are sitting outside of Juno's house, singing together, their bicycles next to them.

Not since *Rosemary's Baby* in 1968 has an American movie taken the audience along through every stage of pregnancy.[19] We are with Juno from the beginning, when she tells us how she conceived, and beyond the baby's birth. As we experience Juno's physical problems—she hurls

Vanessa Loring (Jennifer Garner) says hello to Juno MacGuff's (Ellen Page) unborn baby in *Juno* (2007), one of the recent films in which a pregnancy narrative respects the pregnant teen, revealing facets of her character that reflect her maturity and integrity.

into her stepmother's home décor, she struggles with clothing—we also experience her emotional turmoil as her due date approaches. Behind the wisecracks and nonsense that come out of Juno's mouth, stands a loyal and steadfast pregnant girl, who, when tested on her value system, reveals her fortitude and integrity. We learn early that Juno's own biological mother abandoned her and her father years earlier, and she has articulated very clearly to everyone that she wants this baby to have a stable home environment. When Mark comes on to Juno, telling her that he is leaving Vanessa, Juno is horrified, but smart enough to realize that Mark is more immature than she. Within hours of learning that the Lorings are breaking up, Juno vows to carry through with the adoption regardless of Vanessa's impending status as a single mother. She may be a screwed-up pregnant teenage girl, but she sees very clearly that Vanessa represents the parent she has projected for her baby. "If you're still in, I'm still in," she writes to Vanessa.

Juno opened to critical acclaim in 2007, but also quickly became the center of controversy. "The *Juno* effect," a term coined during the 2008 U.S. election cycle, referred to the glamorization of teen pregnancy that made headlines that year. The film became the center of an argument about teenage pregnancy: Was *Juno* an anti-choice film? A pro-choice film? An anti–pro-choice film? Even the filmmakers seemed flabbergasted by the attention. The controversy about abortion rights intensified with the release of the indie drama *Precious*. The jarring contrast between pregnancy in *Juno* and in *Precious* "contributes to a larger canvas of film in which middle-class white pregnant teens are represented as cute, funny, and end up warmly embraced by friends and family" (Oliver, *Knock*, 98–99). Both *Juno* and *Precious* "reinforce stereotypes" in American culture (99). For countless reasons and in countless ways, both *Juno* and *Precious* were appropriated, reframed, and re-presented by those who would have us shift our gazes away from the narratives of these teenage girls.

In a confluence of race, gender, and class issues, these films became lightning rods for public consumption, used by cable networks to launch reality television shows about teen mothers, race, and family values, and mentioned by cable network talking heads with any number of political agendas.[20] The characters Juno and Precious would both be surprised to know how powerful they had become (reminding us of the power of one handmaiden who escaped into history, perhaps?). They would also both figure out quickly that their pregnancy stories were being appropriated by those who probably did not want to know what we know: that these remarkable young women can tell their own pregnancy stories, which are theirs and belong to no one else. Like most pregnancy narratives, *Juno* is not about a baby. *Juno* is about Juno. *Precious* is about Precious. Their pregnancies, wrong for both teenagers on so many different levels, reveal the most profound characteristic of a pregnancy narrative: pregnancy stories are self-reflexive. They have almost nothing to do with an infant, but reflect back onto the person who carries the baby, whose pregnancy becomes a story.

The *Juno-Precious* teenage pregnancy controversies were not new. Those of us who recognize the ways that pregnancy works in their narratives, however, might have anticipated how their pregnancies might be used in public discourse. Fictional pregnancy had been the site of multiple controversies twenty years earlier in 1987, the year that a teen abortion slipped through Hollywood's grasp and appeared in *Dirty Dancing*. Alice Walker's Pulitzer Prize–winning novel *The Color Purple*, also a pregnancy narrative, had been recently adapted as a mainstream Hollywood production by Steven Spielberg, and critics and scholars fussed about everything from how the movie portrayed men, to the controversial incest and same-sex subplots, to the racial makeup of the crew, especially Spielberg. Not everyone was sold on Spielberg as director, writes Mark Anthony Neal: "That a white director—and one that specialized in fantasy at that—helmed *The Color Purple*, was arguably a secondary thought for those who felt that Walker had colluded with 'White Hollywood' to further demonize black men. In the parlance of the day, Alice Walker was a dirty feminist" ("Critical Noir").[21]

Both *Dirty Dancing* and *The Color Purple*—along with two independent British films, *Wish You Were Here* (1987) and *Hope and Glory* (1987), in which teen girls are the heroes of their own unintended pregnancy narratives during the 1940s and 1950s—caught the attention of American critics and televangelists in the late 1980s. The Moral Majority, by now a well-funded and high-profile American movement, cited these and other films as examples of a critical decline in "traditional family values" in America. Their rant became even shriller five years later, in 1992, when single—and fictional—journalist Murphy Brown (Candace

Bergen), the title character on a network television sitcom, became pregnant and decided to keep her fictional baby.

This sitcom pregnancy inspired a vice-presidential candidate to invoke Murphy Brown as an example of moral decay and an affront to traditional families. "It doesn't help matters," speechified Dan Quayle, "when primetime TV has Murphy Brown, a character who supposedly epitomizes today's intelligent, highly paid professional woman, mocking the importance of fathers by bearing a child alone and calling it just another lifestyle choice." Quayle's reference to *Murphy Brown* did not do for him what he probably hoped it would do. He learned too late what we know about a pregnancy story: it moves around on its own, in spite of our best efforts to control it. A pregnancy narrative does not always mean what we want it to mean, or what we think it should mean. Whether we experience a pregnancy story through a written text, in a dark movie theater, or through public airwaves, we are at the mercy of the narrative, which has its own autonomy and never stops moving. Narrative pregnancy has its own internal structures, its own rules, its own timing. In fact, pregnancy behaves like language.

Pregnancy as Language

Like a language, pregnancy itself is never static; the technologies of photography and moving pictures reveal the ways in which a real pregnancy begins its dance from the second the egg and sperm meet. In perhaps the most lyrical of all descriptions of pregnancy ever written, feminist philosopher Julia Kristeva describes how a pregnancy begins to move: "Cells fuse, split, and proliferate; volumes grow, tissues stretch, and body fluids change rhythm, speeding up or slowing down" (quoted in Hanson, 12). Kristeva describes how pregnancy depends on a set of rules—a grammar—of opposites in order to structure movement and growth. These opposing structures are defined by the known and the unknown, the outer and the inner, the one and the many: "Within the body, growing as a graft, indomitable, there is an other. And no one is present within that simultaneously dual and alien space, to signify what is going on" (12).

So Juno is really onto something when she refers to her pregnant self as "a planet." Her metaphor represents both an internal world and a space projected outside of herself. Like language, pregnancy develops in stages, always moving, always encouraging new definitions of old concepts, so that we can grow into the ever-expanding universe of constant movement of pregnancy. We learn to read by metaphor: Mary Shelley's monster; Sylvia Plath's "cow in calf"; Sharon Olds's "glistening verb," and cinematic metaphors: a stolen look at a profile in a mirror, a spacecraft teeming with life; a close-up of the sweating face of a woman in labor. Also like language, narrative pregnancy demands that we respect necessary boundaries: those of our bodies, our landscapes—and then pregnancy moves the boundaries without us, forcing us to shift our gazes, to consider the insignificant aspects like we do parts of speech. We need not know their names, but we need to know how to recognize and use them, to recognize the larger structures of pregnancy: adjective, adverb, conjunction, conception, creation, trimester, quickening. The language of narrative pregnancy moves, projects, displaces, reproduces. Like Frida Kahlo's paintings, pregnancy can take itself apart so that we can experience its components, and it then helps us rebuild—and rebirth—how we value our own worlds.

As Elissa Marder points out in *The Mother in the Age of Mechanical Reproduction*, mechanical reproduction simulates birth. Photographs and motion pictures are the offspring of pregnant devices that have the power to duplicate "sensory memories"; "photography and the mother are not accidentally related" (181). Of all of the languages by which we read the world, the language of narrative—moving stories in print and moving pictures on film—becomes the most effective way to read pregnancy because narrative and pregnancy are twin discourses. Each uses generic components, but each time they do, we have a different result; reproduction requires specific components, but no two reproductions are alike. Each human pregnancy begins with the language of an old story that we all know, and each resolves distinctively and organically.

The language of pregnancy, like that of narrative, moves us through genres, through centuries, through planets, through our own bodies. Narrative pregnancy on film especially reveals how collaboration of pregnancy enriches our understanding of the push and pull of gender; suggests the ways in which we use and abuse power; and projects those fears and hopes for which we may have no other language. Narrative pregnancy can mirror an entire set of experiences that all people understand against a singular experience—each individual pregnancy—that we may not get at all. Because pregnancy creates its own unknown planet, it allows us to become an Other. Telling our own pregnancy stories, and hearing those stories we cannot even imagine—gives us all the capacity to reframe our own gazes. Pregnancy stories have the power to change our ways of seeing. If we listen and watch, any of us can grow some new idea, expression, understanding, inside us.

Daughters of the Dust

In the independent film *Daughters of the Dust* (1991), American filmmaker Julie Dash brings to life a two-day family reunion of four generations of the Peazants, a Gullah family who gathers on St. Helena

Pregnant Eula (Alva Rogers), Trula (Trula Hoosier) and Yellow Mary (Barbara O) walk along the beach of Ibo Landing during the Peazant 1902 family reunion in *Daughters of the Dust* (1991). Eula's unborn daughter narrates the movie for us—invisible to her relatives.

Island just before several of them are to migrate north in 1902. Dash does not tell this story as a conventional narrative; instead, as Toni Cade Bambera points out, Dash "asks that the spectator honor multiple perspectives rather than depend on the 'official' story offered by a hero" (881).[22] We weave through the stories of the Peazant family, learning about their lives, their mistakes, their dreams. They all have their own pasts complete with regrets, grudges, fears, and longings. Some of them are tired of the old ways, and eschew the matriarch Nana (Cora Lee Day) for her reliance on African ways. Others cling to their heritage, even as they prepare to move away from it into the 20th century. All of them have stories to tell. Some of them have pregnancy stories: one of the most poignant is told by Nana's granddaughter Yellow Mary (Barbara O), who describes how her baby died in her arms.

Nana remembers slave days, and we see one of her memories of herself as a girl, attending to the indigo deep in the woods, among other slaves, her hands and clothing purple with bruises and berries. In contrast to Nana's memory of purple darkness, her granddaughters and great granddaughters all radiate light and air at this reunion. They are dressed in beautiful flowing clothes, all wearing billowing white dresses, especially lovely in scenes where they are frolicking and running on the beach. We watch one of the women in white, Eula (Alva Rogers), pregnant wife of Nana's grandson Eli (Adisa Anderson), as she tries to talk with her husband, who runs from her. Slowly their story comes out: Eula was raped by a plantation owner, and Eli fears that the baby Eula carries is not his baby. But we already know that the baby Eula carries belongs to Eli because the baby herself tells us. She is credited as the "Unborn Child" (Kai-Lynn Warren), and we had heard the voice of a little girl who narrates *Daughters of the Dust* before we had met any of the Peazants: "My story begins on the eve of my family's migration north." The Unborn Child presents us with one of the most engaging and magical pregnancy narratives on film as she guides us through *Daughters of the Dust*.[23]

We see the Unborn Child several times in the film, as she weaves in and out, sometimes talking to other characters who do not see her, sometimes talking to us, sometimes just frolicking on the beach. Although she also wears a billowing white dress, we can always distinguish her because she wears a singular indigo ribbon in her hair. She is always moving, whether in close-up or far away along the waterfront. She jumps around in the water, and sits by the bonfire with her cousins, none of whom know that she is there. When photographer Mr. Snead (Tommy Redmond Hicks) gathers the entire Peazant family together on the beach for a final photograph, the Unborn Child sits among them, posing. She haunts many of the scenes where the adult characters are struggling to work things out. She lets us listen to even the most private conversations, as when Nana confronts Eli about his fear of his wife's pregnancy.

Occasionally the Unborn Child lights near her pregnant mother, who does not see her. But we see her, and we follow her, listening in on conversations that are none of our business. We listen, for instance, to her parents as they gradually begin to reconcile. Eventually, the Unborn Child abandons her parents and the other adults. She goes her own way, returning to play on the beach, laughing among her other relatives as they all begin to return to the boats that will carry them away to their new Northern lives. After the departing Peazants have said their good-byes, and the other adults have returned to their homes, the Unborn Child remains with us on the beach, looking out on the water. She has moved us through this narrative as only pregnancy can, delivering us from ourselves and enriching the ways we see the selves of others. Her final words act as a lyrical coda to the story: "We remain behind, growing older, wiser, stronger." Only a pregnancy narrative can move us so gracefully. Only a pregnancy narrative can deliver such promise, such hope.

Chapter Notes

Preface

1. Fessler, Ann. *The Girls Who Went Away: The Hidden History of Women Who Surrendered Children for Adoption in the Decades Before Roe v. Wade*. New York: Penguin, 2006.

2. Tina Fey hosted *Saturday Night Live* on May 7, 2011. Poehler on October 18, 2008. Both skits are accessible online.

Introduction

1. All technical information about film titles is referenced from the Internet Movie Database: www.imdb.com

2. For more on pregnancy in women's writing, see Podnieks, *Mediating Moms*; Cosslett's *Women writing childbirth*; Tharp and MacCallum-Whitcomb, *This Giving Birth*; Doyle, *Bordering on the Body*; Leavitt, *Brought to Bed*.

3. The Motion Picture Production Code is accessible at several websites, including http://www.artsreformation.com/a001/hays-code.html. A great resource for the Code and pre–Code film is http://www.lib.berkeley.edu/MRC/precode.html. For valuable insight into the Hays Code, see the following: Leff & Simmons; Vieira; Lewis; Wittern-Keller; and Timmer.

4. Still the most useful sources on the consequences of exclusive female pregnancy are Hélène Cixous, *The Laugh of the Medusa*; and Shulamith Firestone, *The Dialectic of Sex*.

5. Plath, Sylvia, *Collected Poems*.

There are many helpful sources on Plath. Most valuable to this aspect of my study have been Kalfopoulou, Lant, Brennan, Bundtzen, Kendall, Mitchell, Wagner-Martin, and Park.

6. See especially Park, "I Could Kill a Woman or Wound a Man"; and Gill.

7. See especially Susan MacCallum-Whitcomb's "Claiming Our Birth-Write" for a good overview of poetry about birth and mothers.

8. Adrienne Rich's foreword to *The Works of Anne Bradstreet* (Hensley, ed.) remains the most lucid and thoughtful treatment of Bradstreet. Rich's extraordinary *Of Woman Born* is essential reading for anyone interested in anything about pregnancy, mothering, and motherhood.

9. Ellen Argyros's essay "Some Epic Use for My Excellent Body" is a very fine study of Olds's poem.

10. For more on Harold Pinter's screenplays, see Klein, *Making Pictures* (1985), and Gale, *Sharp Cut* (2003); for more on Jack Clayton, see Sinyard, *Jack Clayton* (2000).

11. Many of these "social-realism" films, sometimes referred to as "kitchen sink dramas," include plots in which we see or hear about unintended pregnancy. See Heilpern, *John Osborne: The Many Lives of the Angry Young Man*; and Tucker, *British Social Realism in the Arts Since 1940*.

12. There are many good studies of post–World War II women writers. Most helpful to this introduction have been Turner, *Post-War British Women Novelists*

and the Canon; Maroula, *Contemporary Women's Writing: From* The Golden Notebook *to* The Color Purple; and Greene, *Doris Lessing*. Also see Dowson, *Women's Writing, 1945–1960*.

Chapter 1

1. I am indebted to my beloved late teacher and mentor Agnes McNeill Donohue, whose chapter on *The Scarlet Letter*, "'A' Is for Apple," in her wonderful book *Hawthorne: Calvin's Ironic Stepchild*, has inspired and enriched much more than the title of my first chapter. All quotations from and references to *The Scarlet Letter* are from Murfin, ed., *The Scarlet Letter* by Nathaniel Hawthorne, NY: Bedford Books, 1991.

2. The best overview of American women's health issues of the 19th century remains Ehrenreich and English, *For Her Own Good*. See especially Chapter Two, "Witches, Healers, and Gentlemen Doctors." Also see Barlowe, chapter 5.

3. There are *so many* good sources on *The Scarlet Letter*. All of the essays in Murfin, ed., have been useful, especially Joanne Feit Diehl, "Re-reading *The Letter*" and Michael Ragussis, "Silence, Family Discourse, and Fiction in *The Scarlet Letter*." All of Nina Baym's work on Hawthorne has been helpful, as have the amazing insights of David Leverenz. See also Barlowe's discussion of the 1995 film adaptation in "Demi's Hester and Hester's Demi(se)."

4. See especially Stephen Railton's excellent essay, "The Address of *The Scarlet Letter*," in which he explains Hawthorne's "narrative delay" strategies.

5. "The scarlet letter had not done its office" is not just baffling, but also one of the most famous of all of Hawthorne's lines in *The Scarlet Letter*.

6. See especially Diehl and Ragussis for good discussions of Pearl's power and significance to the novel.

7. Laura Doyle discusses some of the similarities between *Charlotte Temple* and *The Scarlet Letter* in her interesting essay

on Hawthorne's work as commentary on Great Britain in "'A' for Atlantic."

8. Angela Davis's writings are especially helpful on this point. Also see Anne B. Dalton's excellent essay "The Devil and the Virgin," and John Ernest, "Motherhood Beyond the Gate: Jacobs's Epistemic Challenge in *Incidents in the Life of a Slave Girl*."

9. All quotations from, and references to *Incidents in the Life of a Slave Girl* are from Henry Louis Gates, Jr., ed., *The Classic Slave Narratives*, New York: Penguin, 2012.

10. The best and most useful works on the relationship between *The Scarlet Letter* and *Incidents in the Life of a Slave Girl* are Jean Fagan Yellin, "*The Scarlet Letter* and the Antislavery Feminists"; and Leland S. Person, "The Dark Labyrinth of Mind: Hawthorne, Hester, and the Ironies of Racial Mothering." Person points out that Hester's "mothering rights" associate her "to her slave sisters," but that Hester "is not a slave mother" (48).

11. The best collection of essays on the rise and importance of women's popular fiction in the U.S. is Lisa Botshon and Meredith Goldsmith's *Middlebrow Moderns: Popular American Women Writers of the 1920s*.

12. Elaine Showalter's essay "Tradition and the Female Talent" has been especially helpful here because she explores the ways in which Chopin's novel was *not* part of the literary landscape of her own time.

13. Gail Lippincott's essay "Thirty-Nine Weeks: Pregnancy and Birth Imagery in Kate Chopin's *The Awakening*" was a most valuable resource for my work. Especially helpful has been her scrupulous documentation. See also Wolter's excellent essay on Hester Prynne and Edna Pontellier.

14. All quotations from and references to *Summer* are from Denise D. Knight, ed., *Ethan Frome and Summer*. By Edith Wharton. Boston: Houghton Mifflin, 2004.

15. Whenever Wharton mentions race, we are somewhere we ought not to be. See especially Ammons, "Edith Wharton and Race."

16. Hermione Lee discusses *Summer* in her excellent biography of Wharton, aptly suggesting that Dr. Merkle is one of Wharton's Jewish characters (512). See also Skillern, "Law, Language and Ritual in *Summer*"; Elbert, "The Politics of Maternality in *Summer*"; and especially Walker, "'Seduced and Abandoned': Convention and Reality in Edith Wharton's *Summer*."

17. *The Scarlet Letter* and *Summer* share many characteristics, noticed by scholars, among them Hermione Lee, who notes that Mr. Royall resembles "Hawthorne's dark, obsessional old husband Chillingworth" (512). Wharton also recognized that the two texts had much in common, including out-of-wedlock pregnancies (Lee, 596).

18. For more on the film adaptation of *The Old Maid*, see Boswell, *Edith Wharton on Film* (Carbondale: Southern Illinois University Press, 2007).

19. All quotations from and references to *The Age of Innocence* are from Candace Waid, ed., *The Age of Innocence*. By Edith Wharton. New York: W.W. Norton, (2003).

20. Martin Scorsese's treatment of this important scene is beautifully realized in his remarkable adaptation of *The Age of Innocence*. See Boswell.

21. Showalter's chapter "The Great Depression," a discussion of women fiction writers in the 1930s, in *Jury of Her Peers*, has been especially helpful.

22. *Jennie Gerhardt* was heavily censored in 1911. Editors cut at least 25,000 words, including any reference to Jennie's point of view. In the censored version, we never hear her decide to keep her baby. The full text was not published until 1992.

23. The most useful works on Morrison for this study have been Gates and Appiah, *Toni Morrison*, and Harris, *Fiction and Folklore*.

24. Wolter's essay on Hester and Sethe has been very helpful with this work. Also see Woidant.

25. For more on the significance of the body, see Nana.

26. Besides William Faulkner, there are many 20th-century male fiction writers who incorporate pregnancy into their work. Notable among them are John Irving (*The World According to Garp*, *The Ciderhouse Rules*), Tennessee Williams (*Cat on a Hot Tin Roof*, *A Streetcar Named Desire*), and Kurt Vonnegut (*Slaughterhouse 5*). The number of fiction writers who include pregnancy is daunting. The best source for lists of these novels would be the Internet.

27. See especially Brenda Daly, "Seeds of Shame or Seeds of Change? When Daughters Give Birth to Their Fathers' Children" in Tharp.

Chapter 2

1. It is no coincidence that melodrama became worthy of film studies about the same time that women began participating in film scholarship. There are some excellent works on melodrama, especially in the classic collection *Imitations of Life*, edited by Marcia Landy. Jackie Byar's *All That Hollywood Allows* has been especially helpful to my study.

2. Griffith, as in all of his films, also served as an anonymous screenwriter on *Way Down East*. For more on Griffith, see Gunning, *D. W. Griffith and the Origins of American Narrative Film*; and Schickel, *D. W. Griffith: An American Life*. Also see Griffith and Mayer's *The Movies* for some great still photos from Griffith's films.

3. Another likely impetus for the Code in the 1930s was the threat to decency posed by Mae West. Doherty, in *Hollywood's Censor* and *Pre-Code Hollywood*; Jacobs in *The Wages of Sin*; and LaSalle in *Complicated Women* all provide insightful scholarship about West's role in the growing power of the Production Code in the early 1930s.

4. Many good sources on women's films during the pre–Code era have enriched my work, especially those which explore a close relative of the pregnancy narrative, the maternal melodrama. The two most influential essays on the maternal melodrama are Doane, "The Moving Image," and Williams, "Something Else

Besides a Mother." The most clever and intimate is LaSalle's *Complicated Women*; Jacobs's *The Wages of Sin* is thoughtful and thorough, especially her chapter "Something Other Than a Sob Story"; Haskell's *From Reverence to Rape*; Viviani's "Who Is Without Sin"; Doherty, *Hollywood's Censor*; and Cook, "Melodrama and the Women's Picture."

5. Basinger includes a wonderful listing of unwed mother films from the pre–Code era in *A Woman's View*, a most lively, focused, and valuable discussion about pregnancy films of the early 1930s.

6. Mick LaSalle discusses *Men in White* (1934), a Hollywood production in which a character has an off-screen abortion. Perhaps "the only pre–Code [film] whose plot centers around an abortion," *Men in White* was one of the last pre–Code films which did not require of women a "last-minute conversion, apology, or reversion to happy subservience" (166).

7. For a wonderful pictorial display of Constance Bennett and other Hollywood stars in their roles as Depression-era mothers, see Griffith and Mayer, *The Movies*. More beautiful stills from a variety of pre–Code Hollywood films are in Vieira's *Sin in Soft Focus*.

8. Jeanine Basinger has a really fine discussion of *The Great Lie* in her chapter on motherhood in *A Woman's View*, explaining that it's one of the best representations of the "missing father" film (411–14).

9. See Chapter 1, "A Is for Pregnant," for a discussion of Kitty Foyle's abortion in the popular novel of the same name. The Production Code would never have allowed for that plot line in the film.

10. There are good discussions of *Miracle of Morgan's Creek* in Doherty and Leff and Simmons. See also Sturges's autobiography, *Preston Sturges*, and Neibaur's essay on *Miracle*.

11. Throughout this work, I have relied on several good sources on the Production Code and censorship. The most useful sources have been Leff and Simmons; Lewis; and especially Doherty's work on Joseph Breen.

12. Noir is perhaps the most robust of all the scholarly areas of film studies that engage film scholars. Among the most accessible and valuable works to my study have been Naremore's *More Than the Night*; Kolker's *Cinema of Loneliness*; and especially Leitch's *Crime Films*, which is an especially ambitious, well-crafted and thoughtful work.

13. That film scholars who write endlessly about both melodrama and noir cannot agree on how to identify films that include characteristics of both seems especially significant (noir melodramas? melodramatic noirs? melonoirs? melonoiriques?).

14. The study of noir has only been enriched by the study of women and women's noir. Especially useful to this study have been the exceptional essays in Kaplan, *Women in Film Noir*, especially "Women in Film Noir" by Janey Place. Mary Ann Doane's *The Desire to Desire* remains essential to any study of noir.

15. See especially Sylvia Harvey's discussion of noir women as barren or childless in "Woman's Place: The Absent Family of Film Noir."

16. Basinger includes a very fine discussion of the *Four Daughters* series in her chapter "The Woman Herself," in *A Woman's View*.

17. François Truffaut's interview with Hitchcock on *Strangers on a Train* is especially interesting. Also helpful have been the essays in Allen and Gonzáles, *Hitchcock: Past and Future*.

18. Alfred Hitchcock acknowledged the affinity between Theodore Drieser's *An American Tragedy* and Highsmith's *Strangers on a Train* in his interview with Truffaut. See Truffaut, 193–207.

19. My study of *Beyond the Forest* has been enriched by the works of Basinger, Doane, and especially Place.

20. The trip to the ladies' room in *No Man of Her Own* takes a few minutes longer than it should. In a perversely funny sequence, Helen and Patrice must wait while an older woman takes her time primping in the lounge mirror. Anyone who knows anything about pregnancy

cannot watch this scene without laughing. Mark Osteen's *Nightmare Alley* includes an especially thoughtful discussion of *No Man of Her Own*.

21. This film—and the novel by Ben Ames Williams from which it was adapted—have also been cited as inspiration for Patricia Highsmith's *Strangers on a Train*.

22. Director George Stevens privileges Montgomery Clift's face in *A Place in the Sun* as well, although he must compete in many frames with one of the most stunning of all Hollywood faces, that of Elizabeth Taylor. See Hatch, "1951: Movies and the New Faces of Masculinity."

23. Byars has an especially insightful chapter on male melodramas of the 1950s in *All That Hollywood Allows*.

24. The film adaptation deviates from James Jones's novel on the point of Karen's childlessness. In the book, she has a son. See especially Byars and Bell-Metereau.

25. The Big Five Hollywood Studios were MGM, Warner Bros., Twentieth Century–Fox, Paramount, and RKO.

26. Doherty refers to the television production of *Fearful Decision*, produced for the *U.S. Steel Hour* in 1955, a drama about a kidnapping, as an example of the difference between television and film censorship. Plots involving kidnapping were forbidden by the Production Code.

27. Ball and Arnaz had to negotiate aggressively with CBS to get their pregnancy story on the air. The best source for more information about Desilu is Sanders's and Gilbert's excellent *Desilu: The Story of Lucille Ball and Desi Arnaz*.

Chapter 3

1. For more on Grace Metalious and the history of her novel *Peyton Place*, see Emily Toth's biography of Metalious, *Inside Peyton Place*; and Callahan, "Peyton Place's Real Victim," in the March 2006 issue of *Vanity Fair* magazine.

2. Ruth Pirsig Wood's *Lolita in Peyton Place* is especially respectful of the novel and insightful as well. Also helpful have

been Pomerance, "1957: Movies and the Search for Proportion," and Byars, *All That Hollywood Allows*.

3. *Lolita* is a daunting novel, and I am indebted to some really fine studies. Among the most important to my work have been Kincaid, Ahlberg, and Goldman's "'Knowing *Lolita*.'" Also see Brian Boyd's *Vladimir Nabokov: The American Years* and Wood's *Lolita in Peyton Place*. Especially good is Ellen Pifer, "The *Lolita* phenomenon from Paris to Tehran."

4. There is also a 1997 film adaptation, more faithful to Nabokov's book: *Lolita*, directed by Adrian Lyne. In this adaptation, we are told in an epilogue that Lolita died in childbirth on Christmas Day.

5. My own reading of Kubrick's *Lolita* has been enriched by Phillips's interviews with Kubrick, and by the fine work of Walker, Taylor and Ruchti in *Stanley Kubrick, Director*. Walker, Taylor and Ruchti have an especially valuable discussion of fidelity in Kubrick's *Lolita*.

6. In Nabokov's novel, Humbert does tell us about Lolita's poor taste in movies, but there is no drive-in scene.

7. The plot of *The Curse of Frankenstein* involves a scientist who is betrayed and attacked by the monster that he creates. This choice by Kubrick cannot have been a coincidence.

8. In the stage drama of *Blue Denim* Janet does have the abortion.

9. Film director Allison Anders has a wonderful entry in the YouTube *Trailers from Hell* for *Blue Denim*, in which she discusses the art and craft of the film, as well as how an illegal abortion would have been arranged in the 1950s. She also discusses the film's original introduction by—of all people—Joan Crawford, who "legitimized the movie." Several of Anders's films include teen pregnancy narratives, including *Gas Food Lodging* (1992) and *Grace of My Heart* (1996). See http://www.youtube.com/watch?v=ptx wuuVJesI

10. There was an entire subgenre of pregnancy films, sometimes called "pulp pregnancy films," which dealt with

graphic details about pregnancy and abortion. With titles like *Street Corner, Because of Eve, You've Ruined Me Eddie, The Scum of the Earth,* and *Lost, Lonely and Vicious,* these films had a loyal following. Some of them are well made and interesting; some are difficult to locate. However, the web provides several sources, the best of which is www.Rottentomatoes.com

11. In *American Jezebel,* Eve LaPlante points out that Hutchinson's condition was most likely a "hydatidiform mole," an uncommon "birth anomaly" occurring "most often in women older than forty-five" (217).

12. There are many good biographies and studies of Mary Shelley. My work here has been enriched especially by Clemit and Walker's edition of William Godwin's *Memoirs of the Author;* St. Clair's *The Godwins and the Shelleys;* and especially Mellor's *Mary Shelley: Her Life, Her Fiction, Her Monsters.* See also Vivien Jones's "The Death of Mary Wollstonecraft" and Miranda Seymour's *Mary Shelley.* Also helpful has been Elissa Marder's discussion of *Frankenstein* in *The Mother in the Age of Mechanical Reproduction.*

13. All references to and quotations from *Frankenstein* are from the 2000 Penguin edition.

14. The 1931 Universal film is adapted from a stage play by Peggy Webling, with further input by James Whale and others. For more, see Alex Jones, *The Rough Guide to Horror Movies;* and especially David Skal's excellent history of horror, *The Monster Show.*

15. Elsa Lanchester plays two roles in *Bride of Frankenstein,* ensuring that we associate the Bride with the author of *Frankenstein:* she plays Mary Shelley, who appears in the introduction of the film, and she plays the Bride.

16. David Cronenberg has always had a special affinity with pregnancy narratives. Besides *The Brood,* his film on twin gynecologists, *Dead Ringers* (1988), is another horror classic. See especially Lianne McLarty, "'Beyond the Veil of the Flesh': Croneneberg and the Disembodiment of Horror."

17. Skal's *The Monster Show* has been indispensable to my discussion on pregnancy horror. He writes especially well about both *The Exorcist* and *Carrie.* Also see Lindsey, "Horror, Femininity, and *Carrie.*"

18. *Rosemary's Baby* seems to be a favorite among film scholars. Among the most helpful to my work have been Skal's *The Monster Show;* Fischer's "Birth Traumas"; and Oliver's *Knock Me Up, Knock Me Down.* Also helpful has been Paul Cronin's *Roman Polanski: Interviews.*

19. Polanski's frequent shots of the long hallway are very interesting, and certainly must have been helpful to Stanley Kubrick when he was filming *The Shining* (1980), where the long hallway of the Overlook Hotel also provides a sort of birth canal.

20. I am especially indebted to Vivien Sobchack's essay "Family Economy and Generic Exchange" on this point. She begins her fine essay with this sentence: "Two very special babies were born to the American cinema in 1968: Rosemary's and Stanley Kubrick's" (143).

Chapter 4

1. Ira Levin wrote a sequel to *Rosemary's Baby* in 1997, entitled *Son of Rosemary,* which was much less successful than the original.

2. See Cranny-Francis, "Feminist Future," for an excellent discussion of feminist science fiction.

3. For an especially insightful discussion of the nature and historical contexts of science fiction, see Thomas Doherty, "Genre, Gender, and the *Aliens* Trilogy." Doherty points out that if "a machine can steal what is most immutably man's ... then his human status is no longer unique and privileged. In the era of artificial intelligence, woman retains her reproductive and generative prerogatives; man loses his intellectual superiority" (183).

4. The *Alien* franchise includes the original trilogy, *Alien Resurrection* (1997), *Alien vs. Predator* (2004), *Aliens vs. Pred-*

ator: Requiem (2007), and *Prometheus* (2012), which is a prequel to the *Alien* series. Scripts for another *Prometheus* film are under consideration (IMDb.com).

5. There are probably enough good sources about the *Alien* movies to constitute a scholarship franchise. Among the most helpful to my discussion have been all of the works by Vivian Sobchack, whose thoughtful essays and book on science fiction have enriched my studies of science fiction. Especially helpful to *Alien* has been her essay "Bringing It All Back Home" and *Screening Space*. Also useful have been Booker, *Alternate Americas*; Doherty, "Genre, Gender, and the *Aliens* Trilogy"; Creed, "Horror and the Monstrous-Feminine"; and all of the essays in the excellent collection *Alien Zone*, edited by Annette Kuhn, especially Byers, "Commodity Futures"; Dervin, "Primal Conditions and Convention" and Newton, "Feminism and Anxiety in *Alien.*"

6. http://www.guardian.co.uk/film/2006/aug/20/features.review

7. *Blade Runner* is an important film, and has inspired some very fine scholarship. See especially Sobchack, *Screening Space*; Bruno, "Ramble City"; Ryan and Kellner, "Technophobia'" and Booker, *Alternate Americas*. Also especially helpful to my work on pregnancy has been Sidney Perkowitz's chapter "Solid Science and Quantum Loopiness" in *Hollywood Science*. See Marder's wonderful discussion of *Blade Runner* as replicant film, in *The Mother in the Age of Mechanical Reproduction*. See also Byars, "Commodity Futures," and Telotte, "The Doubles of Fantasy and the Space of Desire."

8. The most helpful work on cloning and reproduction is Mundy's *Everything Conceivable*. Another good source is Perkowitz's "Genes and Germs Gone Bad" in the wonderful *Hollywood Science*. For a thoughtful discussion of *Never Let Me Go* as memoir, see McDonald, "Days of Past Futures."

9. *The Handmaid's Tale* has been adapted several times, and in several media. The 1990 film, with a screenplay

by Harold Pinter and directed by Volker Schlondorff, stars Natasha Richardson as Offred, Faye Dunaway as Serena Joy, Aidan Quinn as Nick, and Robert Duvall as the Commander. The film is not completely faithful to the novel; Offred stabs the Commander in the neck with scissors at the end of the film before she escapes. The last shot of Offred reveals that she has escaped, and that she is indeed pregnant. *The Handmaid's Tale* has also been adapted to radio by the BBC in 2000; the stage (2002); and as an opera in 2003. For more on the opera, see Neuman, "Just a Backlash."

10. Also see the definitive study of 1980s backlash against women: Susan Faludi's *Backlash*.

11. Neuman's essay "Just a Backlash" is a very thorough contribution to works on *The Handmaid's Tale*, and has been especially helpful. See also Chadha, "Woman as Metaphor in Margaret Atwood's *Handmaid's Tale*"; Cosslett, *Women Writing Childbirth*; Finigan, "Into the Memory Hole"; Freibert, "Control and Creativity"; and Wagner-Lawler, "The Play of Irony." All of the essays in Nicholson, ed., *Margaret Atwood*, have been helpful, especially Evans.

12. All quotations from and references to *The Handmaid's Tale* are from the 1986 Anchor Books edition.

13. The best essay on the correspondence between the colonial Puritan culture and Gilead is Evans, "Versions of History," in Nicholson.

14. Through the years, Steven Spielberg has released three versions of *Close Encounters of the Third Kind*. All of my references refer to the original 1977 production.

15. For more on the Library of Congress National Film Registry, go to: http://www.loc.gov/film/filmnfr.html. For more on *Close Encounters* and the American Film Institute, go to: http://www.afi.com/.

16. Sobchack's work, once again, has been especially valuable to me. She discusses *Close Encounters* in *Screening Space*, and her essays "Bringing It All Back Home" and "The Virginity of Astronauts"

have been useful as well. Booker's *Alternate Americas* includes a good summary of the criticisms of *Close Encounters*, and also a helpful description of the differences among the three versions of the film. Perkowitz's *Hollywood Science* also includes a valuable discussion of the film.

17. Jon Lewis has a thoughtful discussion of the Film School Generation of filmmakers in *American Film*.

18. The best read on this great Hollywood era of insanity is Biskind, *Easy Riders, Raging Bulls*. Much of Biskind's work has enriched my own here. See also *Down and Dirty Pictures*.

19. Bob Balaban's memoir *Spielberg, Truffaut, & Me* is a delightful read about the filming of *Close Encounters*.

20. Barlowe's *The Scarlet Mob of Scribblers* includes a thorough discussion of some of the ways in which Hester and her A have been appropriated in the chapter "What's Black and White and Red/Read All Over?"

21. Lawrence Raw's *Adapting Nathaniel Hawthorne to the Screen* provides a thoughtful, well-written and complete discussion of all the adaptations of Hawthorne, including television productions.

22. Barlowe's *The Scarlet Mob of Scribblers*, in which she sticks it to the mainstream Hawthorne scholarly community, includes a very fine discussion of the 1995 adaptation, in which she addresses both the film and the criticisms of the film by Hawthorne scholars. "My examination of the film," she writes, "allows me to destabilize and recontextualize Hawthorne's novel and his character Hester Prynne" (93). She indeed does both very well, and I am grateful for her work.

Chapter 5

1. Moore has graced the cover of *Vanity Fair* three times, first in 1991 in Liebovitz's *More on Moore*. In 1992 she appeared naked in a trompe-l'œil body painting by Joanne Gair, again photographed by Liebovitz; and in 1993 she appeared on a cover with David Letterman.

2. For more on menstruation and the ancients, see Elaine Fantham et al., *Women in the Classical World*. There is also a very helpful website about the history of menstruation and women's health: http://www.mum.org/

3. The website *Making Visible Embryos* includes valuable information about the history of the unborn, and the relationship of art to pregnancy. This site also features a list of useful resources: http://www.hps.cam.ac.uk/visibleembryos/resources.html#Unborn

4. Two beautiful and useful books on Vermeer are Leidtke and Forty.

5. A traditional *retablo* is a primitive Mexican religious painting, often very small, in which "the holy image—Virgin, Christ, or saint—that saves the sick, wounded, or otherwise endangered person appears in the sky surrounded by an aureole of cloud puffs" (Herrera, 151).

6. Kahlo and Rivera divorced in 1939 and remarried in 1940.

7. There are many fine essays on feminist film theory, and I am indebted to them, especially the work of Laura Mulvey and Linda Williams. Also useful are Teresa de Lauretis's "Rethinking Women's Cinema"; Jane Gaines's "White Privilege and Looking Relations"; and Judith Smith's "The Marrying Kind."

8. Different translations from French to English of the final scene of *Breathless* allow for some very different readings of the scene. The best resource for understanding all of the different translations is the collection of notes provided in the 2007 DVD from the Criterion Collection.

9. I can find no sources on *Breathless* in which Patricia's pregnancy seems important enough to include as part of the coverage. I hope my brief discussion here will inspire further re-readings of *Breathless* as a pregnancy narrative.

10. All comments attributed to Heckerling and Cameron Crowe come from their joint commentary on the *Fast Times at Ridgemont High* DVD.

11. Originally, Vestron Pictures asked the producers of *Dirty Dancing* to edit out the abortion subplot. See Farber.

12. In her essay "Owning Up to Abortion," Barbara Ehrenreich suggests that the best way to break the abortion taboo is for women to talk about their own abortions publicly.

13. Roger Ebert's review of *Greenberg* is wonderful and useful. http://www.rogerebert.com/reviews/greenberg-2010

14. Farber's essay on *Greenberg* has been especially helpful to me. Of all of the sources I have read, Farber's represents the most thorough and thoughtful writing on the great abortion silence.

15. Funding for many independent films made by Americans comes from elsewhere as well. Farber explains that *Greenberg* was funded entirely by European money.

16. *Vera Drake* won awards for Imelda Staunton and director Mike Leigh at the Venice Film Festival, and also won the British Independent Film Awards for Best Actress and Best Director in 2004.

17. Cherbourg is an interesting setting for Giraud's story, especially for those of us who have seen *The Umbrellas of Cherbourg*, Jacques Demy's 1964 musical in which the main character becomes pregnant unintentionally.

18. The Coen Brothers are the subjects of several good works. Especially useful to my work on *Fargo* have been Conard, *The Philosophy of the Coen Brothers*; and Allen, ed., *The Coen Brothers Interviews*.

19. *Juno* shares many characteristics with *Rosemary's Baby*. Besides our experiencing the entire pregnancy with Juno, both Juno's and Rosemary's pregnancies follow the same seasonal pattern: they get pregnant in the fall and deliver in the spring (Rosemary, of course, on June 25). We watch many weather changes in both movies: snow, rain, blossoms. The seasonal changes we see through windows or during exterior scenes help us gauge the timing of both Juno's and Rosemary's pregnancies.

20. Two essays about *Juno* and *Push* have been especially helpful to my study here: McLennan, "Cautionary Whales?" and Luttrell, "Where Inequality Lives in the Body."

21. See Toni Cade Bambera's essay "Reading the Signs" for more on the problems with Spielberg's *The Color Purple*. Spielberg's film, writes Bambera, is "hobbled in fundamental ways—the cartoon view of Africa, for example..." (879).

22. Bambera's excellent essay on *Daughters of the Dust*, "Reading the Signs," has been especially enriching—she shows many affinities among Dash's screenplay and other pregnancy narratives, including *Beloved* and *The Color Purple*, and makes several very helpful comparisons between this film and mainstream Hollywood fare. Also see Gibson-Hudson, "Aspects of Black Feminist Cultural Ideology in Films by Black Women Independent Artists."

23. *Daughters of the Dust* was added to the Library of Congress National Film Registry in 2004.

Filmography

The following represents a comprehensive, chronological listing, by chapter, of all films cited in the text.

Filmography

1964	*Mary Poppins*	Robert Stevenson
1964	*My Fair Lady*	George Cukor
1964	*The Pumpkin Eater*	Jack Clayton
1964	*Santa Claus Conquers the Martians*	Nicholas Webster
1964	*The Umbrellas of Cherbourg*	Jacques Demy
1964	*The Young Lovers*	Samuel Goldwyn, Jr.
1964	*Zorba the Greek*	Michael Cacoyannis
1966	*Who's Afraid of Virginia Woolf?*	Mick Nichols
1968	*Funny Girl*	William Wyler
1968	*Rachel, Rachel*	Paul Newman
1968	*2001: A Space Odyssey*	Stanley Kubrick
1968	*Rosemary's Baby*	Roman Polanski
1970	*A Man Called Horse*	Elliot Silverstein
1972	*Cabaret*	Bob Fosse
1972	*The Carey Treatment*	Blake Edwards
1977	*Close Encounters of the Third Kind*	Steven Spielberg
1977	*The Demon Seed*	Donald Cammell
1977	*Saturday Night Fever*	John Badham
1978	*The Deer Hunter*	Michael Cimino
1979	*Alien*	Ridley Scott
1982	*Fast Times at Ridgemont High*	Amy Heckerling
1990	*Total Recall*	Paul Verhoeven
1991	*Daughters of the Dust*	Julie Dash
1992	*Howards End*	James Ivory
1996	*Fargo*	Joel Coen
1998	*The Opposite of Sex*	Don Roos
1999	*All About My Mother*	Pedro Almodóvar
1999	*The Matrix*	Wachowski Brothers
2000	*Traffic*	Steven Soderbergh
2002	*Balzac and the Little Chinese Seamstress*	Dai Saijie
2002	*The Hours*	Stephen Daldry
2005	*Junebug*	Phil Morrison
2006	*Pan's Labyrinth*	Guillermo del Toro
2007	*Juno*	Jason Reitman
2010	*Never Let Me Go*	Mark Romanek
2012	*The Master*	Paul Thomas Anderson

CHAPTER 1: "A" IS FOR PREGNANT: THE BIRTH OF AMERICAN PREGNANCY LITERATURE

| 1993 | *The Age of Innocence* | Martin Scorsese |

CHAPTER 2: THE WEEPIES: PREGNANCY, MELODRAMA AND NOIR

1920	*Way Down East*	D.W. Griffith
1929	*The Trial of Mary Dugan*	Bayard Veiller
1930	*Common Clay*	Victor Fleming
1931	*Born to Love*	Paul L. Stein
1931	*The Easiest Way*	Jack Conway
1932	*Forbidden*	Frank Capra
1932	*Rockabye*	George Cukor

Filmography

1933	*A Man's Castle*	Frank Borzage
1933	*Baby Face*	Alfred E. Green
1933	*Torch Singer*	Alexander Hall
1934	*Mary Stevens, M.D.*	Lloyd Bacon
1938	*Four Daughters*	Michael Curtiz
1939	*Dark Victory*	Edmund Goulding
1939	*Gone with the Wind*	Victor Fleming
1939	*Goodbye, Mr. Chips*	Sam Wood
1939	*Mr. Smith Goes to Washington*	Frank Capra
1939	*Ninotchka*	Ernst Lubitsch
1939	*The Old Maid*	Edmund Goulding
1939	*The Wizard of Oz*	Victor Fleming
1939	*The Women*	George Cukor
1939	*Wuthering Heights*	William Wyler
1940	*Four Wives*	Michael Curtiz
1940	*Kitty Foyle*	Sam Wood
1941	*Four Mothers*	William Keighley
1941	*The Great Lie*	Edmund Goulding
1943	*Tender Comrade*	Edward Dmytryk
1944	*Double Indemnity*	Billy Wilder
1944	*The Miracle of Morgan's Creek*	Preston Sturges
1945	*Detour*	Edgar G. Ulmer
1945	*Leave Her to Heaven*	John M. Stahl
1946	*Gilda*	Charles Vidor
1946	*To Each His Own*	Mitchell Leisen
1948	*Beyond the Forest*	King Vidor
1948	*Johnny Belinda*	Jean Negulesco
1950	*Father of the Bride*	Vincent Minnelli
1950	*No Man of Her Own*	Mitchell Leisen
1951	*Father's Little Dividend*	Vincente Minnelli
1951	*A Place in the Sun*	George Stevens
1951	*Strangers on a Train*	Alfred Hitchcock
1951	*A Streetcar Named Desire*	Elia Kazan

CHAPTER 3: PREGNANT TEENAGERS AND OTHER MONSTERS

1931	*Dr. Jekyll and Mr. Hyde*	Rouben Marmoulian
1931	*Frankenstein*	James Whale
1931	*Freaks*	Tod Browning
1935	*Bride of Frankenstein*	James Whale
1948	*Because of Eve*	Howard Bretherton
1948	*Street Corner*	Albert H. Kelley
1955	*Rebel Without a Cause*	Nicholas Ray
1955	*Rock Around the Clock*	Fred F. Sears
1956	*The Bad Seed*	Mervyn LeRoy
1956	*Crime in the Streets*	Don Siegel
1957	*Carnival Rock*	Roger Corman
1957	*The Curse of Frankenstein*	Terence Fisher
1957	*I Was a Teenage Werewolf*	Gene Fowler, Jr.
1957	*Motorcycle Gang*	Edward L. Cahn
1957	*Peyton Place*	Mark Robson
1957	*Rockabilly Baby*	William F. Claxton

Filmography

1957	*Sorority Girl*	Roger Corman
1957	*Teenage Thunder*	Paul Helmick
1957	*Young and Dangerous*	William F. Claxton
1958	*Lost, Lonely and Vicious*	Frank Myers
1958	*Joy Ride*	Edward Bernds
1958	*Unwed Mother*	Walter Doniger
1959	*Blue Denim*	Philip Dunne
1959	*Diary of a High School Bride*	Burt Topper
1959	*Ghost of Dragstrip Hollow*	William J. Hole, Jr.
1959	*Imitation of Life*	Douglas Sirk
1959	*A Summer Place*	Delmer Daves
1960	*Because They're Young*	Paul Wendkos
1960	*Psycho*	Alfred Hitchcock
1960	*You've Ruined Me Eddie*	R. John Hugh
1961	*Splendor in the Grass*	Elia Kazan
1961	*Susan Slade*	Delmer Daves
1962	*Lolita*	Stanley Kubrick
1963	*The Scum of the Earth*	Herschell Gordon Lewis
1968	*Funny Girl*	William Wyler
1968	*Rachel, Rachel*	Paul Newman
1968	*Rosemary's Baby*	Roman Polanski
1968	*2001: A Space Odyssey*	Stanley Kubrick
1973	*Andy Warhol's Frankenstein*	Andy Warhol
1973	*The Exorcist*	William Friedkin
1974	*Young Frankenstein*	Mel Brooks
1976	*The Brood*	David Cronenberg
1976	*Carrie*	Brian DePalma
1976	*The Omen*	Richard Donner
1977	*Eraserhead*	David Lynch
1978	*Halloween*	John Carpenter
1980	*The Shining*	Stanley Kubrick
1984	*A Nightmare on Elm Street*	Wes Craven
1988	*Dead Ringers*	David Cronenberg
1992	*Gas Food Lodging*	Allison Anders
1996	*Grace of My Heart*	Allison Anders
1996	*Scream*	Wes Craven
1997	*Lolita*	Adrian Lyne
2011	*We Need to Talk About Kevin*	Lynne Ramsey

CHAPTER 4: THE MOTHERSHIP ARRIVES: PREGNANCY IN SCIENCE FICTION

1920	*Way Down East*	D.W. Griffith
1926	*The Scarlet Letter*	Victor Seastrom
1927	*Metropolis*	Fritz Lang
1935	*The Scarlet Letter*	Robert G. Vignola
1956	*Invasion of the Body Snatchers*	Don Siegel
1957	*Peyton Place*	Mark Robson
1958	*The Blob*	Irvin S. Yeaworth, Jr.
1958	*The Fly*	Kurt Neumann
1965	*Dr. Strangelove*	Stanley Kubrick
1968	*Rosemary's Baby*	Roman Polanski
1968	*2001: A Space Odyssey*	Stanley Kubrick

Filmography

1977	*Annie Hall*	Woody Allen
1977	*Close Encounters of the Third Kind*	Steven Spielberg
1977	*The Deep*	Peter Yates
1977	*Eraserhead*	David Lynch
1977	*Julia*	Fred Zinnemann
1977	*The Last Wave*	Peter Weir
1977	*Saturday Night Fever*	John Badham
1977	*Soldier of Orange*	Paul Verhoeven
1977	*Star Wars*	George Lucas
1977	*That Obscure Object of Desire*	Luis Buñuel
1977	*The Turning Point*	Herbert Ross
1978	*Rabbit Test*	Joan Rivers
1979	*Alien*	Ridley Scott
1982	*Blade Runner*	Ridley Scott
1982	*E.T. the Extra-Terrestrial*	Steven Spielberg
1982	*Poltergeist*	Tobe Hooper
1986	*Aliens*	James Cameron
1987	*Fatal Attraction*	Adrian Lyne
1989	*Look Who's Talking*	Amy Heckerling
1990	*The Handmaid's Tale*	Volker Schlöndorff
1990	*Look Who's Talking Too*	Amy Heckerling
1990	*Total Recall*	Paul Verhoeven
1992	*Aliens 3*	David Fincher
1993	*Look Who's Talking Now*	Tom Ropelowski
1994	*Junior*	Ivan Reitman
1996	*Multiplicity*	Harold Ramus
1997	*Alien Resurrection*	Jean-Pierre Jeunot
2004	*Alien vs. Predator*	Paul W.S. Anderson
2005	*The Island*	Michael Bay
2006	*Children of Men*	Alfonso Cuarón
2007	*Alien vs. Predator: Requiem*	Colin Strause
2009	*The Road*	John Hillcoat
2010	*Inception*	Christopher Nolan
2010	*Never Let Me Go*	Mark Romanek
2012	*Prometheus*	Ridley Scott

CHAPTER 5: WAYS OF SEEING PREGNANCY

1948	*They Live by Night*	Nicholas Ray
1959	*Blue Denim*	Philip Dunne
1960	*Breathless*	Jean-Luc Godard
1963	*Love with the Proper Stranger*	Robert Mulligan
1964	*The Umbrellas of Cherbourg*	Jacques Demy
1968	*Petulia*	Richard Lester
1968	*Rosemary's Baby*	Roman Polanski
1969	*The Rain People*	Francis Ford Coppola
1970	*Five Easy Pieces*	Bob Rafelson
1971	*The Last Picture Show*	Peter Bogdanovich
1972	*Cabaret*	Bob Fosse
1972	*The Carey Treatment*	Blake Edwards
1973	*Mean Streets*	Martin Scorsese
1974	*The Godfather Part II*	Francis Ford Coppola

Filmography

1976	*Next Stop, Greenwich Village*	Paul Mazursky
1976	*Small Change*	François Truffaut
1977	*Demon Seed*	Donald Cammell
1978	*The Deer Hunter*	Michael Cimino
1979	*Alien*	Ridley Scott
1982	*Blade Runner*	Ridley Scott
1982	*Diner*	Barry Levinson
1982	*Fast Times at Ridgemont High*	Amy Heckerling
1983	*Frida Kahlo and Tina Modotti*	Laura Mulvey
1985	*The Color Purple*	Steven Spielberg
1987	*Dirty Dancing*	Emile Ardolino
1987	*Hope and Glory*	John Boorman
1987	*Wish You Were Here*	David Leland
1988	*Another Woman*	Woody Allen
1988	*Parenthood*	Ron Howard
1988	*The Story of Women*	Claude Chabrol
1991	*Daughters of the Dust*	Julie Dash
1995	*Father of the Bride Part II*	Charles Shyer
1995	*Nine Months*	Chris Columbus
1996	*Fargo*	Joel Coen
1996	*If These Walls Could Talk*	Cher, Nancy Savoca
1997	*Fools Rush In*	Andy Tennant
1998	*The Opposite of Sex*	Don Roos
1999	*The Cider House Rules*	Lasse Hallström
2000	*Where the Heart Is*	Matt Williams
2002	*Frida*	Julie Taymor
2004	*Vera Drake*	Mike Leigh
2006	*The Departed*	Martin Scorsese
2007	*4 Months, 3 Weeks, and 2 Days*	Christian Mungiu
2007	*Juno*	Jason Reitman
2007	*Knocked Up*	Judd Apatow
2008	*Baby Mama*	Michael McCullers
2008	*Revolutionary Road*	Sam Mendes
2009	*Away We Go*	Sam Mendes
2009	*Baby on Board*	Brian Herzlinger
2009	*Labor Pains*	Lara Shapiro
2009	*Precious*	Lee Daniels
2010	*The Back-Up Plan*	Alan Poul
2010	*Greenberg*	Noah Baumbach
2011	*The Ides of March*	George Clooney

Works Cited and Consulted

Affron, Charles. "Identification." In Marcia Landy, ed. *Imitations of Life*. Detroit: Wayne State University Press, 1991 (98–117).

Ahlberg, Sofia. "Scenes of Instruction: Representations of the American Girl in European Twentieth-Century Literature." *Journal of Modern Literature*. Vol. 33, Issue 3 (Spring 2010): 64–77.

Allen, Richard, and Sam Ishi-Gonzáles, eds. *Hitchcock: Past and Future*. London: Routledge, 2004.

Allen, William Rodney, ed. *The Coen Brothers Interviews*. Oxford: Oxford University Press, 2006.

Ammons, Elizabeth. "Cool Diana and the Blood-Red Muse: Edith Wharton on Innocence and Art." In Candace Waid, ed. *The Age of Innocence*. By Edith Wharton. New York: W. W. Norton, 2003 (433–447).

_____. "Edith Wharton and Race." In Millicent Bell, ed. *Cambridge Companion to Edith Wharton*. Cambridge: Cambridge University Press, 1995 (68–86).

Anders, Allison. "On *Blue Denim*." *Trailers from Hell*, http://www.youtube.com/watch?v=ptxwuuVJesI.

Angelou, Maya. *I Know Why the Caged Bird Sings*. New York: Bantam, 1970.

Argyos, Ellen. "'Some Epic Use for My Excellent Body': Redefining Childbirth as Heroic in *Beloved* and 'The Language of the Brag.'" In Julie Tharp and Susan MacCallum-Whitcomb, eds. *This Giving Birth: Pregnancy and Childbirth in American Women's Writing*. Bowling Green, OH: Bowling Green State University Popular Press, 2000 (141–156).

Atwood, Margaret. *The Handmaid's Tale*. New York: Anchor, 1986.

Balaban, Bob. *Spielberg, Truffaut, & Me: An Actor's Diary*. New York: Titan, 2003.

Bambara, Toni Cade. "Reading the Signs, Empowering the Eye: *Daughters of the Dust* and the Black Independent Cinema Movement." In Timothy Corrigan, Patricia White and Meta Mazaj, eds. *Critical Visions in Film Theory*. New York: Bedford/St. Martin's, 2011 (871–886).

Barlow, Jamie. *The Scarlet Mob of Scribblers: Rereading Hester Prynne*. Carbondale: Southern Illinois University Press, 2000.

Basinger, Jeanine. *A Woman's View: How Hollywood Spoke to Women, 1930–1960*. New York: Alfred A. Knopf, 1993.

Baym, Nina, ed. *The Norton Anthology of American Literature*, 7th ed., Vol. E. New York: W. W. Norton, 2007.

_____. "Plot in *The Scarlet Letter*." In Seymour Gross, Sculley Bradley, Richmond Croom Beatty, and E. Hudson Long, eds. *The Scarlet Letter: An Authoritative Text; Essays in Criticism and Scholarship*, 3d. ed. By Nathaniel Hawthorne. New York: W. W. Norton, 1988 (402–407).

Bell, Millicent, ed. *The Cambridge Companion to Edith Wharton*. Cambridge: Cambridge University Press, 1995.

Bell-Metereau, Rebecca. "1953: Movies and Our Secret Lives." In Murray Pomerance, ed. *American Cinema of the 1950s:*

Themes and Variations. New Brunswick, NJ: Rutgers University Press, 2005 (89–110).

Benstock, Shari. *No Gifts from Chance: A Biography of Edith Wharton.* New York: Scribner, 1994.

Bercovitch, Sacvan. "*The Scarlet Letter*: A Twice-Told Tale." *Nathaniel Hawthorne Review* 22, no. 2 (Fall 1996): 1–20.

Berger, John. *Ways of Seeing.* New York: Penguin, 1972.

Biskind, Peter. *Down and Dirty Pictures: Miramax, Sundance, and the Rise of Independent Film.* New York: Simon & Schuster, 2005.

_____. *Easy Riders, Raging Bulls: How the Sex-Drugs-and-Rock'N'Roll Generation Saved Hollywood.* New York: Simon & Schuster, 1999.

Bobo, Jacqueline. "Sifting Through the Controversy: Reading *The Color Purple.*" *Callaloo* 39 (Spring 1989): 332–342.

Booker, M. Keith. *Alternate Americas: Science Fiction Film and American Culture.* Westport, CT: Praeger, 2006.

Bordwell, David. *The Poetics of Cinema.* New York: Routledge, 2007.

Boswell, Parley Ann. *Edith Wharton on Film.* Carbondale: Southern Illinois University Press, 2007.

Boyd, Brian. *Vladimir Nabokov: The American Years.* Princeton, NJ: Princeton University Press, 1991.

Braudy, Leo, and Marshall Cohen, eds. *Film Theory and Criticism,* 6th ed. Oxford: Oxford University Press, 2004.

Brennan, Claire, ed. *The Poetry of Sylvia Plath.* New York: Columbia University Press, 2001.

Bruno, Giuliana. "Ramble City: Postmodernism and Blade Runner." In Annette Kuhn, ed. *Alien Zone: Cultural Theory and Contemporary Science Fiction Cinema.* London: Verso, 2003 (183–195).

Bundtzen, Lynda K. *The Other Ariel.* Amherst: University of Massachusetts Press, 2001.

Byars, Jackie. *All That Hollywood Allows: Re-reading Gender in 1950s Melodrama.* Chapel Hill: University of North Carolina Press, 1991.

Byers, Thomas B. "Commodity Futures." In Annette Kuhn, ed. *Alien Zone: Cultural Theory and Contemporary Science Fiction Cinema.* London: Verso, 2003 (39–50).

Callahan, Michael. "*Peyton Place*'s Real Victim." *Vanity Fair,* March 2006. Online.

Carson, Diane, Linda Dittmar, and Janice R. Welsch, eds. *Multiple Voices in Feminist Film Criticism.* Minneapolis: University of Minnesota Press, 1994.

Cawelti, John G. "The Evolution of Social Melodrama." In Marcia Landy, ed. *Imitations of Life.* Detroit: Wayne State University Press, 1991 (33–49).

Chadha, Sonia. "Woman as a Metaphor in Margaret Atwood's *The Handmaid's Tale.*" *Journal of English Studies* Vol. 4, Issue 3/4 (Sept. 2009): 28–34.

"Cinema: A Wife's Tale." *Time Magazine,* Nov. 13, 1964 (125).

Cixous, Hélène. *The Hélène Cixous Reader.* Susan Sellers, ed. Foreword by Jacques Derrida. New York: Routledge, 1994.

Clegg, Christine. *Vladimir Nabokov, Lolita: A Reader's Guide to Essential Criticism.* Cambridge: Icon, 2000.

Clemit, Pamela, and Gina Luria Walker, eds. *Memoirs of the Author of A Vindication of the Rights of Woman.* By William Godwin. Peterborough: Broadview Press, 2001.

Conard, Mark T. *The Philosophy of the Coen Brothers.* Lexington: University Press of Kentucky, 2012.

Connolly, Julian W., ed. *The Cambridge Companion to Nabokov.* Cambridge: Cambridge University Press, 2005.

Corrigan, Timothy, Patricia White, with Meta Mazaj, eds. *Critical Visions in Film Theory: Classic and Contemporary Readings.* New York: Bedford/St. Martin's, 2011.

Cosslett, Tess. *Women Writing Childbirth: Modern Discourses of Motherhood.* New York: Manchester University Press, 1994.

Cranny-Francis, Anne. "Feminist Futures: A Generic Study." In Annette Kuhn, ed. *Alien Zone: Cultural Theory and Contemporary Science Fiction Cinema.* London: Verso, 2003 (219–227).

Creed, Barbara. "Horror and the

Monstrous-Feminine: An Imaginary Abjection." In Barry Keith Grant, ed. *The Dread of Difference: Gender and the Horror Film*. Austin: University of Texas Press, 1996 (35–65).

Cronin, Paul. *Roman Polanski: Interviews*. Jackson: University Press of Mississippi, 2005.

Crowther, Bosley. "The Screen: 'Kisses for My President': Fred MacMurray and Polly Bergen Star." http://movies.ny times.com/movies/critics/Bosley-Crowther.

Dalton, Anne B. "The Devil and the Virgin: Writing Sexual Abuse in *Incidents in the Life of a Slave Girl*." In Deidre Lashgari, ed. *Violence, Silence, and Anger: Women's Writing as Transgression*. Charlottesville: University Press of Virginia, 1995 (38–61).

Daly, Brenda. "Seeds of Shame or Seeds of Change? When Daughters Give Birth to Their Father's Children." In Julie Tharp and Susan MacCallum-Whitcomb, eds. *This Giving Birth: Pregnancy and Childbirth in American Women's Writing*. Bowling Green, OH: Bowling Green State University Press, 2000 (103–123).

Davis, Angela Y. "Reflections on the Black Woman's Role in the Community of Slaves." *Black Scholar* 3, no. 4 (1971): 2–15.

_____. *Women, Race, and Class*. New York: Vintage Classics, 1981.

De Lauretis, Teresa. *Alice Doesn't: Feminism, Semiotics, Cinema*. Bloomington: Indiana University Press, 1984.

_____. "Rethinking Women's Cinema: Aesthetics and Feminist Theory." In Diane Carson et al., eds. *Multiple Voices in Feminist Film Criticism*. Minneapolis: University of Minnesota Press, 1994 (140–161).

Dervin, Daniel. "Primal Conditions and Conventions: The Genre of Science Fiction." In Annette Kuhn, ed. *Alien Zone: Cultural Theory and Contemporary Science Fiction Cinema*. London: Verso, 2003 (96–102).

Diawara, Manthia. "Black Spectatorship: Problems of Identification and Resist-

ance." In Leo Braudy and Marshall Cohen, eds. *Film Theory and Criticism*, 6th ed. New York: Oxford University Press, 2004 (892–900).

Diehl, Joanne Feit. "Re-Reading *The Letter*: Hawthorne, the Fetish, and the (Family) Romance." In Ross C. Murfin, ed. *The Scarlet Letter*. Boston: Bedford Books of St. Martin's Press, 1991 (235–251).

DiLillo, Don. "That Day in Rome: Movies and Memory." *The New Yorker*, Oct. 20, 2003 (76–78).

Doane, Mary Ann. "The Moving Image: Pathos and the Maternal." In Marica Landy, ed. *Imitations of Life*. Detroit: Wayne State University Press, 1991 (283–306).

_____. "The 'Woman's Film': Possession and Address." In Mary Ann Doane, Patricia Mellencamp, and Linda Williams, eds. *Re-Vision*. Frederick, MD: University Publications of American, 1984 (67–82).

Doane, Mary Ann, Patricia Mellencamp, and Linda Williams, eds. *Re-Vision: Essays in Feminist Film Criticism*. Frederick, MD: University Publications of America, 1983.

Doherty, Thomas. "Genre, Gender, and the *Aliens* Trilogy." In Barry Keith Grant, ed. *The Dread of Difference: Gender and the Horror Film*. Austin: University of Texas Press, 1996 (181–199).

_____. *Hollywood's Censor: Joseph I. Breen & the Production Code Administration*. New York: Columbia University Press, 2007.

_____. *Pre-Code Hollywood: Sex, Immorality, and Insurrection in American Cinema 1930–1934*. New York: Columbia University Press, 1999.

Donohue, Agnes McNeill. *Hawthorne: Calvin's Ironic Stepchild*. Kent, OH: Kent State University Press, 1985.

Dowson, Jane, ed. *Women's Writing, 1945–1960: After the Deluge*. New York: Palgrave Macmillan, 2004.

Doyle, Laura. "'A' for Atlantic: The Colonizing Force of Hawthorne's *The Scarlet Letter*." *American Literature* Vol. 79, Issue 2 (June 2007): 243–273.

_____. *Bordering on the Body: The Racial Matrix of Modern Fiction and Culture*. New York: Oxford University Press, 1994.

Dreiser, Theodore. *Jennie Gerhardt*. New York: Penguin, 1992.

Dyer, Richard. "White." In Corrigan, ed. *Critical Visions in Film Theory*. New York: Bedford/St. Martin's, 2011 (822–839).

Ehrenreich, Barbara. "Owning Up to Abortion." In *This Land Is Their Land: Reports from a Divided Nation*. New York: Holt Paperbacks, 2009 (183–186).

Ehrenreich, Barbara, and Deirdre English. *For Her Own Good: Two Centuries of the Experts' Advice to Women*. New York: Anchor, 2005.

Elsaesser, Thomas. "Tales of Sound and Fury: Observations on the Family Melodrama." In Marcia Landy, ed. *Imitations of Life*. Detroit: Wayne State University Press, 1991 (68–91).

Ernest, John. "Motherhood Beyond the Gate: Jacobs's Epistemic Challenge in *Incidents in the Life of a Slave Girl*." In Deborah M. Garfield and Rafia Zafar, eds. *Harriet Jacobs and Incidents in the Life of a Slave Girl: New Critical Essays*. Cambridge: Cambridge University Press, 1996 (179–198).

Evans, Mark. "Versions of History: *The Handmaid's Tale* and Its Dedicatees." In Colin Nicholson, ed. *Margaret Atwood: Writing and Subjectivity: New Critical Essays*. New York: St. Martin's Press, 1994 (77–88).

Faludi, Susan. *Backlash: The Undeclared War Against Women*. New York: Doubleday Anchor, 1992.

Fantham, Elaine, Helene Peet Foley, Natalie Boymel Kampen, Sarah B. Pomeroy, and H.A. Shapiro. *Women in the Classical World: Image and Text*. Oxford: Oxford University Press, 1994.

Farber, Stephen. "A Movie Breaks the Abortion Taboo." *The Daily Beast*, April 10, 2010. http://www.thedailybeast. com/articles/2010/04/12/the-taboo-breaking-abortion-in-greenberg.html.

Faulkner, William. *Absalom, Absalom!* New York: Random House, 1964.

_____. *Light in August*. New York: Random House, 1985.

Ferriss, Suzanne, and Mallory Young, eds. *Chick Flicks: Contemporary Women at the Movies*. New York: Routledge, 2008.

Fessler, Ann. *The Girls Who Went Away: The Hidden History of Women Who Surrendered Children for Adoption in the Decades Before Roe v. Wade*. New York: Penguin, 2006.

Finigan, Theo. "'Into the Memory Hole': Totalitarianism and Mal D'Archive in *Nineteen Eighty-Four* and *The Handmaid's Tale*." *Science Fiction Studies* 38.3 (2011): 435–459.

Firestone, Shulamith. *The Dialectic of Sex: The Case for a Feminist Revolution*. New York: Farrar, Straus and Giroux, 2003.

Forty, Sandra. *Vermeer*. Surrey: TAJ, 2002.

Freidenfields, Lara. *The Modern Period: Menstruation in Twentieth-Century America*. Baltimore: Johns Hopkins University Press, 2009.

Gaines, Jane. "*The Scar of Shame*: Skin Color and Caste in Black Silent Melodrama." In Marcia Landy, ed. *Imitations of Life*. Detroit: Wayne State University Press, 1991 (331–348).

_____. "White Privilege and Looking Relations: Race and Gender in Feminist Film Theory." In Carson, et al., eds. *Multiple Voices in Feminist Film Criticism*. Minneapolis: University of Minnesota Press, 1994 (176–190).

Gale, Steven H. *Sharp Cut: Harold Pinter's Screenplays and the Artistic Process*. Lexington: University Press of Kentucky, 2003.

Garfield, Deborah M., and Rafia Zafar, eds. *Harriet Jacobs and Incidents in the Life of a Slave Girl; New Critical Essays*. Cambridge: Cambridge University Press, 1996.

Gates, Henry Louis, Jr., ed. *The Classic Slave Narratives: The Life of Olaudah Equiano; The History of Mary Prince; Narrative of the Life of Frederick Douglass; Incidents in the Life of a Slave Girl*. New York: Signet Classics, 2002.

Gates, Henry Louis, Jr., and K. A. Appiah, eds. *Toni Morrison: Critical Perspectives*

Past and Present. New York: Amistad, 1993.

Gibson, Donald B. "Text and Countertext in *The Bluest Eye.*" In Henry Louis Gates, Jr., and K.A. Appiah, eds. *Toni Morrison: Critical Perspectives Past and Present.* New York: Amistad, 1993 (159–174).

Gibson-Hudson, Gloria. "Aspects of Black Feminist Cultural Ideology in Films by Black Women Independent Artists." In Diane Carson, Linda Dittmar, and Janice R. Welsch, eds. *Multiple Voices in Feminist Film Criticism.* Minneapolis: University of Minnesota Press, 1994 (365–379).

Gilbert, Sandra M., and Susan Gubar. *The Madwoman in the Attic: The Woman Writer and the Nineteenth-Century Literary Imagination.* New Haven: Yale University Press, 1984.

Gill, Jo. "Influence of Nathaniel Hawthorne's *The Scarlet Letter* on Sylvia Plath's "Daddy." *Notes & Queries* Vol. 52., Issue 1 (Mar. 2005): 107–108.

Gilman, Charlotte Perkins. *The Herland Trilogy.* Blacksburg, VA: Wilder Publications, 2011.

Goldman, Eric. "'Knowing' Lolita: Sexual Deviance and Normality in Nabokov's *Lolita.*" *Nabokov Studies* 8 (2004): 87–104.

Grant, Barry Keith, ed. *The Dread of Difference: Gender and the Horror Film.* Austin: University of Texas Press, 1996.

Greene, Gayle. *Doris Lessing: The Poetics of Change.* Ann Arbor: University of Michigan Press, 1994.

Griffith, Richard, and Arthur Mayer. *The Movies.* New York: Simon & Schuster, 1970.

Gunning, Tom. *D. W. Griffith and the Origins of American Narrative Film.* Urbana: University of Illinois Press, 1991.

Hanson, Clare. *A Cultural History of Pregnancy: Pregnancy, Medicine and Culture, 1750–2000.* New York: Palgrave Macmillan, 2004.

Harris, Trudier. *Fiction and Folklore: The Novels of Toni Morrison.* Knoxville: University of Tennessee Press, 1991.

Harvey, Sylvia. "Woman's Place: The Absent Family of Film Noir." In E. Ann Kaplan, ed. *Women in Film Noir.* London: BFI, 2003 (35–46).

Haskell, Molly. *From Reverence to Rape: The Treatment of Women in the Movies.* Chicago: University of Chicago Press, 1987.

Hatch, Kristen. "1951: Movies and the New Faces of Masculinity." In Murray Pomerance, ed. *American Cinema of the 1950s: Themes and Variations.* New Brunswick, NJ: Rutgers University Press, 2005 (43–64).

Hecht, Anthony. *Selected Poems.* J.D. McClatchy, ed. New York: Alfred A. Knopf, 2011.

Heilpern, John. *John Osborne: The Many Lives of the Angry Young Man.* New York: Alfred A. Knopf, 2007.

Hendler, Jane. *Best Sellers and Their Film Adaptations in Postwar America.* New York: Peter Lang, 2001.

Hensley, Jeannine, ed. *The Works of Anne Bradstreet.* Foreword by Adrienne Rich. New York: Belknap Press of Harvard University, 2010.

Herrera, Hayden. *Frida: A Biography of Frida Kahlo.* New York: Harper Perennial, 1983.

Hirsch, Marianne. "Maternal Narratives: 'Cruel Enough to Stop the Blood.'" In Henry Louis Henry Gates, Jr., and K.A. Appiah, eds. *Toni Morrison: Critical Perspectives Past and Present.* New York: Amistad, 1993 (261–273).

Hollinger, Karen. *In the Company of Women: Contemporary Female Friendship Films.* Minneapolis: University of Minnesota Press, 1998.

Houston, Beverle. "Missing in Action: Dorothy Arzner." In Diane Carson, Linda Dittmar, and Janice R. Welsch, eds. *Multiple Voices in Feminist Film Criticism.* Minneapolis: University of Minnesota Press, 1994 (271–279).

Huxley, Aldous. *Brave New World.* New York: Harper Perennial Modern Classics, 2010.

Ishiguro, Kazuo. *Never Let Me Go.* New York: Vintage, 2006.

Jacobs, Lea. *The Wages of Sin: Censorship and the Fallen Woman Film, 1928–1942.*

Works Cited and Consulted

Berkeley: University of California Press, 1997.

James, P.D. *The Children of Men.* New York: Vintage, 2006.

Jenkins, Greg. *Stanley Kubrick and the Art of Adaptation: Three Films.* Jefferson, NC: McFarland, 2007.

Jones, Alan. *The Rough Guide to Horror Movies.* New York: Rough Guides, 2005.

Jones, Vivien. "The Death of Mary Wollstonecraft." *British Journal for Eighteenth-Century Studies* 20.2 (1997): 187–205.

Kalfopoulou, Adrianne. "Sylvia Plath's Emersonian I/Eye." *Women's Studies* Vol. 40, Issue 7 (Oct./Nov. 2011): 890–909.

Kaplan, E. Ann, ed. *Feminism and Film.* Oxford: Oxford University Press, 2000.

_____, ed. *Women in Film Noir.* London: BFI, 2003.

Kashner, Sam, and Jennifer MacNair. *The Bad and the Beautiful: Hollywood in the Fifties.* Old Saybrook, CT: Konecky & Konecky, 2002.

Kendall, Tim. *Sylvia Plath: A Critical Study.* London: Faber & Faber, 2001.

Kettenmann, Andrea. *Frida Kahlo 1907–1954: Pain and Passion.* Köln: Benedikt Taschen, 1993.

Kincaid, James R. *Erotic Innocence: The Culture of Child Molesting.* Durham: Duke University Press, 1998.

_____."Lolita at Middle Age." *Chronicle of Higher Education* 55.8 (2008): B18-B19.

Klein, Joanne. *Making Pictures: The Pinter Screenplays.* Columbus: Ohio State University Press, 1985.

Kolker, Robert. *A Cinema of Loneliness.* Oxford: Oxford University Press, 2011.

Kristeva, Julia. "Motherhood According to Giovanni Bellini." In Kelly Oliver, ed. *The Portable Kristeva.* New York: Columbia University Press, 1997 (301–307).

Kuhn, Annette, ed. *Alien Zone: Cultural Theory and Contemporary Science Fiction Cinema.* London: Verso, 2003.

Landy, Marcia, ed. *Imitations of Life: A Reader on Films & Television Melodrama.* Detroit: Wayne State University Press, 1991.

Lant, Kathleen Margar. "The Big Strip Tease: Female Bodies and Male Power in the Poetry of Sylvia Plath." *Contemporary Literature* Vol. 34, Issue 4 (Winter 1993): 620–670.

LaPlante, Eve. *American Jezebel: The Uncommon Life of Anne Hutchinson, the Woman Who Defied the Puritans.* San Francisco: HarperSanFrancisco, 2005.

LaSalle, Mick. *Complicated Women: Sex and Power in Pre-Code Hollywood.* New York: St. Martin's Press, 2000.

Lashgari, Deirdre, ed. *Violence, Silence, and Anger: Women's Writing as Transgression.* Charlottesville: University Press of Virginia, 1995.

Lauter, Paul, ed. *The Heath Anthology of American Literature,* 5th ed., Vols. D, E. New York: Houghton Mifflin, 2006.

Lee, Hermione. *Edith Wharton.* New York: Alfred A. Knopf, 2007.

Leff, Leonard J., and Jerold L. Simmons. *The Dame in the Kimono: Hollywood, Censorship, and the Production Code from the 1920s to the 1960s.* New York: Grove Weidenfeld, 1990.

Liebovitz, Annie. *More on Moore.* Cover photograph. *Vanity Fair,* August 1991.

Lessing, Doris. *The Fifth Child.* New York: Vintage, 1989.

_____. *The Golden Notebook.* New York: Harper Perennial Classics, 1999.

_____. *A Proper Marriage.* New York: Harper Perennial, 1995.

Leverenz, David. "Mrs. Hawthorne's Headache: Reading *The Scarlet Letter.*" In Ross C. Murfin, ed. *The Scarlet Letter* by Nathaniel Hawthorne. Boston: Bedford Books of St. Martin's Press, 1991 (263–274).

Lewis, Jon. *American Film: A History.* New York: W. W. Norton, 2008.

_____. *Hollywood v. Hard Core: How the Struggle Over Censorship Saved the Modern Film Industry.* New York: New York University Press, 2000.

Lewis, R. W. B. *Edith Wharton: A Biography.* New York: Macmillan, 1988.

Liedtke, Walter. *Vermeer: The Complete Paintings.* New York: Harry M. Abrams, 2012.

Lindsey, Shelley Stamp. "Horror, Femininity, and Carrie's Monstrous Puberty." In Barry Keith Grand, ed. *The Dread of Difference: Gender and the Horror Film*. Austin: University of Texas Press, 1996 (279–295).

Lucas, Rose. "Radical Parturition and Literary Labours of Mourning: The Case of Mary Shelley's *Frankenstein*." *Hecate* 32.2 (2006): 58–67.

Lury, Celia. *Consumer Culture*. Cambridge: Polity Press, 1996.

Luttrell, Wendy. "Where Inequality Lives in the Body: Teenage Pregnancy, Public Pedagogies, and Individual Lives." *Sport, Education, and Society* Vol. 16, Issue 3 (June 2011): 295–308.

Lynch, Joan Driscoll. "Incest Discourse and Cinematic Representation." *Journal of Film & Video* Vol. 54, Issue 2/3 (Summer/Fall 2002): 43–55.

Maguire, Gregory. *Wicked: The Life and Times of the Wicked Witch of the West*. New York: ReganBooks, 1995.

Making Visible Embryos. http://www.hps.cam.ac.uk/visibleembryos/resources.html#Unborn.

Marder, Elissa. *The Mother in the Age of Mechanical Reproduction: Psychoanalysis, Photography, Deconstruction*. New York: Fordham University Press, 2012.

Maroula, Joannou. *Contemporary Women's Writing: From* The Golden Notebook *to* The Color Purple. New York: St. Martin's Press, 2000.

Matthews, Sandra, and Laura Wexler. *Pregnant Pictures*. London: Routledge, 2000.

Mayne, Judith. "Paradoxes of Spectatorship." In Timothy Corrigan, Patricia White, and Meta Mazaj, eds. *Critical Visions in Film Theory*. New York: Bedford/St. Martin's, 2011 (88–110).

_____. "The Woman at the Keyhole: Women's Cinema and Feminist Criticism." In Mary Ann Doane, Patricia Mellencamp, and Linda Williams, eds. *Re-Vision*. Frederick, MD: University Publications of American, 1984 (49–66).

McCarthy, Cormac. *The Road*. New York: Vintage, 2007.

McCarthy, Mary. *The Group*. New York: Signet, 1963.

McDonald, Keith. "Days of Past Futures:

Kazuo Ishiguro's *Never Let Me Go* as 'Speculative Memoir.'" *Biography* 30.1 (Winter 2007): 74–83.

McLarty, Lianne. "'Beyond the Veil of the Flesh': Cronenberg and the Disembodiment of Horror." In Barry Keith Grant, ed. *The Dread of Difference: Gender and the Horror Film*. Austin: University of Texas Press, 1996 (231–252).

McLennan, Rachael. "'Cautionary Whales?' Adolescence and Genre in *Juno* and *Push*." *Mosaic* Vol. 46, no. 2 (June 2013): 105–121.

Mellor, Anne K. *Mary Shelley: Her Life, Her Fiction, Her Monsters*. New York: Routledge, 1989.

Metalious, Grace. *Peyton Place* and *Return to Peyton Place*. New York: Gramercy, 1954.

Miller, Jordan Y., ed. *The Heath Introduction to Drama*, 5th ed. Lexington, MA: D.C. Heath, 1996.

Mitchell, Paul. "Reading (and) the Late Poems of Sylvia Plath." *Modern Language Review* Vol. 100, Issue 1 (Jan. 2005): 37–49.

Morley, Christopher. *Kitty Foyle*. Philadelphia: J. B. Lippincott, 1939.

Morrison, Toni. *A Mercy*. New York: Alfred A. Knopf, 2008.

_____. *Beloved*. New York: Penguin, 1987.

_____. *The Bluest Eye*. New York: Washington Square Press, 1970.

_____. *Home*. New York: Alfred A. Knopf, 2012.

_____. *Jazz*. New York: Alfred A. Knopf, 1992.

_____. *Love*. New York: Alfred A. Knopf, 2003.

_____. *Paradise*. New York: Alfred A. Knopf, 1998.

_____. *Song of Soloman*. New York: Penguin, 1987.

_____. *Sula*. New York: Plume, 1973

_____. *Tar Baby*. New York: Vintage, 2004.

Mulvey, Laura. "Visual Pleasure and Narrative Cinema." In Timothy Corrigan, Patricia White, and Meta Mazaj, eds. *Critical Visions in Film Theory*. New York: Bedford/St. Martin's, 2011 (715–726).

Works Cited and Consulted

Mundy, Liza. *Everything Conceivable: How Assisted Reproduction is Changing Men, Women, and the World.* New York: Alfred A. Knopf, 2007.

Murfin, Ross C., ed. *The Scarlet Letter* by Nathaniel Hawthorne. Boston: Bedford Books of St. Martin's Press, 1991.

Museum of Menstruation: http://www.mum.org/.

Nabakov, Vladamir. *The Annotated Lolita.* Edited with preface, introduction and notes by Alfred Appel, Jr. New York: Vintage, 1991.

Nafisi, Azar. *Reading Lolita in Tehran: A Memoir.* New York: Random House, 2008.

Nana, Meri, and Ama Danquah, eds. *The Black Body.* New York: Seven Stories Press, 2012.

Naremore, James. *More Than the Night: Film Noir in Its Contexts.* Berkeley: University of California Press, 2008.

Naylor, Gloria. *Mama Day.* New York: Vintage, 1989.

_____. *The Women of Brewster Place.* New York: Penguin, 1982.

Neal, Mark Anthony. "Critical Noir: *The Color Purple* Controversy Revisited." *Cinematic Representations of Blackness.* May 12, 2012. http://ces335summer12.wordpress.com/2012/05/12/critical-noir-the-color-purple-controversy-revisited-the-color-purple/.

Neibaur, James L. "The Miracle of Morgan's Creek." *Senses of Cinema,* Issue 58 (March 2011). http://sensesofcinema.com/2011/cteq/the-miracle-of-morgan%E2%80%99s-creek/.

Neuman, Shirley. "'Just a Backlash': Margaret Atwood, Feminism, and *The Handmaid's Tale.*" *University of Toronto Quarterly* 75.3 (2006): 857–868.

Newton, Judith. "Feminism and Anxiety in *Alien.*" In Annette Kuhn, ed. *Alien Zone: Cultural Theory and Contemporary Science Fiction Cinema.* London: Verso, 2003 (82–87).

Nicholson, Colin, ed. *Margaret Atwood: Writing and Subjectivity: New Critical Essays.* New York: St. Martin's Press, 1994.

Nilsson, Lennart. *A Child is Born.* London: Penguin, 1967.

Olds, Sharon. *Satan Says.* Pittsburgh: University of Pittsburgh Press, 1980.

Oliver, Kelly. *Knock Me Up, Knock Me Down: Images of Pregnancy in Hollywood Films.* New York: Columbia University Press, 2012.

_____. *The Portable Kristeva.* New York: Columbia University Press, 1997.

Orr, Christopher. "Closure and Containment: Marylee Hadley in *Written on the Wind.*" In Marcia Landy, ed. *Imitations of Life.* Detroit: Wayne State University Press, 1991 (380–387).

Orwell, George. *Nineteen Eighty-Four.* New York: Plume, 2003.

Osteen, Mark. *Nightmare Alley: Film Noir and the American Dream.* Baltimore: Johns Hopkins University Press, 2013.

Park, Jooyoung. "'I Could Kill a Woman or Wound a Man': Melancholic Rage in the Poems of Sylvia Plath." *Women's Studies* Vol. 31, Issue 4 (July/Aug. 2002): 467–498.

Perkowitz, Sidney. *Hollywood Science: Movies, Science, and the End of the World.* New York: Columbia University Press, 2007.

Person, Leland. "The Dark Labyrinth of the Mind: Hawthorne, Hester, and the Ironies of Racial Mothering." *Studies in American Fiction* 29 (Spring 2001): 33–48.

Petrie, Dennis, and Joseph Boggs. *The Art of Watching Films,* 8th ed. New York: McGraw-Hill, 2012.

Phillips, Gene D., ed. *Stanley Kubrick: Interviews.* Jackson: University of Mississippi Press, 2001.

Pifer, Ellen. "The *Lolita* Phenomenon from Paris to Tehran." In Julian W. Connolly, ed. *The Cambridge Companion to Nabokov.* Cambridge: Cambridge University Press, 2005 (185–199).

Place, Janey. "Women in Film Noir." In E. Ann Kaplan, ed. *Women in Film Noir.* London: BFI, 2003 (47–68).

Plath, Sylvia. *Collected Poems.* New York: Buccaneer, 1998.

Podnieks, Elizabeth. *Mediating Moms: Mothers in Popular Culture.* Montreal: McGill-Queens University Press, 2012.

Poli, Doretta Davanzo. *Maternity Fashion.* Modena, Italy: Zandi Editori s.r.l., 1988.

Pomerance, Murray. "1957: Movies and the Search for Proportion." In Murray Pomerance, ed. *American Cinema of the 1950s: Themes and Variations.* New Brunswick, NJ: Rutgers University Press, 2005.

_____, ed. *American Cinema of the 1950s: Themes and Variations.* New Brunswick, NJ: Rutgers University Press, 2005.

Ragussis, Michael. "Silence, Family Discourse, and Fiction in *The Scarlet Letter.*" In Ross C. Murfin, ed. *The Scarlet Letter* by Nathaniel Hawthorne. Boston: Bedford Books of St. Martin's Press, 1991 (316–329).

Railton, Stephen. "The Address of *The Scarlet Letter.*" In Leland S. Person, ed. *The Scarlet Letter and Other Writings.* New York: W.W. Norton, 2005 (481–500).

Rae, Catherine. *Edith Wharton's Old New York Quartet.* Lanham, MD: University Press of America, 1984.

Raw, Laurence. *Adapting Nathaniel Hawthorne to the Screen; Forging New Worlds.* Lanham, MD: Scarecrow Press, 2008.

Renov, Michael. "*Leave Her to Heaven*: The Double Bind of the Post-War Woman." In Marcia Landy, ed. *Imitations of Life.* Detroit: Wayne State University Press, 1991 (227–235).

Rich, Adrienne. *Of Woman Born: Motherhood as Experience and Institution.* New York: W. W. Norton, 1995.

Riss, Arthur. *Race, Slavery, and Liberalism in Nineteenth-Century American Literature.* Cambridge: Cambridge University Press, 2006.

Robertson, Ben P. *Inchbald, Hawthorne and the Romantic Moral Romance.* London: Pickering & Chatto, 2010.

Rubenstein, Roberta. "Pariahs and Community." In Henry Louis Gates, Jr., and K.A. Appiah, eds. *Toni Morrison: Critical Perspectives Past and Present.* New York: Amistad, 1993 (126–158).

Ryan, Michael, and Douglas Kellner. "Technophobia." In Annette Kuhn, ed.

Alien Zone: Cultural Theory and Contemporary Science Fiction Cinema. London: Verso, 2003 (58–65).

St. Clair, William. *The Godwins and the Shelleys: The Biography of a Family.* New York: W.W. Norton, 1989.

Sanders, Coyne, and Tom Gilbert. *Desilu: The Story of Lucille Ball and Desi Arnaz.* New York: It, 2011.

Sapphire. *Push.* New York: Vintage, 1996.

Schatz, Thomas. "The Family Melodrama." In Marcia Landy, ed. *Imitations of Life.* Detroit: Wayne State University Press, 1991 (148–167).

Schickel, Richard. *D. W. Griffith: An American Life.* New York: Limelight Editions, 2004.

Seymour, Miranda. *Mary Shelley.* New York: Grove Press, 2002.

Shelley, Mary. *Frankenstein or, The Modern Prometheus.* New York: A Signet Classic, 2005.

Showalter, Elaine. *A Jury of Her Peers: American Women Writers from Anne Bradstreet to Annie Proulx.* New York: Alfred A. Knopf, 2009.

_____. "Tradition and the Female Talent: *The Awakening* as a Solitary Book." In Nancy A. Walker, ed. *The Awakening.* Boston: Bedford Books of St. Martin's Press, 1993 (169–189).

Sinyard, Neil. *Jack Clayton. British Film Makers.* Manchester: Manchester University Press, 2000.

Skal, David J. *The Monster Show: A Cultural History of Horror.* New York: Faber and Faber, 2001.

Skillern, Rhonda. "Law, Language, and Ritual in *Summer.*" In Millicent Bell, ed. *Cambridge Companion to Edith Wharton.* Cambridge: Cambridge University Press, 1995 (117–136).

Smith, Judith E. "The Marrying Kind: Working-Class Courtship and Marriage in 1950s Hollywood." In Diane Carson, Linda Dittmar, and Janice R. Welsch, eds. *Multiple Voices in Feminist Film Criticism.* Minneapolis: University of Minnesota Press, 1994 (226–242).

Sobchack, Vivian. "Bringing It All Back Home: Family Economy and Generic

Works Cited and Consulted

Exchange." In Barry Keith Grant, ed. *The Dread of Difference: Gender and the Horror Film.* Austin: University of Texas Press, 1996 (143–163).

_____. *Screening Space: The American Science Fiction Film*, 2d ed. New Brunswick, NJ: Rutgers University Press, 1998.

_____. "The Virginity of Astronauts: Sex and the Science Fiction Film." In Annette Kuhn, ed. *Alien Zone: Cultural Theory and Contemporary Science Fiction Cinema.* London: Verso, 2003 (103–115).

Steinbeck, John. *The Grapes of Wrath.* New York: Penguin, 1987.

Sterritt, David. "The Pumpkin Eater." http://www.tcm.com/tcmdb/title/27821 /The-Pumpkin-Eater/articles.html# topofpage.

Sturges, Preston. *Preston Sturges by Preston Sturges.* Adapted and edited by Sandy Sturges. New York: Simon & Schuster, 1990.

Telotte, J.P. "The Doubles of Fantasy and the Space of Desire." In Annette Kuhn, ed. *Alien Zone: Cultural Theory and Contemporary Science Fiction Cinema.* London: Verso, 2003 (152–159).

Tharp, Julie, and Susan MacCallum-Whitcomb, eds. *This Giving Birth: Pregnancy and Childbirth in American Women's Writing.* Bowling Green, OH: Bowling Green State University Popular Press, 2000.

Timmer, Joel. "Restricting Portrayals of Film Violence to Reduce the Likelihood of Negative Effects in Viewers: Did the Framers of the MPPC Get It Right?" *Journal of Popular Film and Television* Vol. 39, Issue 1 (Spring 2011): 29–36.

Titus, Mary. "'This Poisonous System': Social Ills, Bodily Ills, and *Incidents in the Life of a Slave Girl.* In Deborah M. Garfield and Rafia Zafar, eds. *Harriet Jacobs and Incidents in the Life of a Slave Girl: New Critical Essays.* Cambridge: Cambridge University Press, 1996 (199–215).

Toth, Emily. *Inside Peyton Place: The Life of Grace Metalious.* Jackson: University of Mississippi Press, 2000.

Truffaut, François. *Hitchcock.* New York: Simon & Schuster, 1985.

Tucker, David, ed. *British Social Realism in the Arts since 1940.* New York: Palgrave Macmillan, 2001.

Turner, Nick. *Post-War British Women Novelists and the Canon.* New York: Continuum, 2010.

Vieira, Mark. *Sin in Soft Focus: Pre-Code Hollywood.* New York: Harry N. Abrams, 1999.

Viviani, Christian. "Who Is Without Sin: The Maternal Melodrama in American Film, 1930–1939." Translated by Dolores Burdick. In Marcia Landy, ed. *Imitations of Life.* Detroit: Wayne State University Press, 1991 (168–182).

Wagenknecht, Edward. *Nathaniel Hawthorne: The Man, His Tales and Romances.* New York: Continuum, 1989.

Wagner-Lawlor, Jennifer A. "The Play of Irony: Theatricality and Utopian Transformation in Contemporary Women's Speculative Fiction." *Utopian Studies* 13.1 (2002): 114.

Wagner-Martin, Linda. *Sylvia Plath: A Literary Life.* New York: St. Martin's, 1999.

Walker, Alexander. *Stanley Kubrick, Director.* New York: W. W. Norton, 1999.

Walker, Alice. *The Color Purple.* New York: Harcourt Brace Jovanovich, 1982.

Walker, Nancy A. *The Awakening.* By Kate Chopin. Boston: Bedford Books of St. Martin's Press, 1993.

Wharton, Edith. *The Age of Innocence.* Candace Waid, ed. New York: W. W. Norton, 2003.

_____. *Ethan Frome* and *Summer.* Denise D. Knight, ed. New York: Houghton Mifflin, 2004.

_____. *Old New York: Four Novellas.* New York: Pocket, 2002.

_____. *Summer.* Intro. Cynthia Griffin Woolf. New York: Harper, 1979.

White, Armond. "Breathless." *Cineaste* 33, No.1 (Winter 2007). Online only.

Williams, Linda. *Playing the Race Card: Melodramas of Black and White from Uncle Tom to O.J. Simpson.* Princeton, NJ: Princeton University Press, 2011.

_____. "'Something Else Besides a Mother': *Stella Dallas* and the Maternal

Works Cited and Consulted

Melodrama." In Marcia Landy, ed. *Imitations of Life*. Detroit: Wayne State University Press, 1991 (307–330).

———. "When the Woman Looks." In Mary Ann Doane, Patricia Mellencamp, and Linda Williams, eds. *Re-Visions*. Frederick, MD: University Publications of America, 1984 (83–99).

Wineapple, Brenda. *Hawthorne: A Life*. New York: Alfred A. Knopf, 2003.

Winter, Jessica. *The Rough Guide to American Independent Film*. New York: Penguin, 2006.

Wittern-Keller, Laura. *Freedom of the Screen: Legal Challenges to State Film Censors, 1915–1981*. Lexington: University Press of Kentucky, 2008.

Woidat, Caroline. "Talking Back to Schoolteacher: Morrison's Confrontation with Hawthorne in *Beloved*." *Modern Fiction Studies* 39 (1993): 527–46.

Wolff, Cynthia Griffin. "*The Age of Innocence* as a Bildungsroman." In Candace Waid, ed. *The Age of Innocence*. By Edith Wharton. New York: W. W. Norton, 2003 (421–433).

Wolter, Jurgen C. "Southern Hesters: Hawthorne's Influence on Kate Chopin, Toni Morrison, William Faulkner, and Tennessee Williams." *Southern Quarterly*, Vol. 50, No. 1 (Fall 2012): 24–42.

Wood, Ruth Pirsig. Lolita *in* Peyton Place: *Highbrow, Middlebrow, and Lowbrow Novels of the 1950s*. New York: Garland, 1995.

Wright, Sarah Bird. *Edith Wharton A to Z: The Essential Guide to the Life and Work*. New York: Checkmark, 1998.

Yellin, Jean Fagan. "*The Scarlet Letter* and the Antislavery Feminists." In Leland Person, ed., *The Scarlet Letter and Other Writings*. New York: W. W. Norton, 2005 (632–655).

———. *Women and Sisters: The Antislavery Feminists in American Culture*. New Haven: Yale University Press, 1989.

Young, Elizabeth. "Here Comes the Bride: Wedding Gender and Race in *Bride of Frankenstein*." In Barry Keith Grant, ed. *The Dread of Difference: Gender and the Horror Film*. Austin: University of Texas Press, 1996 (309–337).

Young, Iris Marion. *Throwing Like a Girl and Other Essays in Feminist Philosophy and Social Theory*. Bloomington: Indiana University Press, 1990.

———. *On Female Body Experience*. New York: Oxford University Press, 2005.

Index

Numbers in **bold italic** indicate pages with photographs.

225

Index

Index

Index

Index

Index

Index

Index

patriarchy: *Close Encounters of the Third Kind* 149–150, 152; *The Great Lie* 71; *The Handmaid's Tale* 142, 146; noir women 76; *Way Down East* 61
Penn, Sean: *Fast Times at Ridgemont High* 176
periods *see* menstruation
pessary 51
Petulia (1968) 173
Peyton Place (Metalious) 92–99, 161, 174
Peyton Place (1957) 9, 98
Peyton Place (1964–1969) 120
Phillips, Gene 104
Phoenix, Joaquin: *The Master* 25
Photofest 5
Picasso, Pablo 163
the pill 116, 117
Pillow Talk (1959) 4
Pinter, Harold: *The Handmaid's Tale* 203n9; *The Pumpkin Eater* 18
A Place in the Sun (1951) 9, 75, 76
Plath, Sylvia: *The Bell Jar* 19; "Metaphors" 13–14; pregnant woman as cliché 161; as woman writer 20
Play It as It Lays (Didion) 20
Poehler, Amy 1, 2, 5
poetry: "agonized poetry" of Frida Kahlo 165; heroic act of pregnancy 14–15; metaphor of pregnancy 13–14; perils of pregnancy 14; resources 197n6
Polanski, Roman: framing of women 184; *Rosemary's Baby* 119–124
Poltergeist (1982) 128
post-war era *see* World War II
Povah, Phyllis: *The Women* 69
power: *The Age of Innocence* 49–50; art context and gender 163–164; backlash against women 140–141; *Carrie* 119; controlling film phantasy 168; exclusively female 10, 197n4; *From Here to Eternity* 88; *Incidents in the Life of a Slave Girl* 39–40; "The Language of the Brag" 14–15; *Lolita* 101–102, 104; monsters reborn 115; power and powerless 45; pregnancy as triumph 36, 50, 55; of pregnancy narrative *24*, 192; *Rosemary's Baby* 120; *The Scarlet Letter* 31, 32, 34, 35–36; women over reproduction 116; *see also* control; vulnerability
Precious (2009) 189–190
pregnancy: in art mirroring real 3, 4, 25, 43, 44, 53, 57, 192; as commodity 161; from conception to birth *123*, 124, 126, 187; as enemy within 127; as enlightenment 56; first obvious in film 69–72, *70*; as heroic act 14–15, 54; as language 191–193; as metaphor 13–15, 187, 191–192;

public vs. private 161–162; as punishment 33, 37, 66, 84, 87; as science fiction 12, 126; space travel language 153; as Trojan horse 5; as unwholesome 66–67; *Vanity Fair* cover 159, 160; as weapon 48, 50, 102, 103
pregnancy narrative: *Alien* 131; *The Awakening* 44–45; *Beloved* 56; *Close Encounters of the Third Kind* 153; description of 12; embedded 172–174; emergence of 9, 43–44; *Fences* 21; films since 2000 23–25; *I Love Lucy* 90–91; *Incidents in the Life of a Slave Girl* 37, 39–40, 40–42; link between text and film 61; menstruation 12, 39, 42; modern 170; musical theater 22–23; pulp pregnancy films 201n10; *Rosemary's Baby* 124; *The Scarlet Letter* 156; *Summer* 47; ubiquitous 50–51; Unborn Child *193*, 193–195; *see also* narrative
pregnant as word: "light in August" 52; 19th century fiction writers 43; pre–Code Hollywood 8–9, 63–64; post–Code Hollywood 9; on television 90
pregnant men 129–130, *130*, 147–149
president pregnant 8
Production Code (1934): abortion 200n9; B studio teenpics 108; emergence of 64; First Amendment protections 89; first obviously pregnant woman 69–72, *70*; Mae West and 199n3; *Peyton Place* 98; post–Code era 9, 21–25, *22*, 124, 169–195; pre–Code era 8–9, 60, 63–66, 83–84, 200nn5–7; Production Code era 9, 16, 66–69, 169; Production Code era changes 68, 73, 75, 79, 91; Production Code era post–WW II 75–91; ratings system for films 124, 155; resources 197n3, 200n11
A Proper Marriage (Lessing) 19
Psycho (1960) 117
pulp pregnancy films 201n10
The Pumpkin Eater (1964) 18–19, 21
punchline pregnancies *see* comedic aspects of pregnancy
punishment via pregnancy: *Charlotte Temple* 37; childless freaks 84, 87; Production Code era 66; *The Scarlet Letter* 33
Push (Sapphire) 56, 161

Quayle, Dan 191

Rabbit Test (1978) 148
race/ethnicity: abortion and 183; black women writers 37–38; characters of Edith Wharton 198n15, 199n16; *The Color Purple* 190; Jewish characters 68, 199n16; *The Scarlet Letter* (1995) 158; teen pregnancy and 189

234

Index

Index

Index

Winslet, Kate: *Revolutionary Road* 180
Winters, Shelley: *Lolita* 105; *A Place in the Sun* 75
Wish You Were Here (1987) 190
Wolff, Cynthia Griffin 49–50
Woman in Blue Reading a Letter (Vermeer) 163
Woman Weighing a Balance (Vermeer) 163
The Women (1939) 68, 69
women as doubles: in art 164, 166–168; *Breathless* 172; double vision of stories 15; grammar of opposites 191; noir women 74–75; *see also* doppelgangers; mirrors
women writers: black women emerging 37–38; female perspective post–WW II 19–20
women's health issues: as commodity 161; 19th century 198*n*2; organ harvesting 135–139; pessary fitting 51; resources 204*n*2
Wonder Boys (Chabon) 184
Wood, Evan Rachel: *The Ides of March* 180

Wood, Natalie: *Love with the Proper Stranger* 175
Wood, Ruth Pirsig 99
Woodward, Joanne: *Rachel, Rachel* 125
word *pregnant* see *pregnant* as word
World War II: female in post-war America 82–83, 88; noir emigration 74; *Peyton Place* as post-war mirror 97; post-war baby boom 84; Production Code changes 68, 73, 75, 79, 91; teen group emergence 107–108; Victory Girls 73, 88
Written on the Wind (1956) 4
Wyman, Jane: *Johnny Belinda* 75

Yao Lu 163
Young, Loretta: *A Man's Castle* 66
Young, Sean: *Blade Runner* 134
Young Frankenstein (1974) 115

Zeta-Jones, Catherine: *Traffic* 23
Zhou Xun: *Balzac and the Little Chinese Seamstress* 23